IMAGES of America
LIGHTHOUSES OF NORTHWEST MICHIGAN

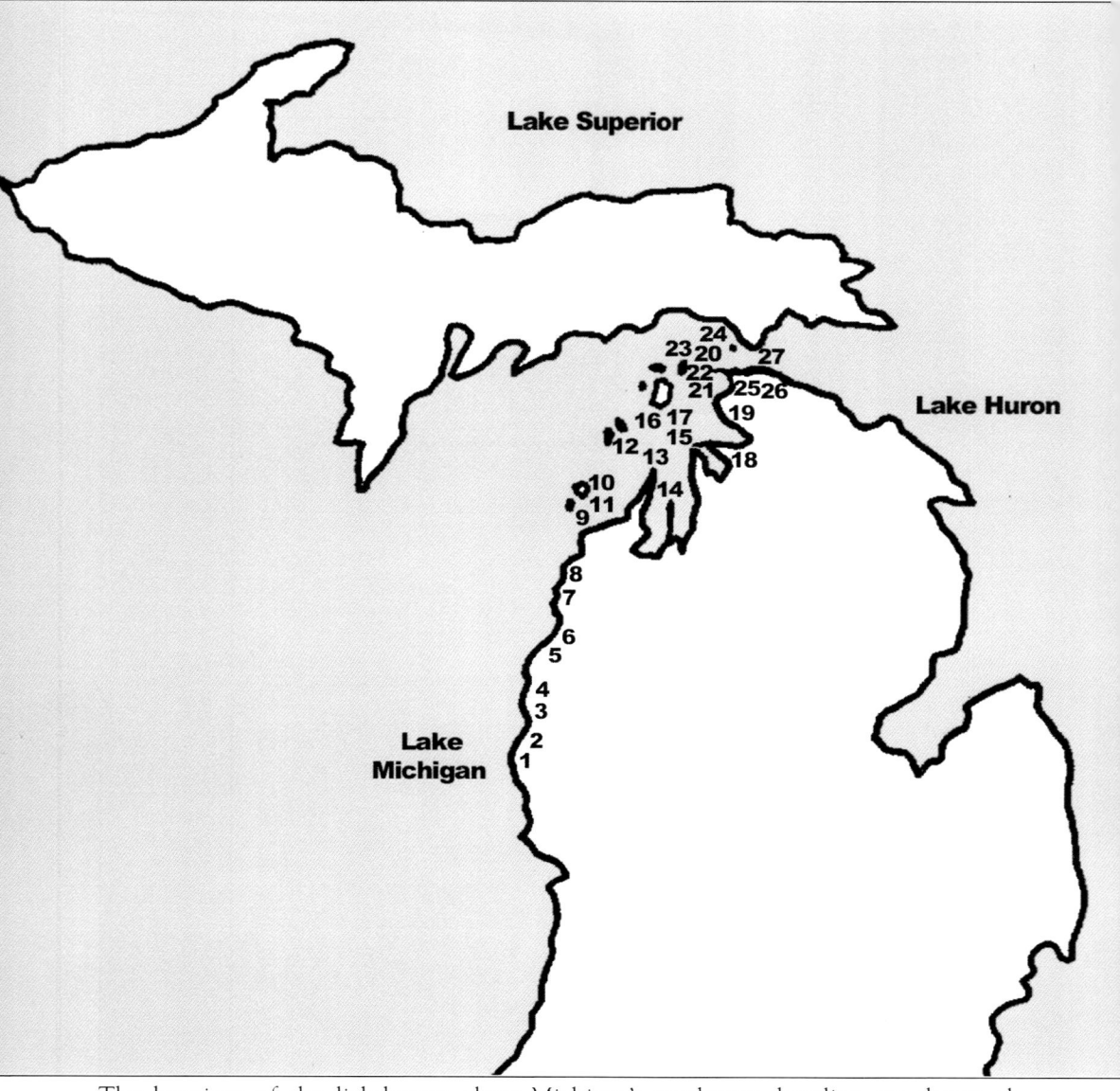

The locations of the lighthouses along Michigan's northwest shoreline are shown above: 1. Little Sable Point, 2. Pentwater, 3. Ludington, 4. Big Sable Point, 5. Manistee, 6. Portage Lake, 7. Frankfort, 8. Point Betsie, 9. South Manitou Island, 10. North Manitou Island, 11. North Manitou Shoal, 12. South Fox Island, 13. Grand Traverse, 14. Old Mission Point, 15. Charlevoix, 16. Beaver Island, 17. St. James, 18. Petoskey, 19. Harbor Springs, 20. Waugoshance Shoal, 21. Skillagalee, 22. Gray's Reef, 23. White Shoal, 24. St. Helena, 25. McGulpin's Point, 26. Old Mackinac Point, 27. Mackinac Bridge.

IMAGES of America
LIGHTHOUSES OF NORTHWEST MICHIGAN

Susan Roark Hoyt

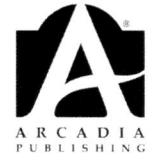

Copyright © 2004 by Susan Roark Hoyt
ISBN 978-0-7385-3313-1

Published by Arcadia Publishing
Charleston, South Carolina

Printed in the United States of America

Library of Congress Catalog Card Number: 2004108331

For all general information contact Arcadia Publishing at:
Telephone 843-853-2070
Fax 843-853-0044
E-mail sales@arcadiapublishing.com
For customer service and orders:
Toll-Free 1-888-313-2665

Visit us on the Internet at www.arcadiapublishing.com

To the Father of Lights who secures our destination.

Contents

Acknowledgments		6
Introduction		7
1.	Lights of the Graveyard of Ships: Little Sable Point Light, Pentwater Pierhead Light, Ludington Pierhead and North Breakwater Lights, and Big Sable Point Light	9
2.	The Lights of Manistee County: Manistee River and Pierhead Lights, Portage Lake North Pier Light	39
3.	Benzie County and the Manitou Island Lights: Frankfort Pierhead and Breakwater Lights, Point Betsie Light, South Manitou Island Light, North Manitou Island Light, North Manitou Shoal Light, and South Fox Island Light	49
4.	The Lights of Grand Traverse Bay: Grand Traverse Light and Old Mission Point Light	73
5.	Charlevoix County and Little Traverse Bay Lights: Charlevoix Pierhead Lights, Beaver Island Light, St. James Light, Petoskey Breakwater Light, and Little Traverse Light	83
6.	Lights of the Mackinac Straits: Waugoshance Shoal Light, Ile Aux Galets Light, Gray's Reef Light, White Shoal Light, and St. Helena Island Light	101
7.	Mackinac Area Lights: McGulpin's Point Light, Old Mackinac Point Light, and Mackinac Bridge	111

Acknowledgments

Unraveling the stories of history cannot be accomplished alone. Each thread contains a part that weaves into the whole. My journey in discovering the history of northwest Michigan lighthouses has led me to many interesting and knowledgeable people who possess fascinating threads of history. Weaving these threads together into the story of this book was made easier by their contributions.

    I would like to thank Nancy Campbell and Phil Ward for freely sharing their stories and pictures. It was a pleasure to spend time with them and to learn from each of them. I am grateful to the wonderful people at Oceana County Historical and Genealogical Society (OCHGS) for their kindness and assistance, to Fred Seaman at the Pentwater Historical Society (PHS) who went the extra mile for me, and to Judy Ranville at Mackinaw Area Public Library (MAPL) for sharing her personal and historical insights.

    Institutions are only as good as the people who manage them. The following institutions contributed significantly to this project and the helpful people on their staffs made my work more enjoyable: Michigan Maritime Museum (MMM), Mason County Historical Society (MCHS), Manistee County Historical Museum (MCHM), Clarke Historical Library CMU (CHL-CMU), Bentley Historical Library (BHL), State Archives of Michigan (SAM), Mackinac State Historic Parks (MSHP), Muskegon County Museum (MCM), Benzonia Public Library (BPL), Walter P. Reuther Library (WPRL), United States Coast Guard (USCG), National Archives (NA), and the Library of Congress (LG).

    I also want to thank my husband Tim for traveling with me on another project, for his unfailing support, and his excellent work on the images. I couldn't have made it without his help. Thanks to Janet Shantz for sharing her computer knowledge and using her superb skills on the maps. Thank you to my friends and family for their support and prayers. And a special thanks to my editor, Maura Brown, who is gifted with words, wonderful to work with, and always encouraging.

    I thank all of you for your part in helping this book come to fruition.

INTRODUCTION

In the early 1800s, northwest Michigan's vast undeveloped pine forests beckoned lumber enthusiasts and settlers to its shores. As the lumber industry emerged, schooners quickly arrived to carry shipments of lumber to ports on Lake Michigan's western side. Unfortunately, channels to Lake Michigan were often little more than shallow rivers or streams that weren't deep enough to receive large vessels. Schooners were forced to drop anchor in the lake and wait in the rolling surf while goods were carried out to them on scows. This process was time-consuming, costly, and often dangerous, if the lake was in a foul mood.

Lumbermen recognized that the improvement of loading conditions was imperative if their businesses were going to flourish. Therefore, they ran piers from the shoreline into the lake, allowing vessels to tie up as they waited for their cargoes to be loaded. This improvement was somewhat effective; however, the piers were difficult for mariners to find during nighttime and in foggy weather, and extensive winter ice damage necessitated expensive repairs each spring.

Vessels traveling the northern waters of Lake Michigan also encountered hidden obstacles, uncommon in the southern waters of the lake. Hidden shoals and reefs stretched for miles beneath the water's surface and threatened to destroy unsuspecting vessels. Safe passages around these areas developed, but their exact locations were difficult to find without the help of navigational aids. It was clear that significant work was essential on many fronts if maritime commerce was going to succeed.

While a few rudimentary lights existed in northern Michigan before 1850, they were often poorly constructed and deteriorated quickly. With the establishment of the Lighthouse Board in 1852, Congress began appropriating significant funds to erect more quality lighthouses and to make necessary harbor improvements. As a result, harbors were dredged to greater depths, they were lined with revetments and piers, and lights were placed at their entrances. Breakwaters were built to calm the waters leading to the channel and coastal lights were placed along the shoreline to mark turning points, safe passages, and points of land that protruded into the water.

A new lighting phenomenon on the Great Lakes also came into existence about this time. Vessels equipped with lights, fog bells, and crews were anchored offshore in the water as temporary lights to mark hidden shoals and reefs. These lightships served for many years until they were replaced with permanent crib lights. Crib lights, which were also new to the lake, consisted of large wooden boxes, filled with stone and concrete, that were sunk in the water directly on the shoal to form a solid foundation for the lighthouse.

The addition of lighthouses significantly cut down on the loss of lives and cargo. However, constant maintenance was required to keep the lights clean and properly functioning. Lighthouse keepers were hired to live in or near the light to handle these tasks. The keeper's life was a tedious one. In addition to lighting and extinguishing the light at the proper times each day, he was given a rigid list of rules that precisely delineated his duties. Included among these rules were 74 general instructions to the keeper, 14 rules on the care of the light and accessories, 36 rules for the use and management of lights, and 15 rules for painting. Various other rules described how the dwelling and grounds were to be kept at all times. These rules were strictly adhered to and enforced by surprise inspections held periodically by the Lighthouse Inspector.

While performing his duties, the keeper also kept a watchful eye on the lake, checking for any vessels that might be in distress. He was always ready to risk his life to help save others and frequently housed and provided for rescued victims, at his own expense, until they had recuperated. Though a keeper could be active in life-saving, it was not his primary duty and he did not have the necessary equipment required to perform large scale rescues. Those rescues did not occur until the government established the United States Life-Saving Service, whose sole purpose was to perform life-saving rescues. As Life-Saving Stations became established along the Lake Michigan shoreline, their crews often worked in tandem with the lighthouse keeper during emergencies.

With the discovery of electricity changes occurred at the lights which ultimately led to full automation and the end of occupied lighthouses. Stations that once bustled with life were left empty to become victims of deterioration and vandalism. While some of these noble structures have disappeared, many are being restored today in an effort to preserve the memory of Michigan's rich maritime history and the valiant men and women who guarded the lake and illuminated the way for future maritime commerce and recreation.

One

LIGHTS OF THE GRAVEYARD OF SHIPS
LITTLE SABLE POINT LIGHT, PENTWATER PIERHEAD LIGHT, LUDINGTON PIERHEAD AND NORTH BREAKWATER LIGHTS, AND BIG SABLE POINT LIGHT

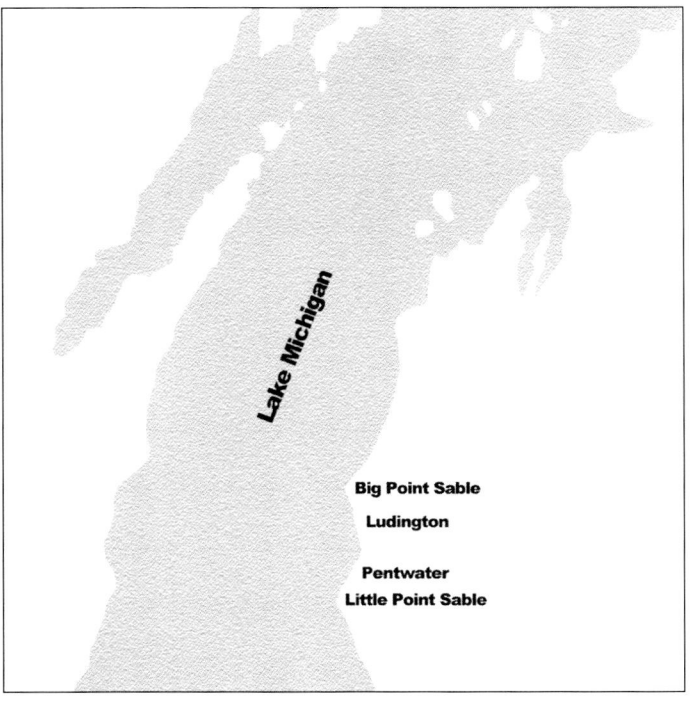

The portion of Lake Michigan that lies between Little Sable Point and Big Sable Point is known as the "Graveyard of Ships." In this 20-mile span of water, over 60 vessels went down between the years 1848–1881. Storm-driven west winds often blew sailing vessels and early model steamers into this bight or concave curve of land between the two points. Lacking sufficient power to overcome the wind and clear the point, many of these vessels became trapped in the bight, blown around helplessly, until they struck bottom and were destroyed. To assist mariners traveling through these perilous waters, the following lighthouses were placed along this short, but dangerous portion of the lake: Little Sable Point Light, Pentwater Pierhead Light, Ludington Pierhead and Breakwater Lights, and Big Sable Point Light.

In c. 1872 Congress appropriated $35,000 and a set aside a 39-acre parcel of land for the construction of a lighthouse on Little Sable Point. Since the construction site was on a remote section of beach, with no roads leading to it, a temporary dwelling was set up for the workers and a dock was built to receive incoming supplies.

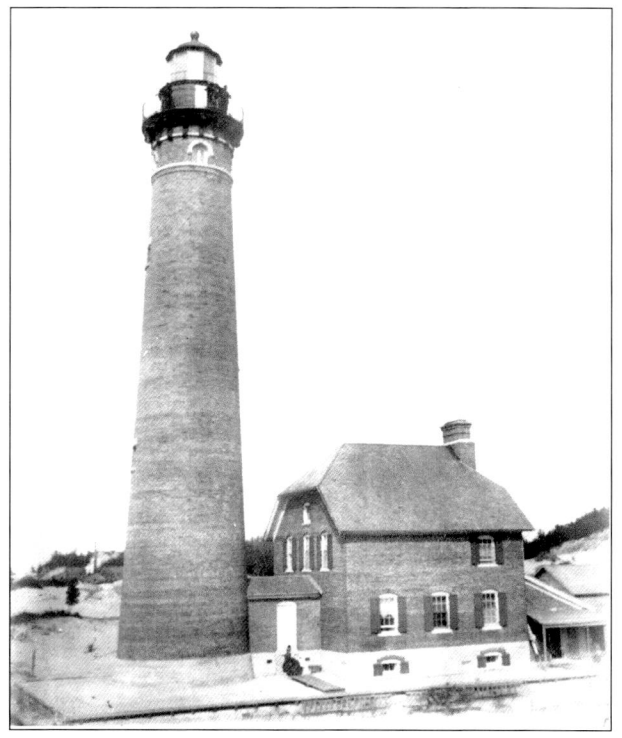

Over 100 pilings one foot in diameter were driven into the sand to form a solid base for the lighthouse tower. Cut stone was then laid over the pilings and a red brick tower was built on top. An enclosed passageway connected the tower to the matching red brick keeper's dwelling. The first floor of the keeper's house contained a living room, kitchen, bedroom, and oil storage room. The second floor contained only bedrooms. (OCHGS)

A lean-to used for wood storage was added to the dwelling on the opposite end of the tower. Since it was decided that the red brick was of good enough quality to withstand the weather, the tower and dwelling were left unpainted. The completed light, named "Petite Pointe Au Sable Lighthouse," began shining at the beginning of the 1874 shipping season. (OCHGS)

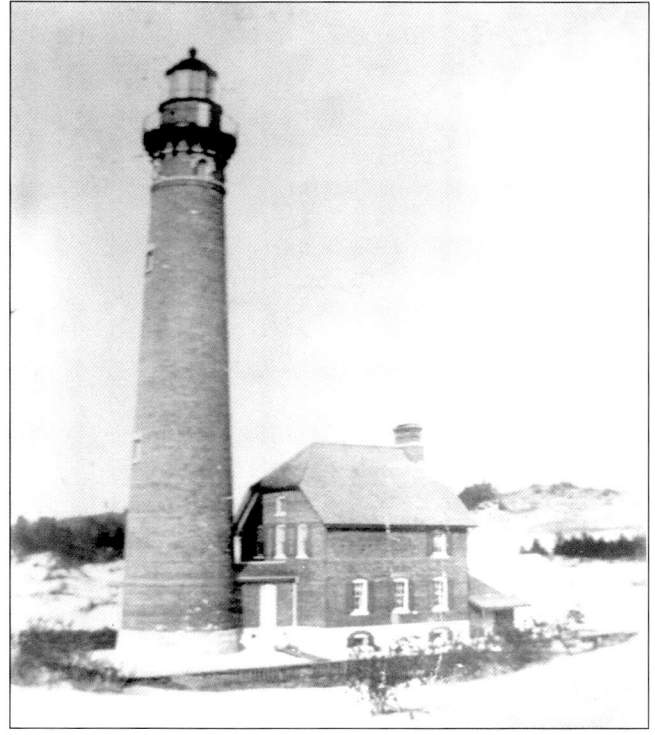

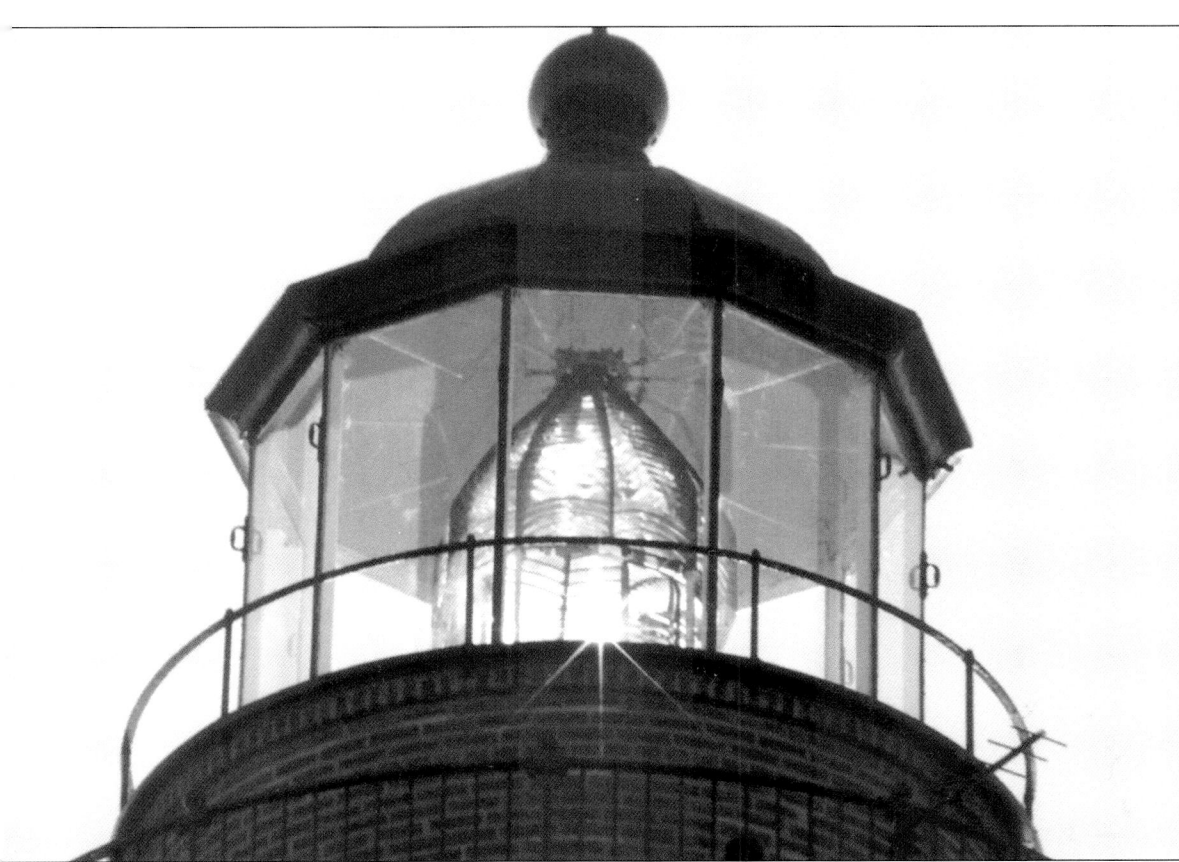

The tower was lighted with a Third Order Fresnel Lens. Developed in 1822 by French physicist Augustin Fresnel, the Fresnel lenses consisted of glass pieces supported by a brass framework that usually took on the shape of a beehive or a bullseye. Lenses ranged from First to Sixth Order depending upon their size and the intensity of their beam. A Sixth Order lens was just under two feet tall, while the First Order lens stood nearly twelve feet tall. The smaller Third and Fourth Order lenses were often used as coastal and harbor lights on the Great Lakes.

Fresnel's design used one large lamp placed in the center of the lens as the light source. A series of mirrors and prisms were then used to reflect and refract the light in order to make its unified beam shine farther across the water. While the Fresnel lens was remarkably advanced for its time and virtually doubled the visible range of light beams, its acceptance was resisted by the U.S. Superintendent of Lighthouses. It seems he was very tight with funds and he was also loyal to his friend who supplied the lighting apparatus for most of the U.S. lights at that time. It took 30 years and the removal of the superintendent from office before American lighthouses were refitted with the life-saving Fresnel lens.

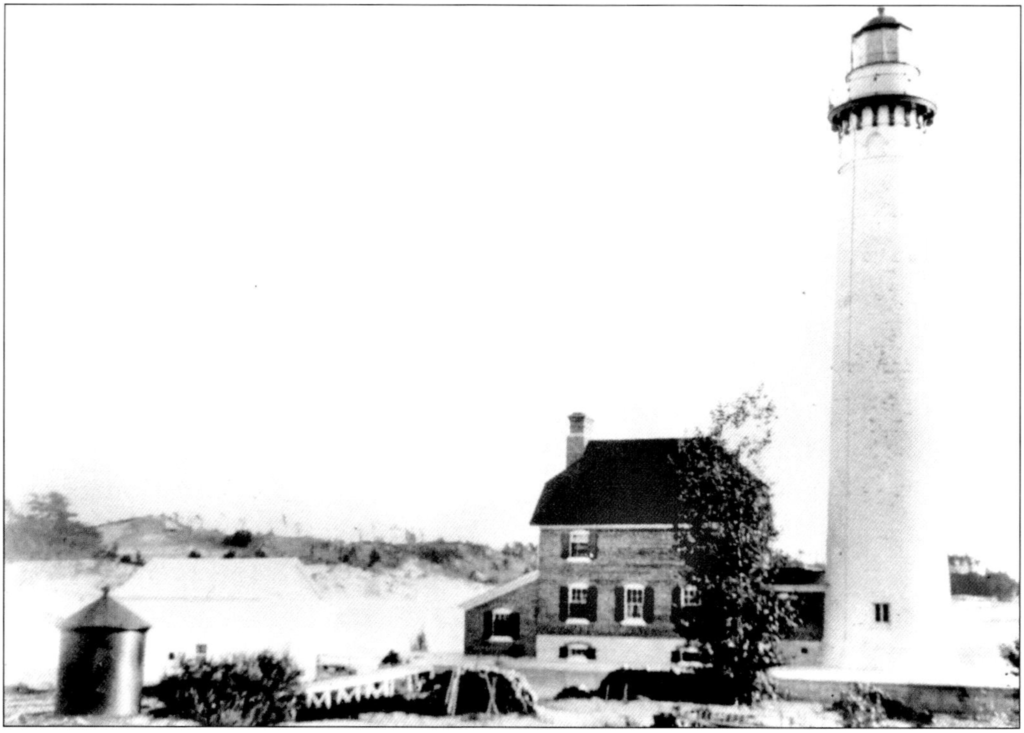

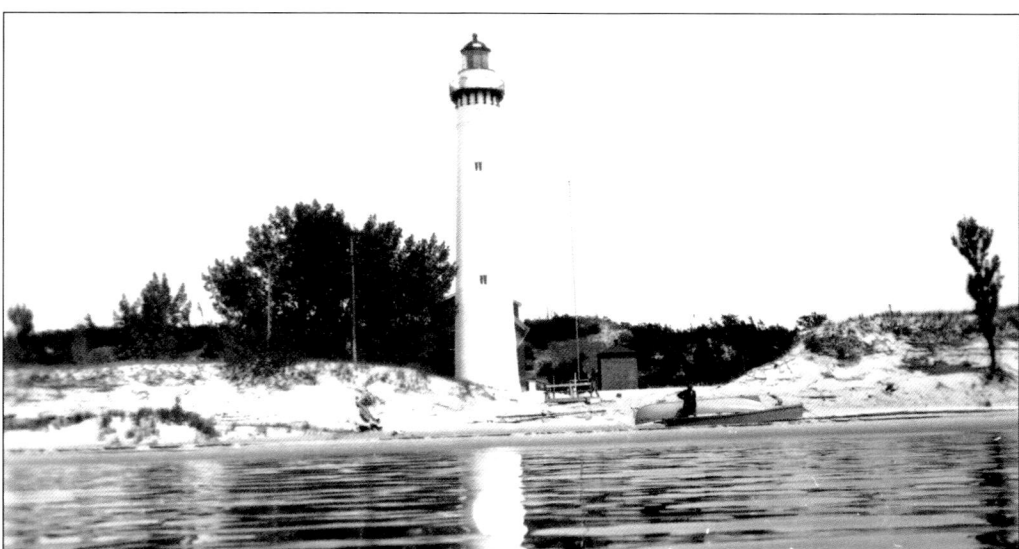

Since the lighthouse was built on a desolate piece of land with no roads leading to it, the oil for the kerosene lamps was delivered offshore by a tugboat. It was retrieved from the tug and brought to shore by rowboat, then carried by hand in five-gallon cans to the storage tank (lower left). It took two hard-working men 12 hours each to accomplish this task. (OCHGS)

The 115-foot tall tower, with 145 steps in its spiral stairway, was one of the tallest lights on Lake Michigan. Standing on the shoreline with little protection from the elements, it is said that the tower could sway as much as 12 inches during severe storms. (OCHGS)

Mariners complained that they could not see the tower during daylight hours because it blended into the landscape. As a result the tower was painted white in 1900, and the keepers from that time on begrudgingly added yearly painting of the tower to their list of duties. Pictured here standing on the parapet are keeper Wallace Hall and his assistant, Henrik Olsen, taking their turn at repainting the tower in 1922. (OCHGS)

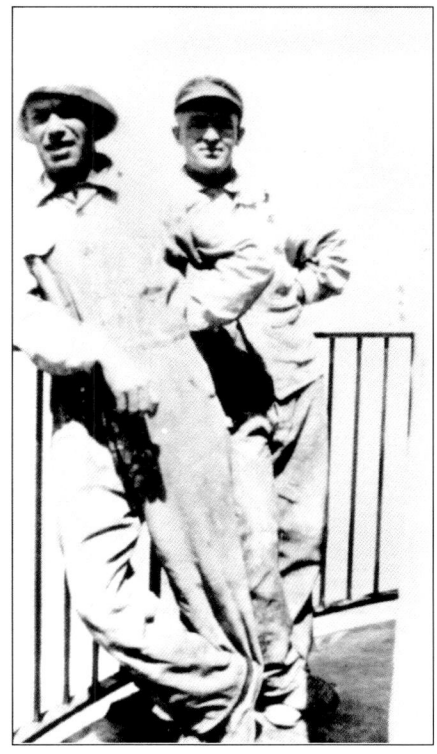

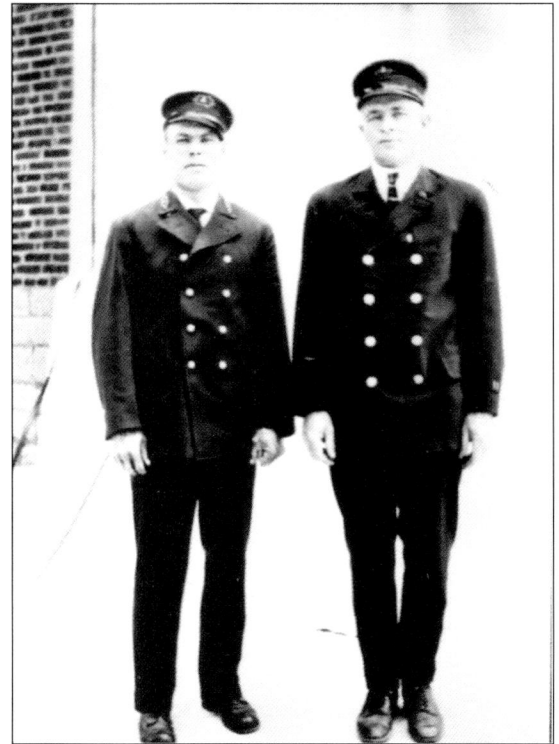

Lighthouse personnel were often transferred or promoted and it was not uncommon for them to serve at more than one lighthouse in their careers. Including Little Sable Point Light, Olsen (right) served at four lighthouses in Michigan and Wisconsin before he became the assistant and eventually the keeper at Old Mackinac Point Light. (OCHGS)

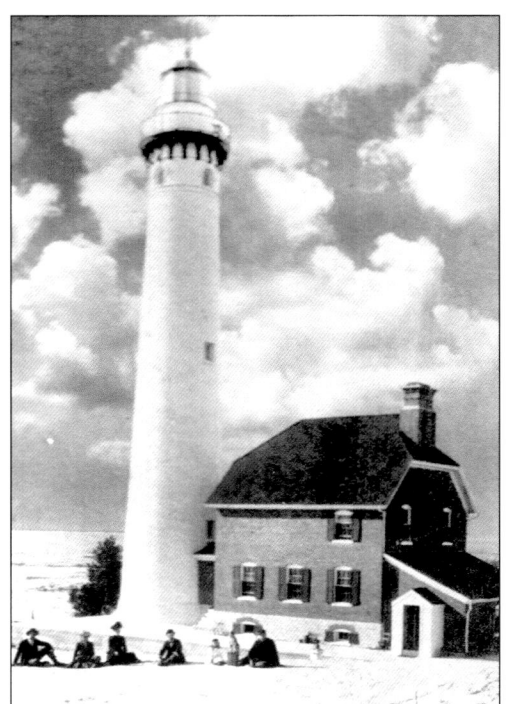 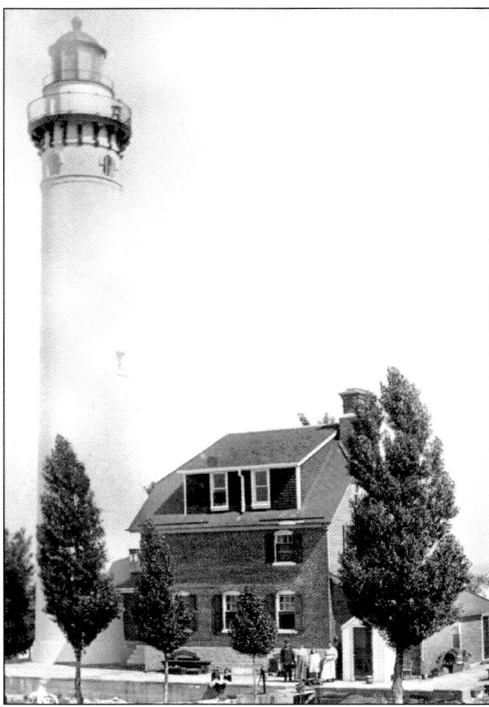

Shortly after the name of the lighthouse was changed to Little Sable Point Light c. 1910, dormers were added to each side of the dwelling to accommodate the keeper's growing family. These pictures, taken a few years apart, show the difference in appearance with the addition of the dormers. (OCHGS, MMM)

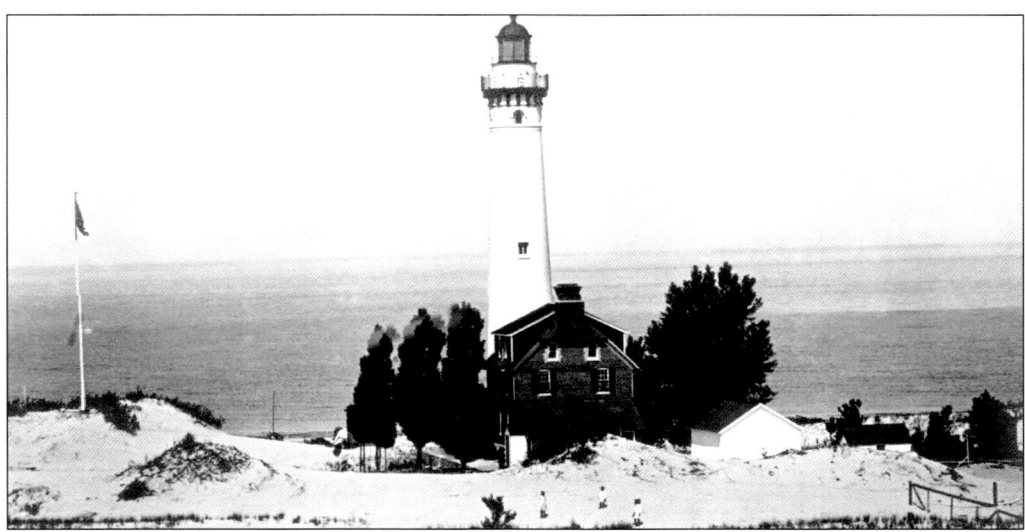

A view looking from the rear of the dwelling toward the lake offers an alternate perspective of the remodeled dwelling and the lighthouse grounds. A brick oil storage shed, a barn, and additional out buildings had been added to the property by the time this picture was taken, c. 1917. A trail with a boardwalk leading to the lighthouse had also been added, which made it possible for some of the supplies to be delivered by land.

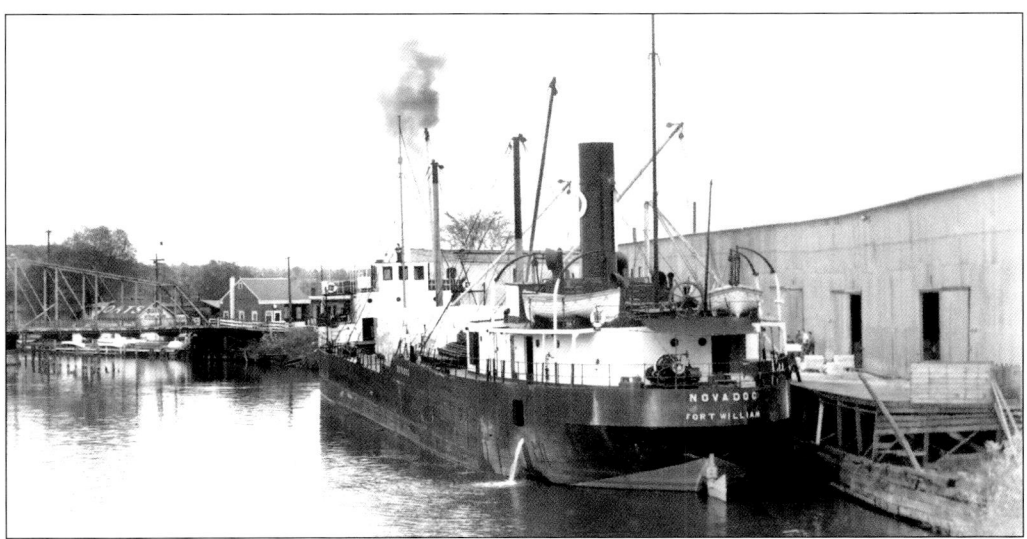

The infamous storm of November 11, 1940, marked a day of tragedy on Lake Michigan. A storm that swept across the nation, killing over 100 people, hit hardest between Little Sable Point and Big Sable Point. With wind gusts up to 110 miles per hour and waves 30–40 feet high, six vessels were lost on the lake that day. The *Novadoc* was one of those vessels.

According to an account given by Lloyd H. Belcher, crewman of the *Novadoc*, the ship left Chicago in the early morning fog. Unable to get a current weather report as they left the harbor, they decided to continue on toward Quebec. As they watched the barometer fall and felt the winds increase, they knew they were headed for a big storm. Attempts to reach the east shore and ride in the lee of the land failed when the wind shifted and grew in intensity. The west shore was too far away by this time to return to through the burgeoning waves. (MMM)

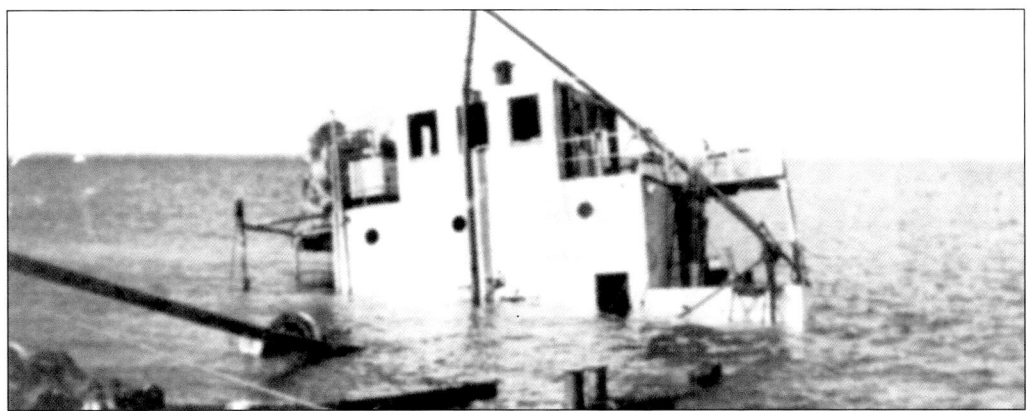

The captain attempted to ride the storm out in the middle of the lake but the powerful waves washed the ship dangerously close to shore near Little Point Sable. The surf of the water returning from shore whirled them around so that they were hit head-on by the waves. Immediately the water crashed into the wheelhouse and broke the windows out. The helpless ship was carried about two miles north of the lighthouse, where she hit bottom and broke in two. As she filled with water, two groups of men huddled together desperately, one group in the captain's office and the other on the opposite end of the ship in the oiler's room. They spent the long cold night listening to the waves pound against the walls and hoping the water wouldn't break through. (MMM)

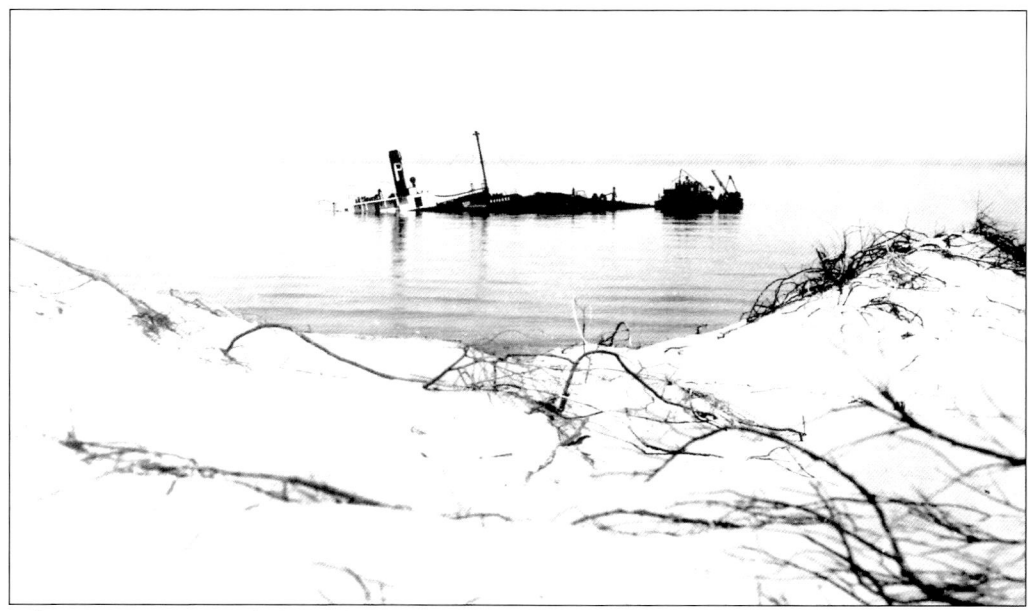

When morning arrived the sailors spotted three men on shore and waved them down. With their hope renewed, they waited through that day and night for help to come. A great crowd had gathered to cheer them on, but no one dared to venture out into the wild surf to try to rescue them. Although they were only 700 feet from shore it seemed like a million miles. (OCHGS)

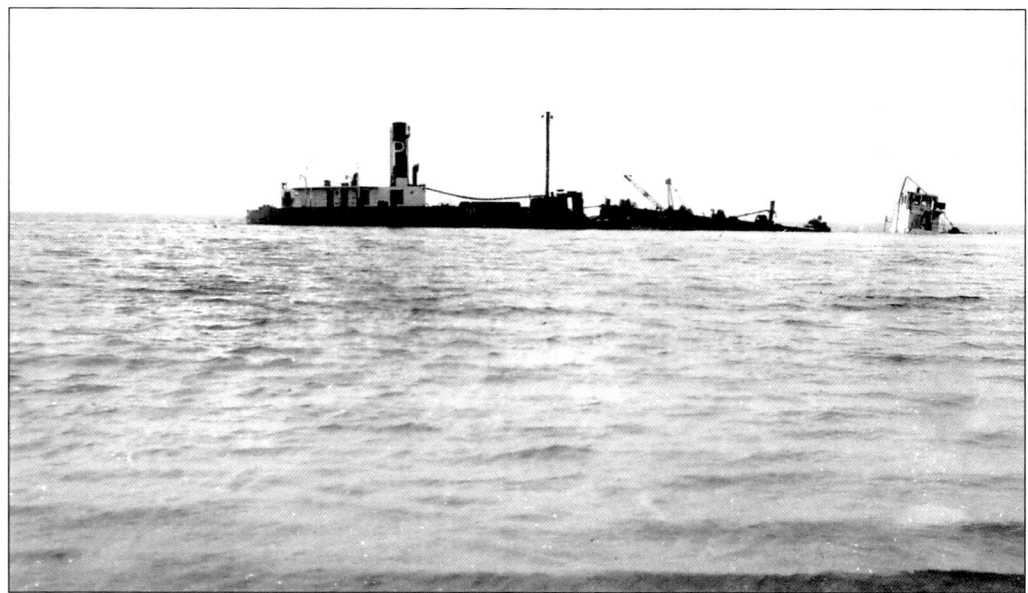

After 36 hours on the crippled ship, the sailors spotted the fishing tug *Three Brothers* coming toward them. As soon as it arrived the crew quickly embarked and were taken eight arduous miles north to the safety of Pentwater Harbor. It was later learned that one of the crewmen of the *Three Brothers* had been among the crowd watching from shore the previous day. Realizing there was life stranded on board, he knew he had to go out and try to rescue them. After two failed attempts the tug successfully reached the weary crew. (OCHGS)

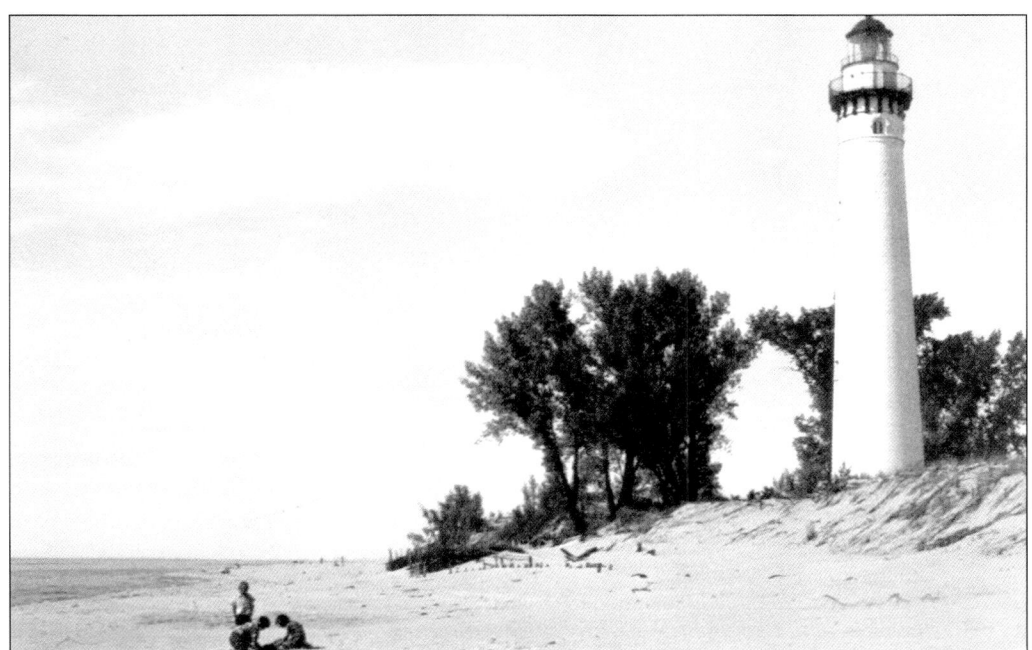

Little Sable Point Light was electrified in 1954 and fully automated in 1955. As a result of these modernizations it was no longer necessary to have a keeper on site. In order to cut maintenance costs, the Coast Guard tore down all the beautiful brick buildings except the tower. A concrete retaining wall was then built and buried in the sand in front of the tower to help combat erosion. (OCHGS)

To further cut expenses, the tower was sand-blasted back to its original red brick in 1974. It remains in that condition today with the original Fresnel lens still secure in the lantern room. With the use of the modern Global Positioning System the day marker is no longer needed by passing vessels.

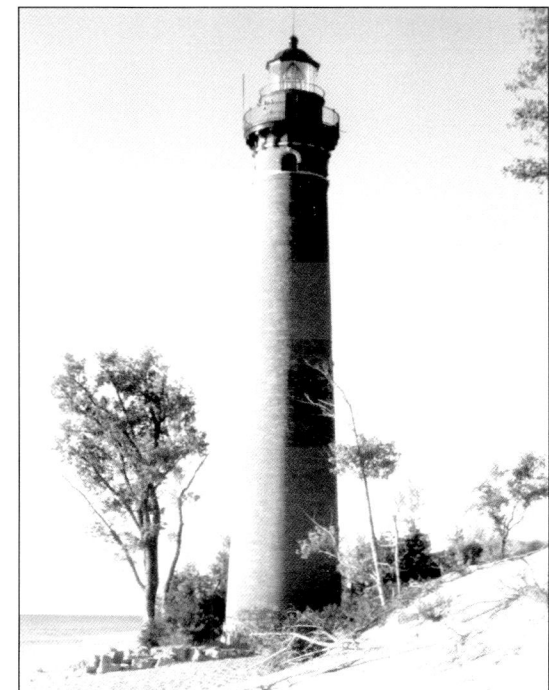

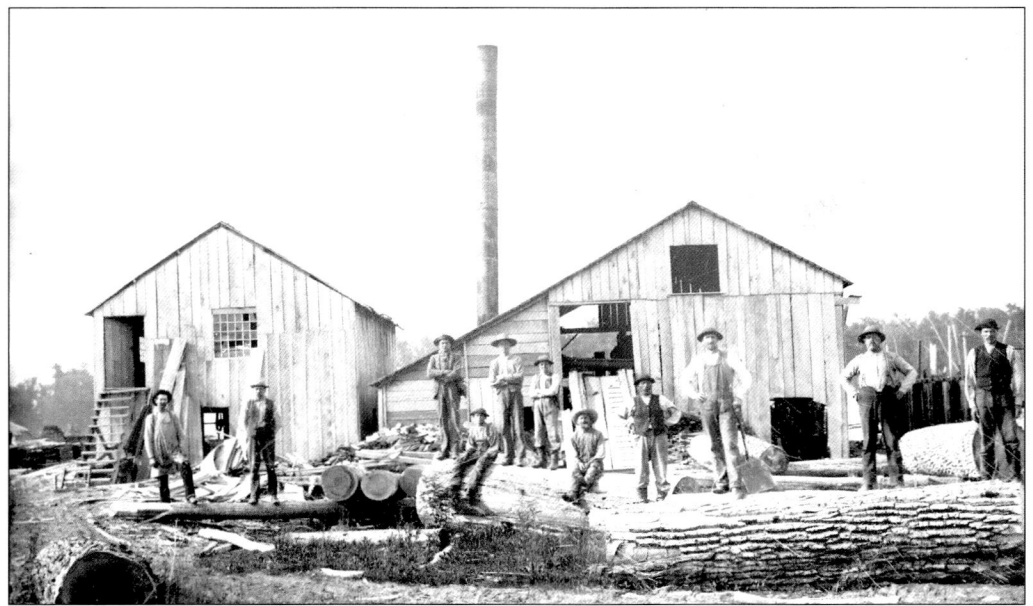

In the early 1800s, western Michigan was covered with vast pine forests. Lumbermen swarmed to the eastern shoreline of Lake Michigan to seek their fortunes by taking advantage of this bounty. One such man was Charles Mears, who arrived to purchase land along the shore from White Hall to the Ludington area. In 1855 he began constructing a sawmill on the north side of the channel in Pentwater. To aid with his lumber business, Mears closed the marshy stream of water that connected Pentwater Lake and Lake Michigan and opened a new, more direct channel south of the stream. The picture above is from a tin type original of one of the early mills in the Pentwater area. (CHL)

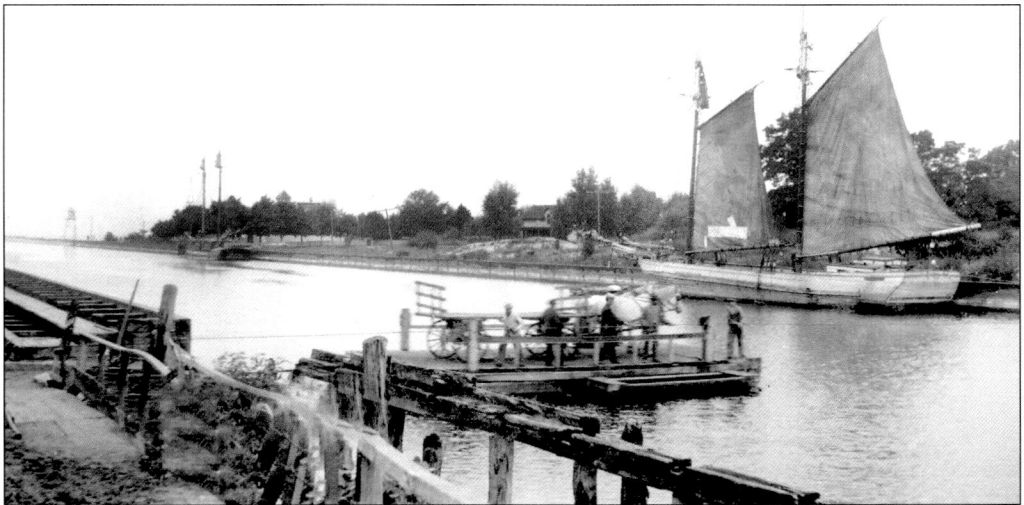

When the new channel was opened, people could no longer wade across the stream as they had done previously. A ferry system was established in 1858 to carry goods, as well as transport passengers crossing the channel to catch the train or to visit friends on the other side. The ferry consisted of a wooden scow that was pulled across the channel on a cable which ran from shore to shore. It remained in service until a swinging bridge was built across the river in 1926. (PHS)

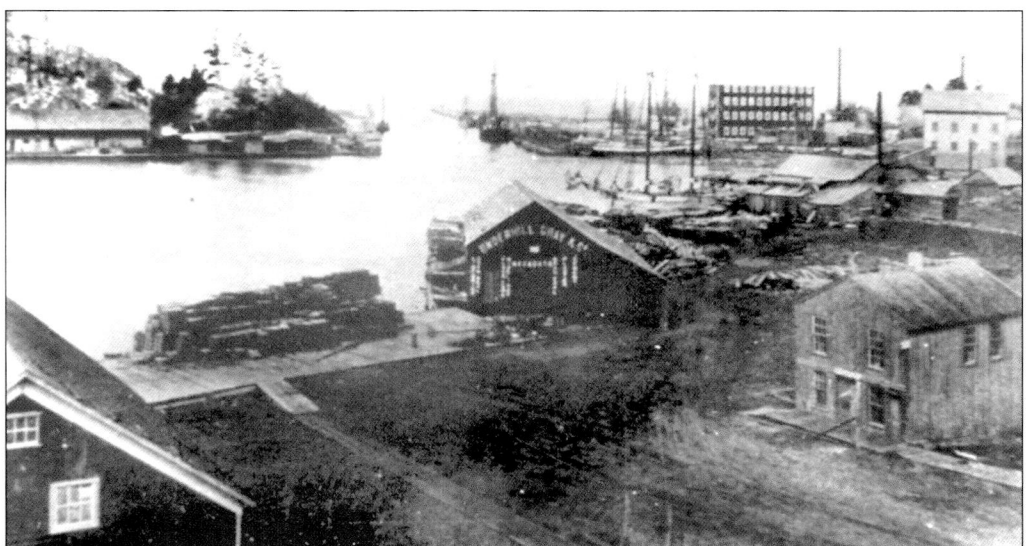

In the early days, sailing vessels could not enter the new channel because it was too shallow. To remedy this situation, Mears built piers out into the lake from which the vessels could be loaded. However, maintenance proved to be very costly, since yearly ice storms caused a great deal of damage to these piers. In 1867, the U.S. Army Corps of Engineers was persuaded to begin a program to widen and deepen the harbor and to line it with piers. (PHS)

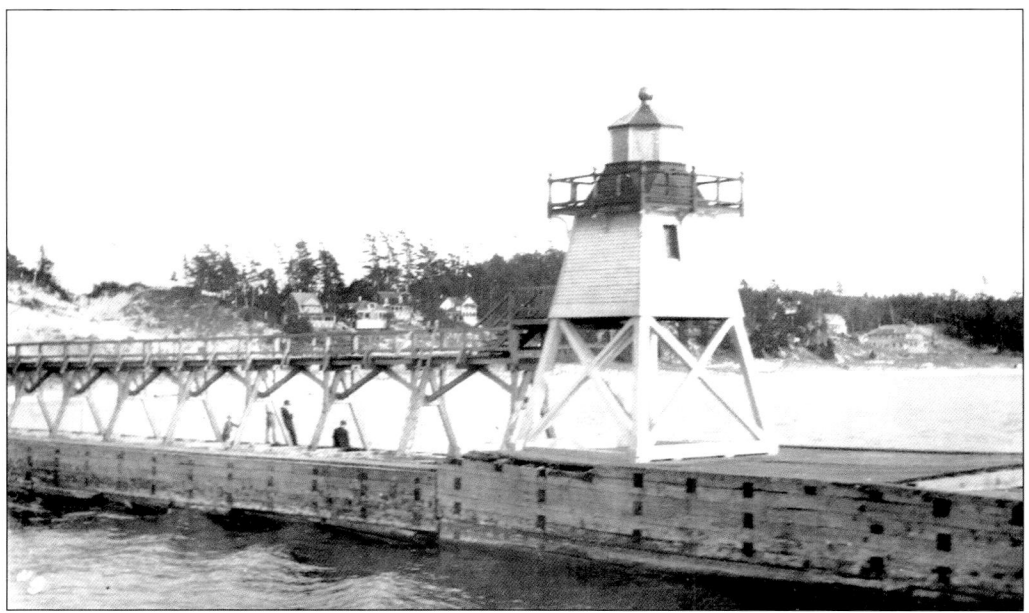

A c. 1912 picture shows the lighthouse that was added to the south pier in 1873. The wooden pyramidal tower had an open framework base and was connected to the shore by a raised catwalk. This light remained operational until it was replaced by a skeletal steel tower in 1937. (PHS)

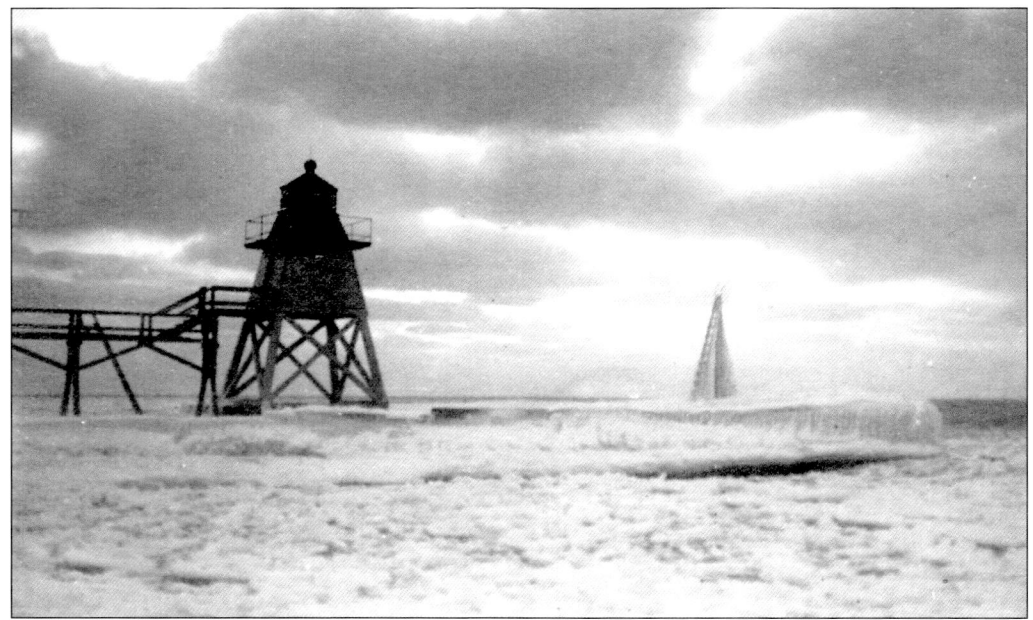

A raised catwalk was necessary to enable the keeper to reach the light in foul weather. During storms, waves often swept over the pier, washing away anything that wasn't fastened down. The catwalk allowed the keeper to walk above most of the storm-driven waves. The handrail was an added benefit when walking on the ice during the winter. (PHS)

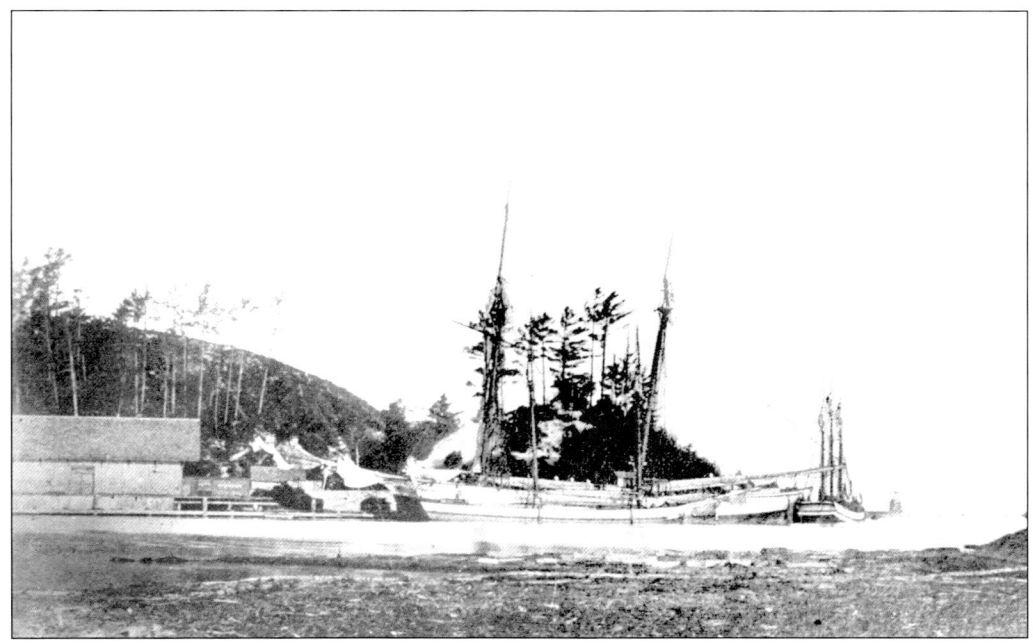

The Pentwater Pierhead Light can be seen on the far right of this 1878 view of the harbor. When lumber supplies were depleted by the early 1900s, the harbor was used primarily by ships serving the agricultural, fishing, and tourist industries. (PHS)

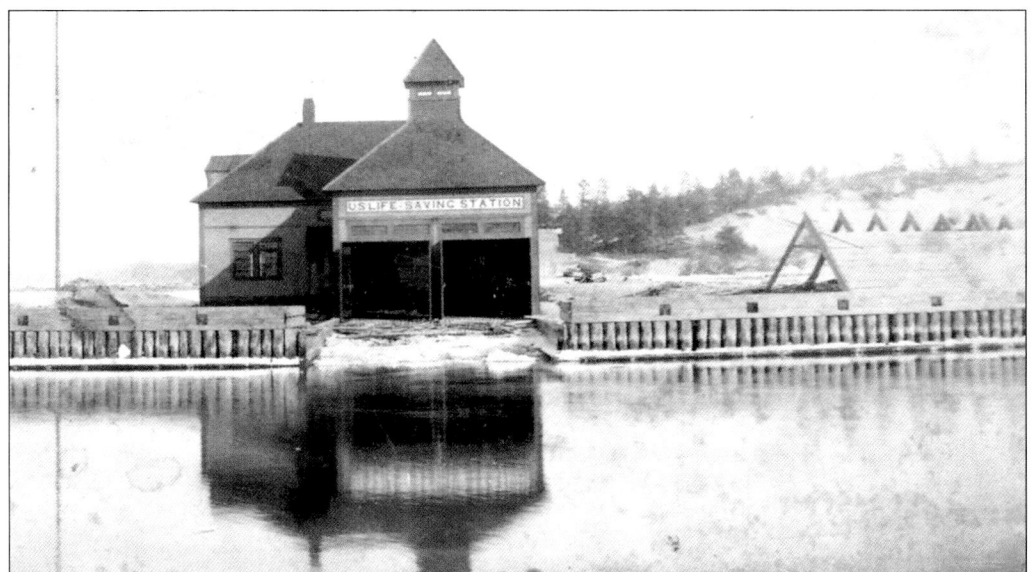

In 1878 the United States adopted the Act to Organize the Life-Saving Service to assist those in peril on the seas and lakes. The Life-Saving Service provided equipment for crews whose sole purpose was to rescue people from distressed vessels. In 1886 a Life-Saving Station was built in Pentwater on the north side of the channel. (PHS)

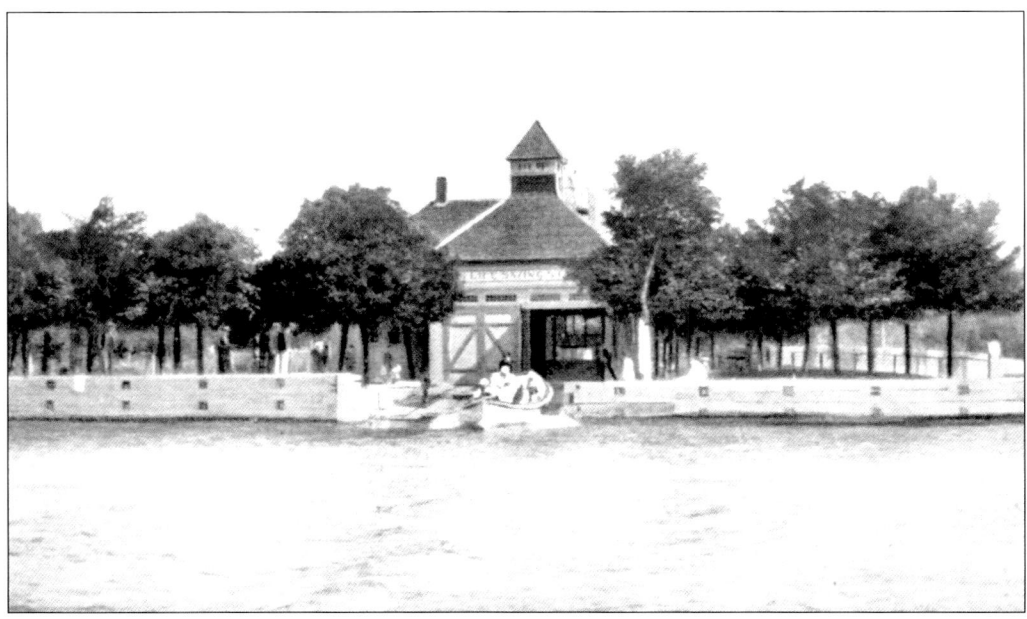

Architect Albert Bibb designed this #3 type station. Eleven stations of this style were known to exist on Lake Michigan in the years 1886–1893. The #3 type station contained a gable-roof dwelling for the crew with a semi-detached boathouse. An enclosed lookout tower with a steeply pitched hip roof sat on top of the boathouse. (MMM)

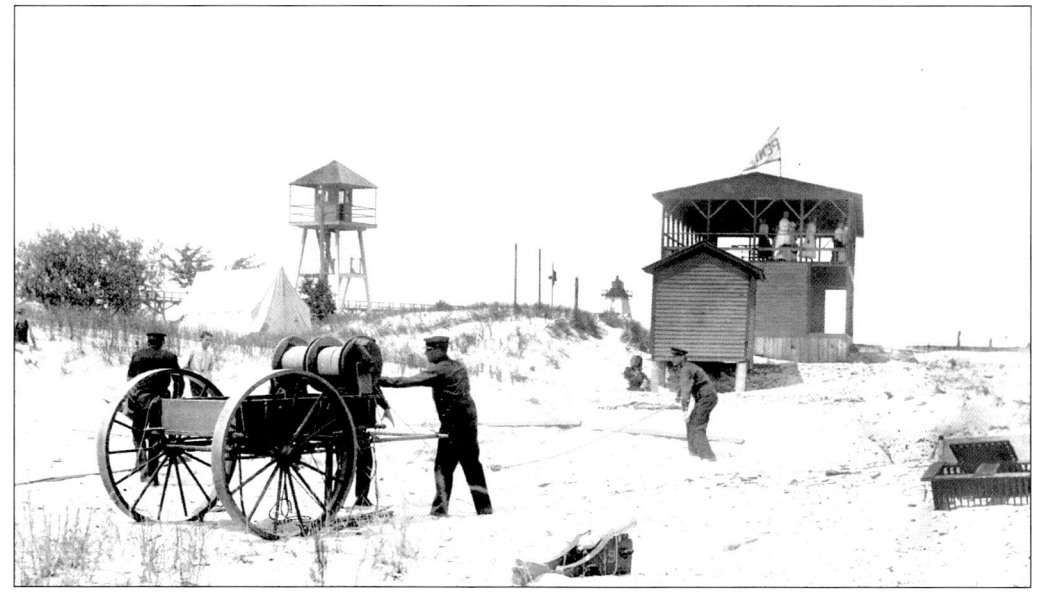

When possible, life-saving rescues were performed from land. The Lyle gun, seen on the bottom of the picture, was used to shoot a line out to the distressed ship. The crew secured the line on the ship and a breeches buoy or seat-like device was tied to it. The "victim" sat in the breeches buoy and was brought to shore along the line using a pulley system. (MMM)

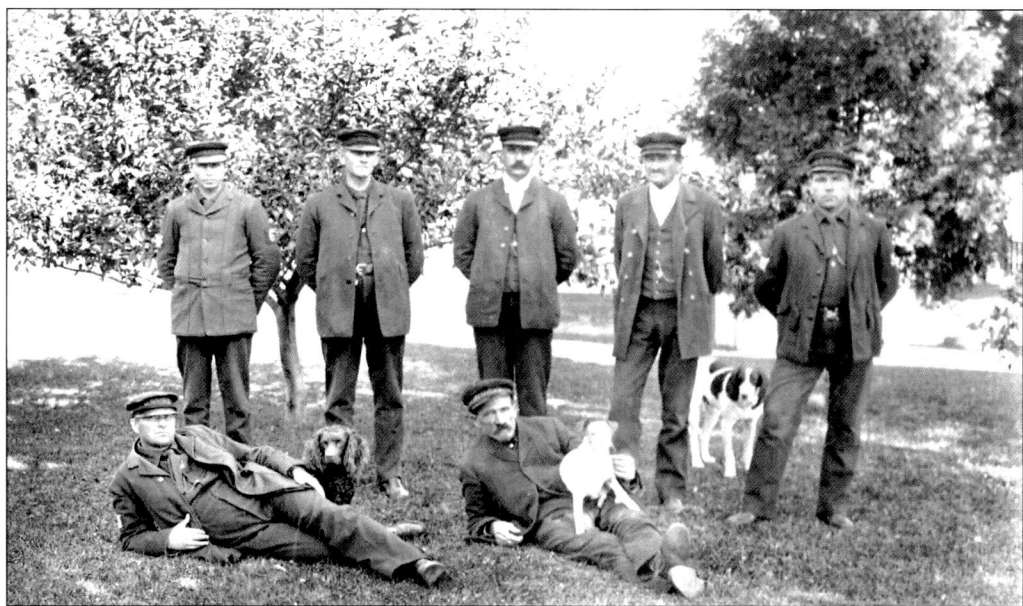

Pictured from left to right are: (front row) A. Peck, G.W. Grant; (back row) Pierson, E.E. Pugh, C.G. Edlund, the station's first keeper, Martin Ewald, and E. Nienhaus, who formed one of the early Pentwater life-saving crews. Crewmen were required to be on duty 24 hours a day during the navigation season, which lasted from April until December. They received one day off per week, weather permitting. In the first eight years of the station's existence, the life-savers were credited with rescuing 35 people. (PHS)

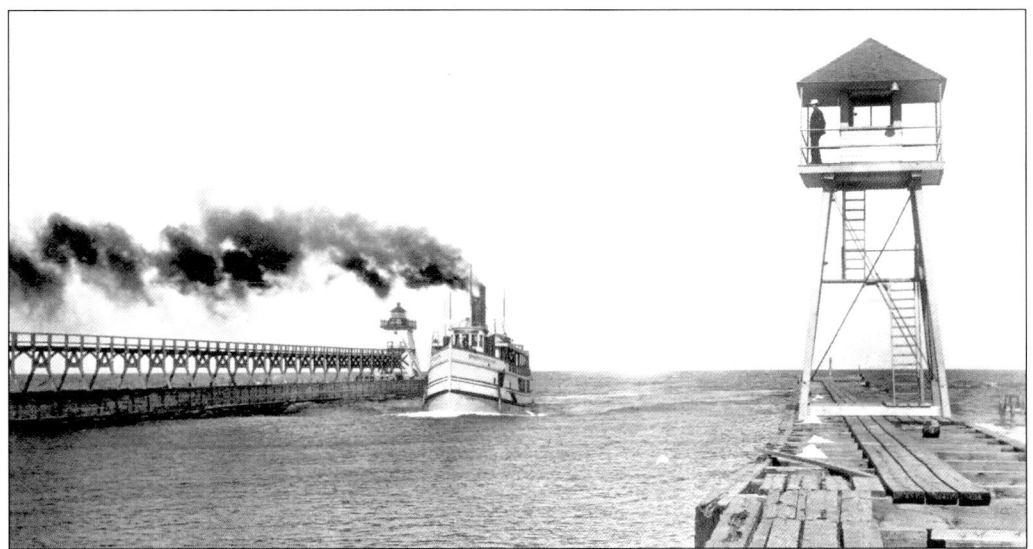

A view looking out toward Lake Michigan shows the channel entrance and both wooden piers. The north pier was a crib-like structure. Stones filled the crib to give it strength and stability while wooden planks formed a walkway along its surface. The Life-Saving Station's lookout tower was added to the extended north pier after the station was built. The location of this tower greatly improved the watchman's ability to monitor lake activity. (PHS)

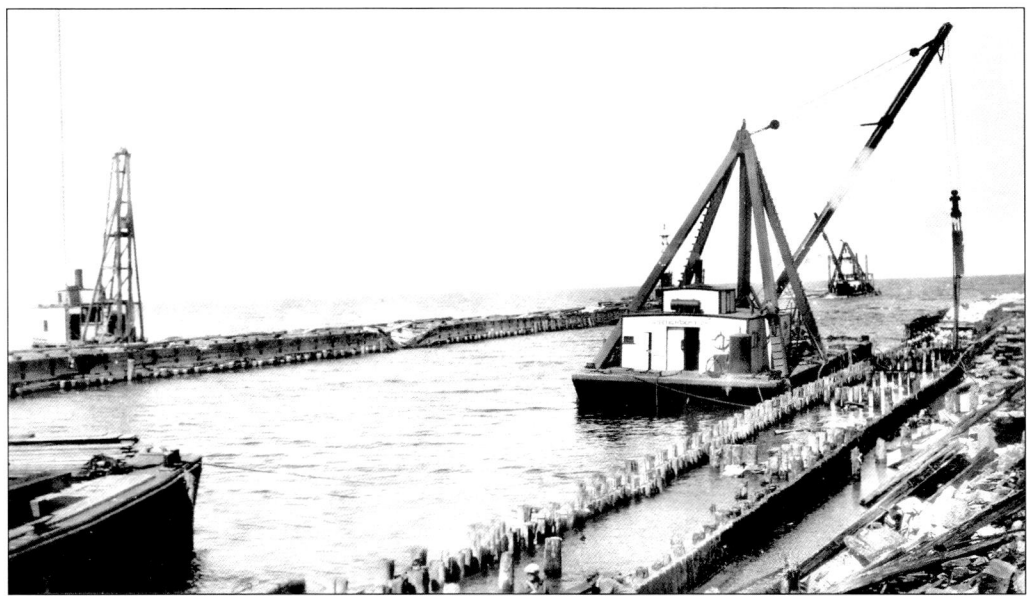

From 1917 until 1931, the federal government abandoned maintenance of the harbor. In 1931 a government dredge returned and removed over 20,000 cubic feet of sand from the channel. Instead of dumping the sand into the lake, it was piled on the sides of the piers, where it constantly seeped back into the channel. Two years later, the government returned to dredge the channel again and resume responsibility for its maintenance. This photograph depicts the 1938 harbor improvement project. The modern skeletal tower that replaced the original light can be seen on the end of the south pier. (MMM)

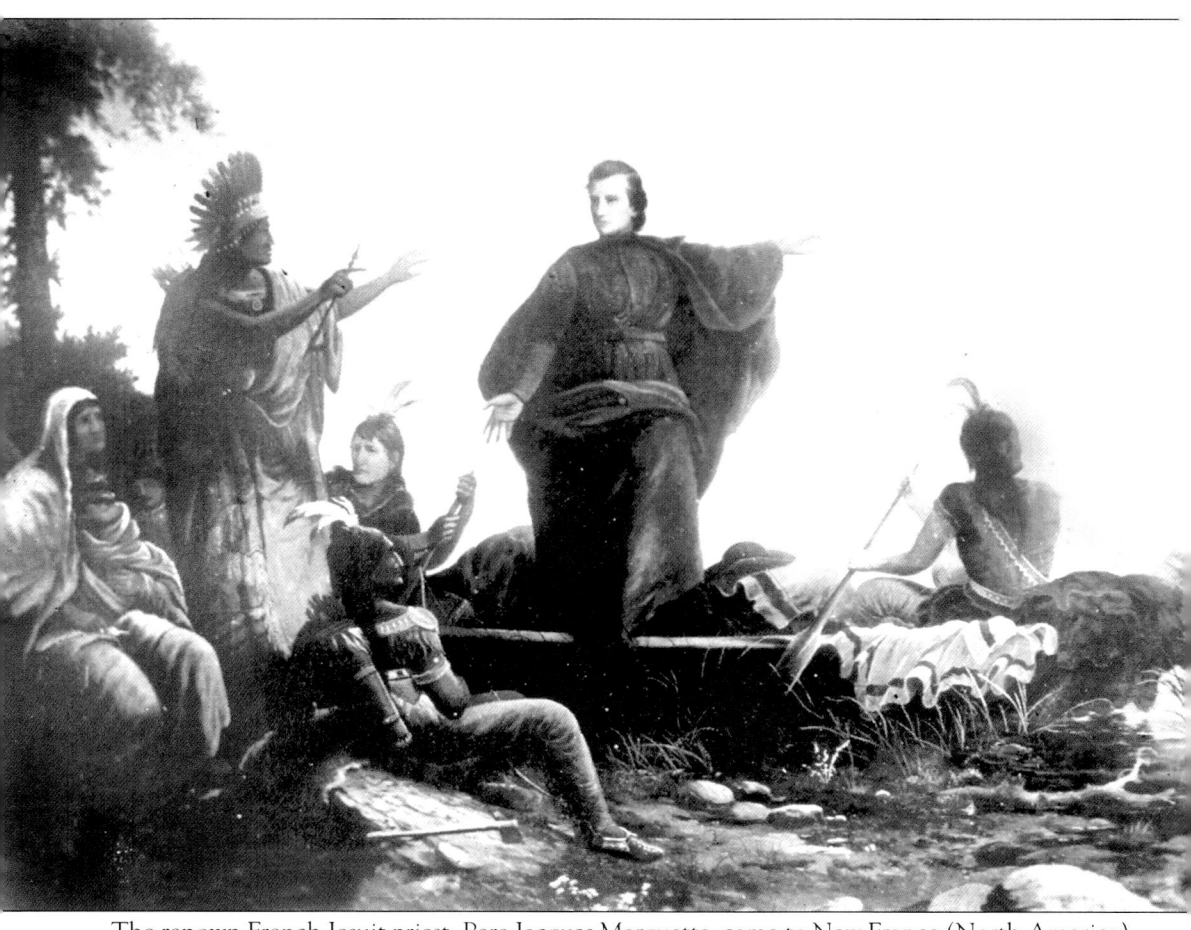

The renown French Jesuit priest, Pere Jacques Marquette, came to New France (North America) in 1666 to bring Christianity to the area. In 1671 he established a mission in the Straits of Mackinac at St. Ignace, Michigan.

After learning of a great river to the south called the Mississippi, he eagerly joined an expedition to explore and map Lake Michigan and the great Mississippi River Valley. However, by the time Pere Marquette and his group approached the Arkansas River, they realized that the Mississippi probably did not lead to the Pacific Ocean, as they had hoped, but rather to the Gulf of Mexico. Consequently, they decided to end their mission and return to Mackinac with the valuable maps they had already made.

Marquette spent the next few months at Mackinac recuperating from the dysentery he had acquired on the trip and then headed south, hoping to establish a mission among the Illini tribes. Unfortunately, he suffered a relapse and died en route on May 18, 1675. Although there is some dispute, it seems likely that Pere Marquette died and was buried in the Ludington/Frankfort area. Two years after his death, his remains were exhumed and taken to his beloved mission in St. Ignace, where they were re-buried.

The city of Ludington was originally named Pere Marquette after this explorer priest. The Pere Marquette Lake at the east end of the Ludington channel and the Pere Marquette River, which flowed through the lake and into Lake Michigan, were also named in his honor. (CHL)

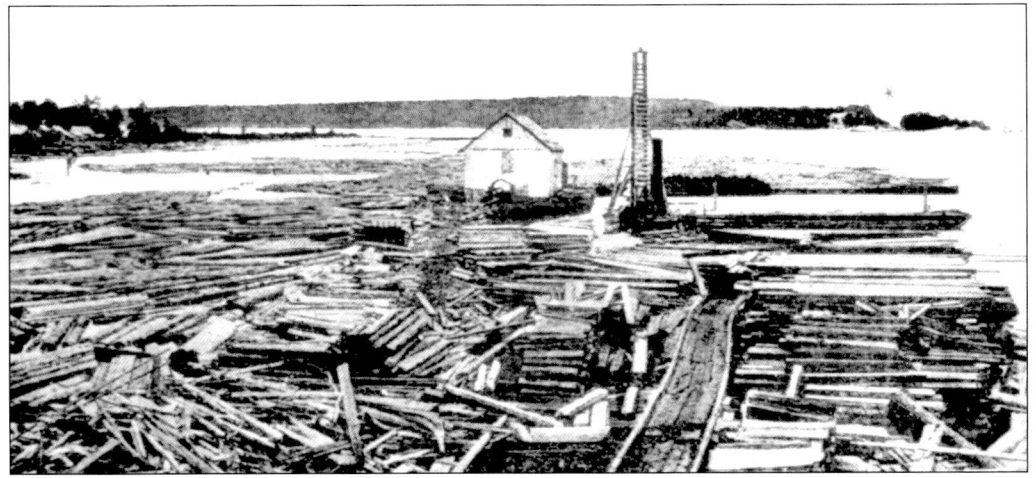

Burr Caswell and his family came to the Ludington area in 1845 and became its first permanent white settlers. A few years later, a sawmill was opened, which marked the beginning of the lucrative lumbering business. Pictured above is Eber Brock Ward's south mill as it looked in 1869. Eber Brock Ward, son of lighthouse keeper Eber Ward of Bois Blanc Island Light in Lake Huron, was an astute businessman who eventually became a multimillionaire. His north and south mills combined gave him one of the largest mills in the world at that time. They supplied much of the lumber used to rebuild Chicago after the fire of 1871. (MCHS)

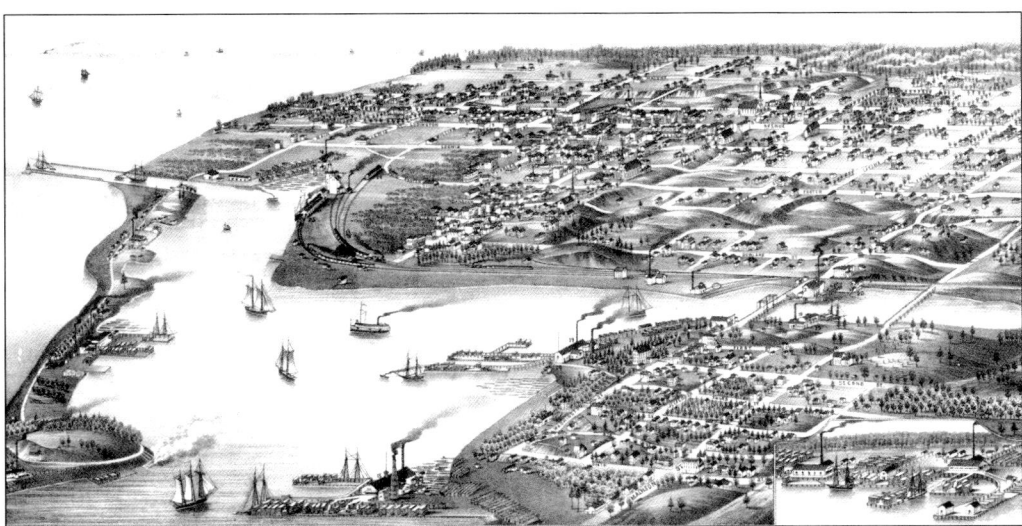

In 1859 a schooner arrived from Chicago to pick up a load of lumber but couldn't navigate the shallow channel. It was forced to drop anchor in Lake Michigan and wait while the lumber was lightered out to it. This was a very slow and costly process. Lumberman Charles Mears knew the channel had to be improved to accommodate large vessels if his business was going to survive, so he hired a crew to begin hand-digging a new channel. This new channel was opened up north of the channel used by Pere Marquette in the 1600s.

By the late 1860s, Congress had become involved in harbor improvements. Piers and revetments were built along the river's edge and a light was placed on the end of the south pier in 1871. In this overview of the harbor, the piers of the new channel and the light can be seen on the left side of the picture. (MCHS)

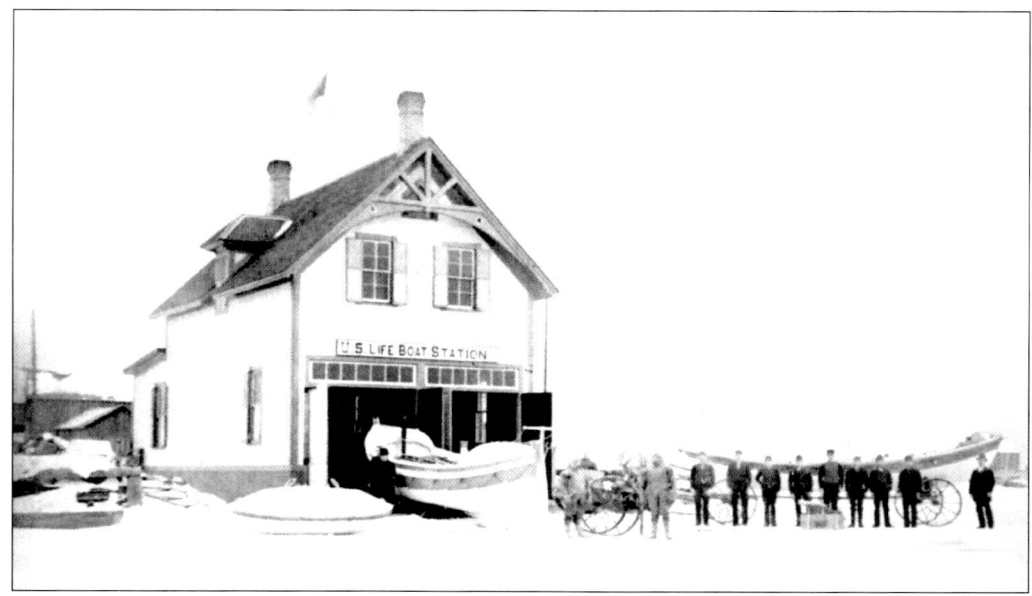

Shipwrecks occurred during all seasons of the year, but the month of November was notorious for being the worst. Violent storms caused such a staggering loss of life and property that sailors referred to it as "the curse of the eleventh month." To help rescue stranded ships and cut down the loss of life, Congress established a Lifeboat Station in Ludington in 1879. (MCHS)

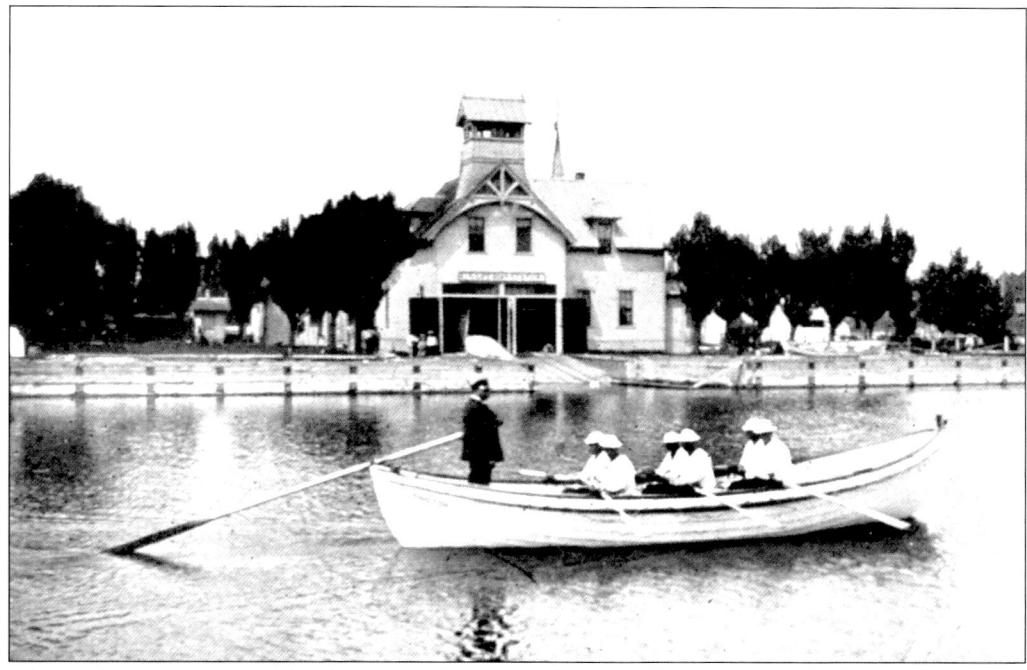

The station was designed by Assistant Superintendent for Construction of life-saving stations, J. Lake Parkinson. Originally built on the south side of the channel on Pere Marquette Lake, the station was moved to the north side in 1884. At this time a lookout tower was also added above the boat room, and a wing was added on the side of the station to increase its size. (MMM)

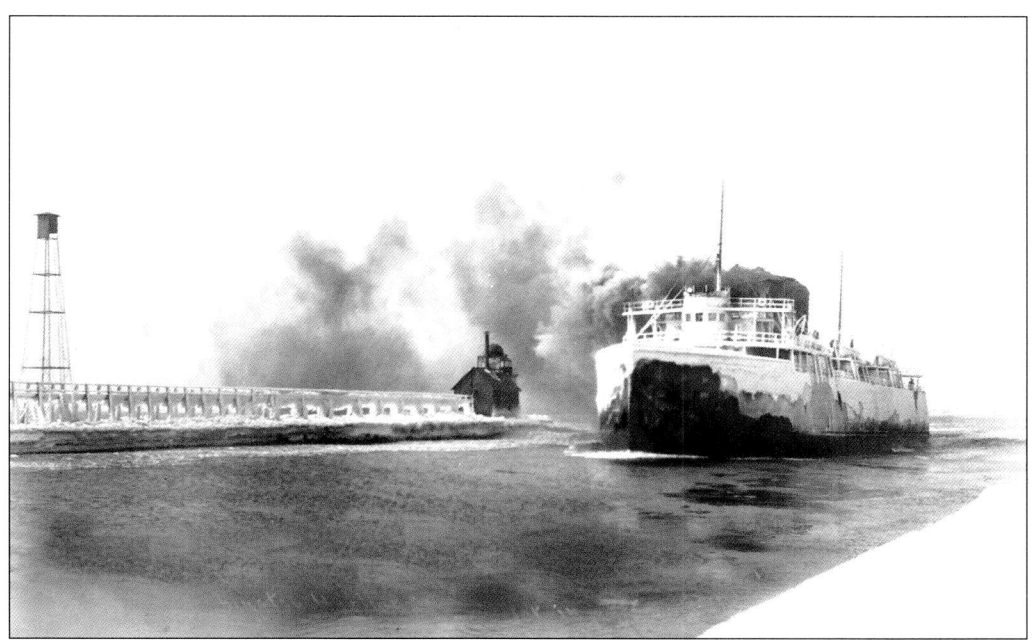

In 1894, an appropriation of funds was requested for the construction of a fog signal building to be placed behind the Ludington Pierhead light. The resulting structure was a wood-framed building sheathed in corrugated iron. It held the equipment used to power a 10-inch fog whistle that sent out a warning signal when the light could not be seen. Three years later a parabolic reflector was installed behind the whistle to direct the signal's sound out toward the lake. In 1904, a steel skeletal tower was added 400 feet behind the light to form a range light system with the lighthouse. (MCHS)

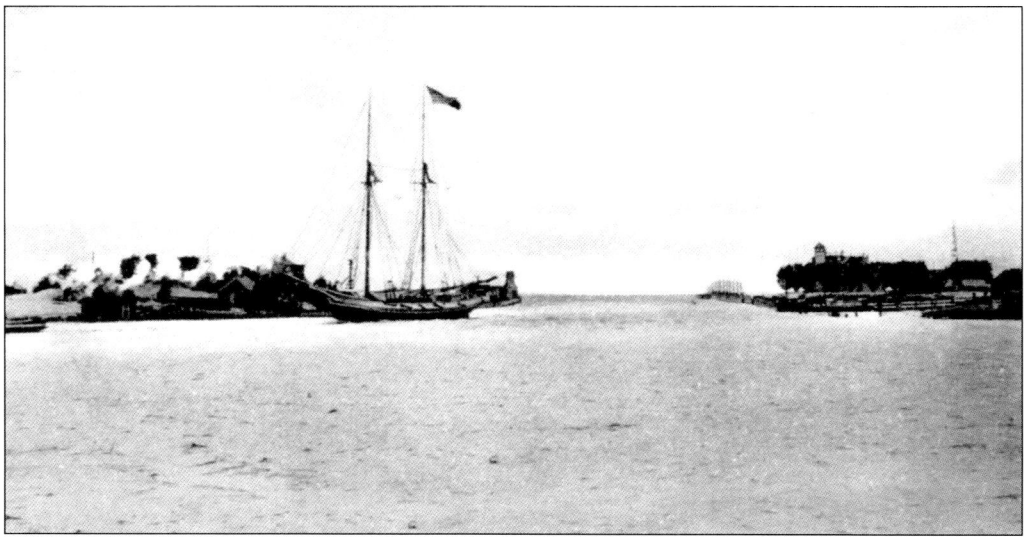

While iron-clad vessels were plying the Great Lakes in the early 1900s, wooden sailing vessels still traveled the Lakes as well. Ludington harbor was open year-round and the deep calm waters of Pere Marquette lake on the east end of the channel offered relative safety to all vessels seeking to escape angry seas. (MMM)

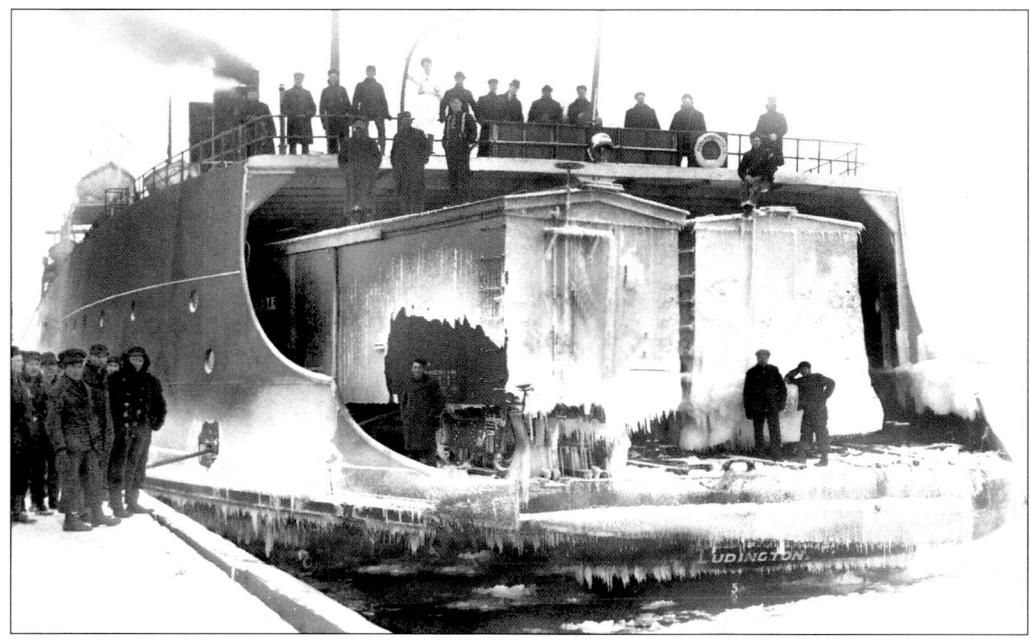

Organized in 1857, the Flint & Pere Marquette Railroad arrived in Ludington in 1874. To help expedite shipping goods from Ludington to Wisconsin, the railroad purchased two wooden steamships that could carry its box cars across the lake, rather than around it. These ships, placed into service in the late 1890s, marked the beginning of a long-standing carferry service that still exists between the ports today. In 1897 the first steel carferry was put into service in Ludington. The #17 steel ferry was built in 1901 and is pictured above with her stern encrusted in ice during the winter of 1909. (MMM)

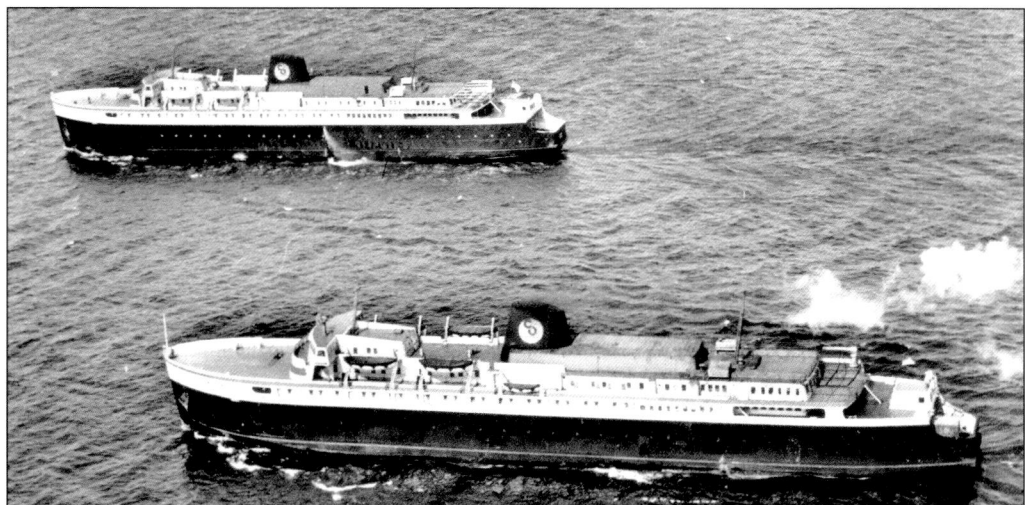

The sister ships S.S. *Badger* and S.S. *Spartan* were purchased for $5 million each and added to the fleet in 1952. Built by the Christy Corporation of Sturgeon Bay, each vessel was designed to carry 34 standard railroad cars. When they ceased carrying railroad cars, the ships continued to transport automobiles and passengers across the lake. The *Spartan* was retired in 1979, but the *Badger* is still in use today as a cross-lake ferry. (MMM)

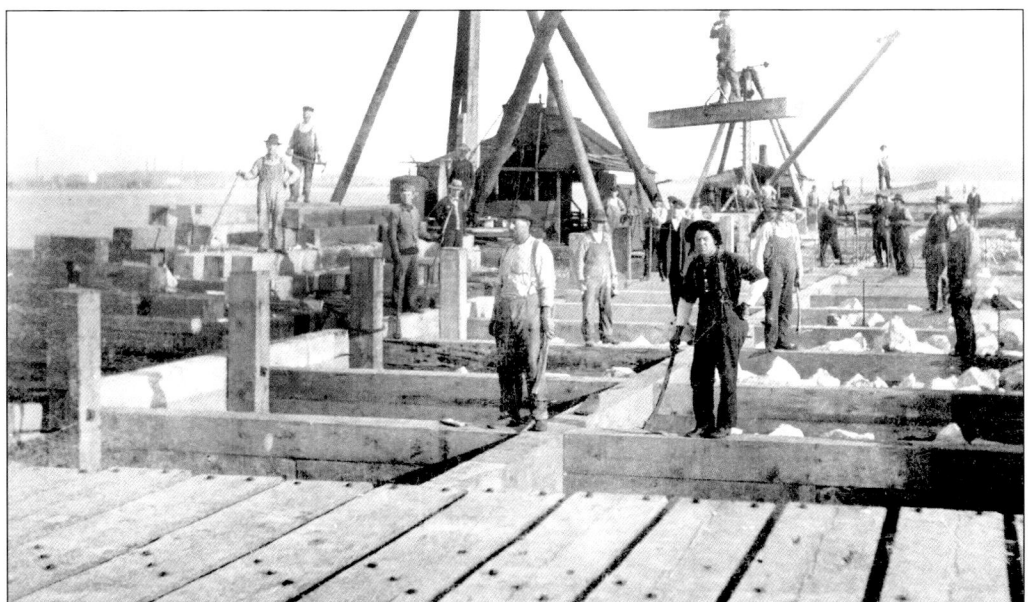

As early as the 1880s, the Ludington community desired to develop the harbor as a Harbor of Refuge, or safe place for ships to tuck in and escape from the fury Lake Michigan produced during storms. The project that grew out of that desire was dubbed "The Million Dollar Harbor," since that was the estimated cost to complete the project. Actual construction began in late 1909 by the Greiling Brothers crew, pictured above. Wooden cribs or box-like structures were sunk in the water and filled with stones, then the breakwaters were built on top. (MCHS)

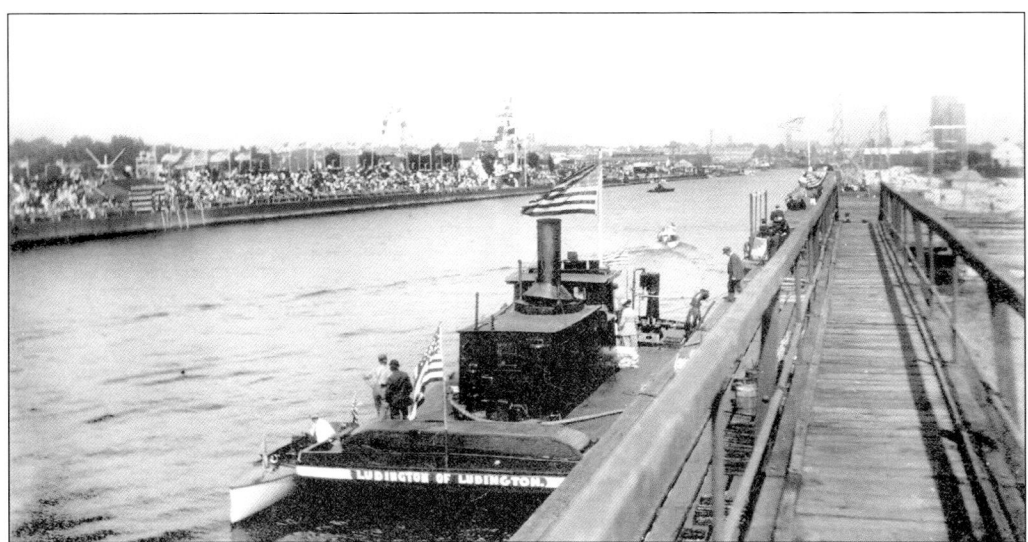

By 1914 the piers and breakwaters were completed on the north and south sides of the channel at a cost of $1.5 million. To celebrate the completion, "The Million Dollar Harbor Jubilee and Water Carnival for a Greater Ludington" was held. An estimated 40,000 people attended the celebration, which consisted of military, motor car, and ship parades, followed by numerous water activities and a giant fireworks display. The new harbor officially marked the end of the lumbering years and ushered in the era of interstate trade. (MCHS)

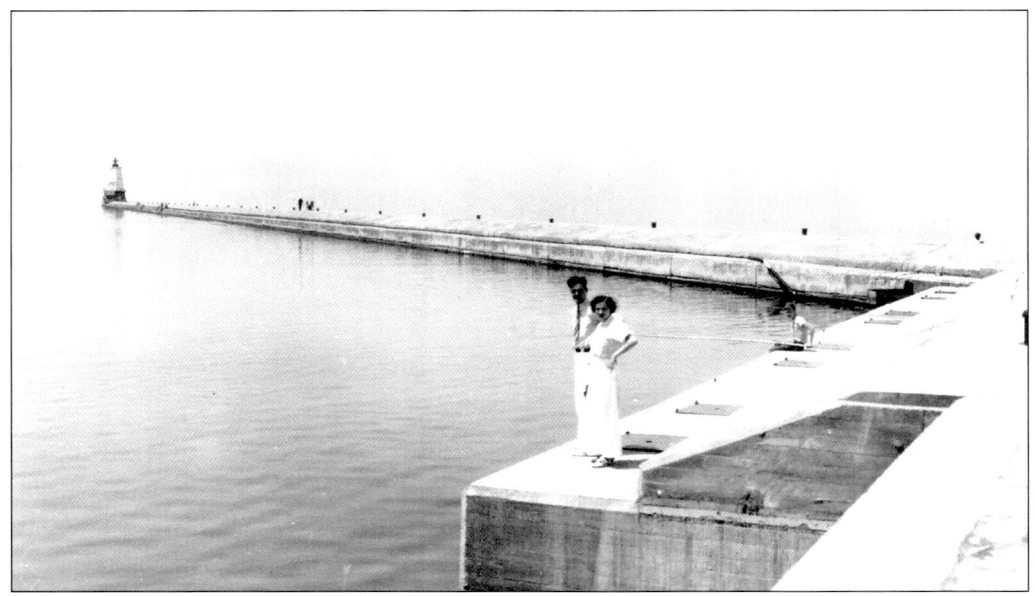

Five years after the completion of the harbor, the wooden piers showed signs of decay. To combat this problem, construction was begun to rebuild the piers with concrete and to replace the fog signal building with a combination light and fog signal. The project's north breakwater was completed in 1925 and the south breakwater was finished in 1931. This 1939 picture shows the completed north breakwater with the new light. (NC)

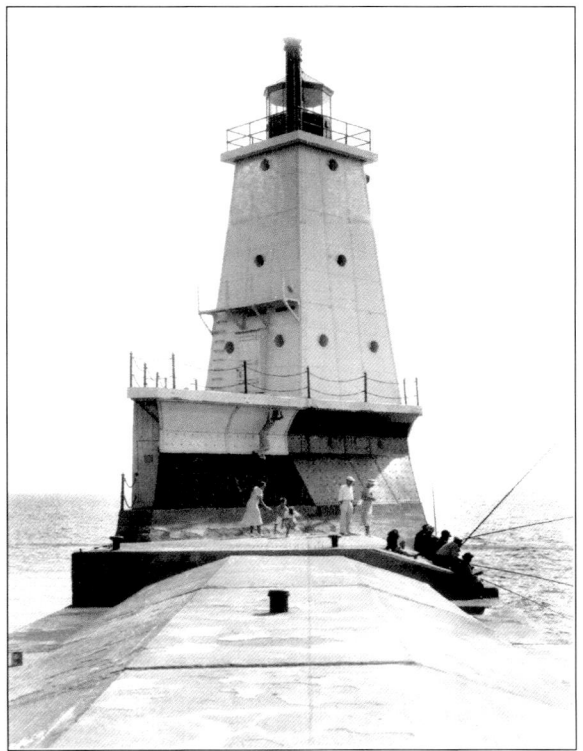

Since the north breakwater was completed before the south breakwater, a decision was made to place the new lighthouse on the north side of the channel. The 57-foot-tall pyramidal steel structure began operating in 1924, and contained both the light and an electrically powered fog signal. The front and rear of the tower base were shaped like the prow of a ship in order to help protect it from the force of incoming waves and ice. (MCHS)

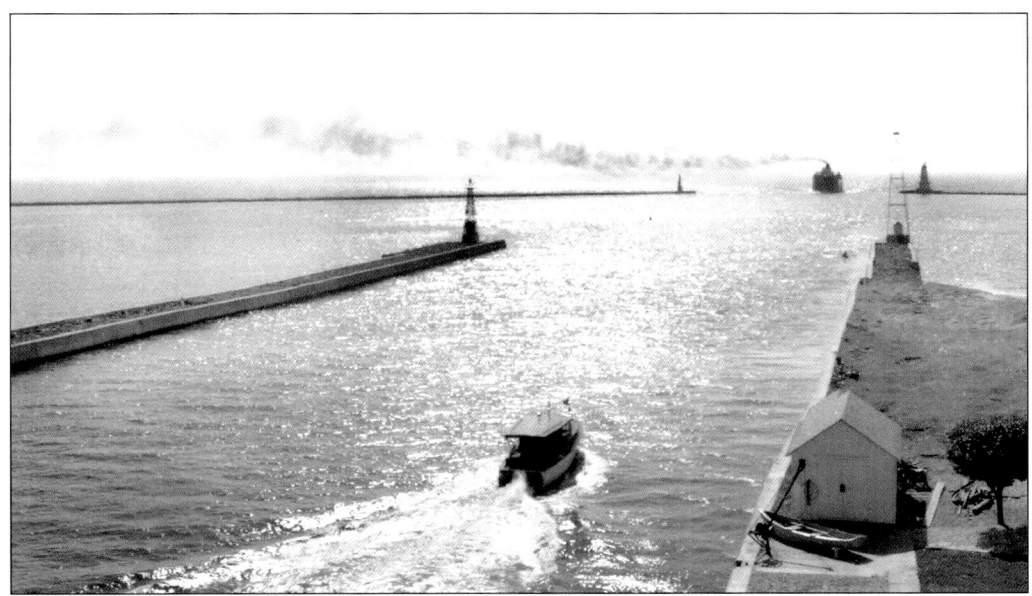

This picture taken sometime after 1924 shows the completed arrowhead design of the "Million Dollar Harbor." Shaped like an Indian arrowhead, the outer breakwaters helped calm the water leading to the channel entrance. This popular design of the early 1900s gave ships more control as they entered the channel and greatly reduced the number of accidents that occurred at the pierheads when vessels tried to enter a narrow channel directly from rough seas. (MCHS)

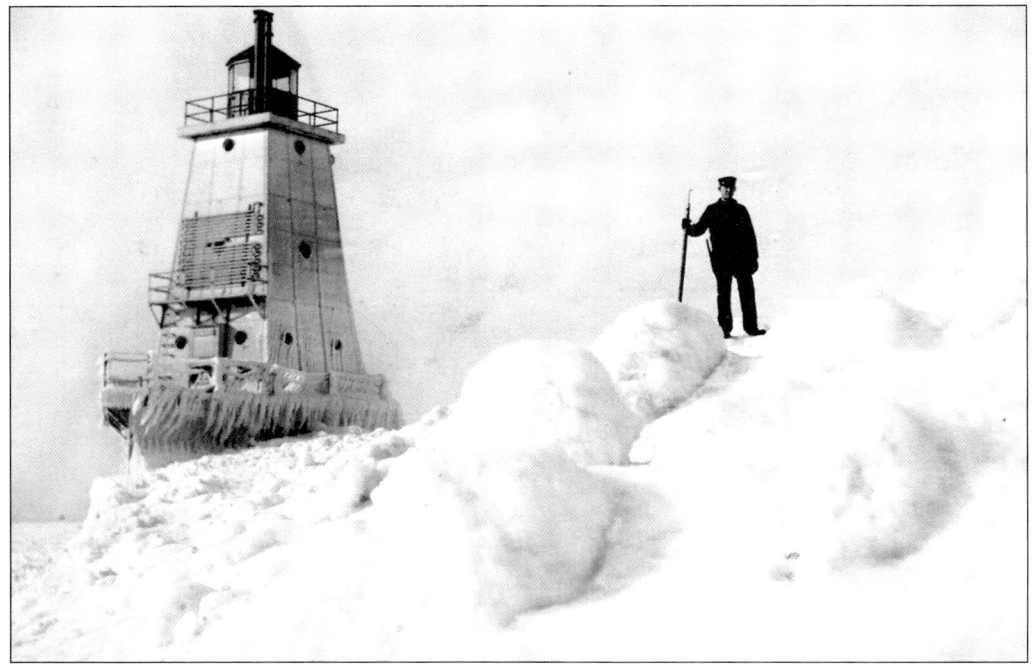

John Paetschow served as first and second assistant at the Ludington North Breakwater light from 1920–1937. In 1937 he was promoted to keeper and served in that capacity for approximately three years. He is pictured above, walking on the ice-covered north pier. (MCHS)

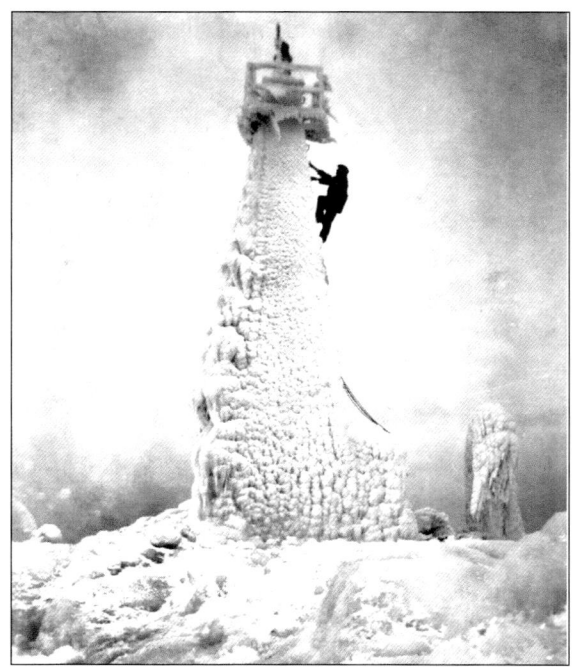

An unidentified man, presumably the lighthouse keeper, is seen climbing the ice encrusted tower of the south breakwater. The tower was destroyed in 1939 when a vessel crashed into the pier. A new 31-foot-tall steel tower with an electric light was then built to replace it. (MCHS)

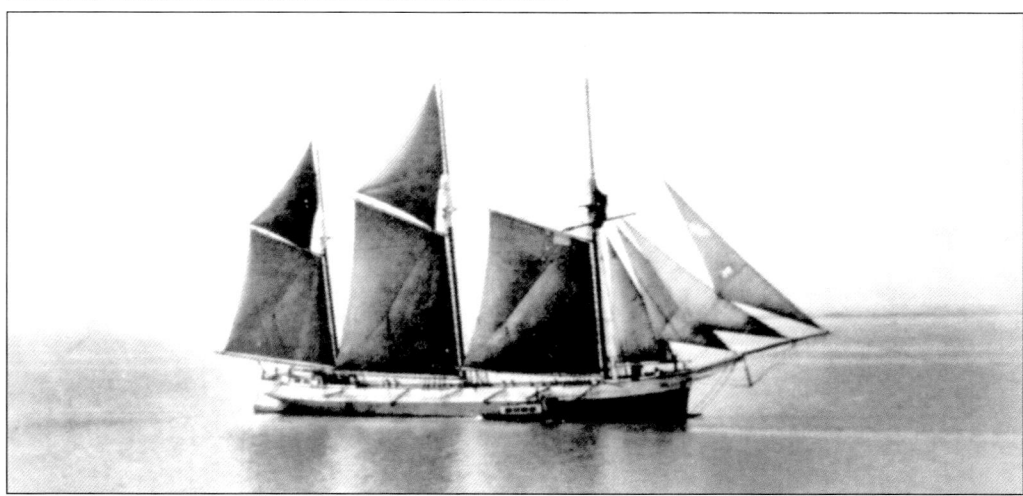

Our Son was the last lumber schooner to sail Lake Michigan. While under construction in 1875, the son of shipbuilder captain Henry Kelly was playing on the ship's deck when he fell overboard and drowned. The captain named the ship in honor of his lost son. This ship sailed the lake for over 50 years, until she foundered on the afternoon of September 26, 1930. Captain Fred Nelson and his six-man crew were going down the Wisconsin side of Lake Michigan when they were caught in a gale that blew them across the lake toward Ludington. At the same time, Captain Mohr of the freighter *William Nelson* was coming down from Mackinac. Mohr came upon them, and using great skill in the midst of the rolling, pounding surf, he maneuvered the bow of his boat close enough to the schooner so that a man could leap across. In less than one minute, all seven crew members jumped safely to the *William Nelson*. *Our Son* stayed afloat for another hour until the water pulled her down, bringing to an end the magnificent era of Lake Michigan lumber schooners. (MCM)

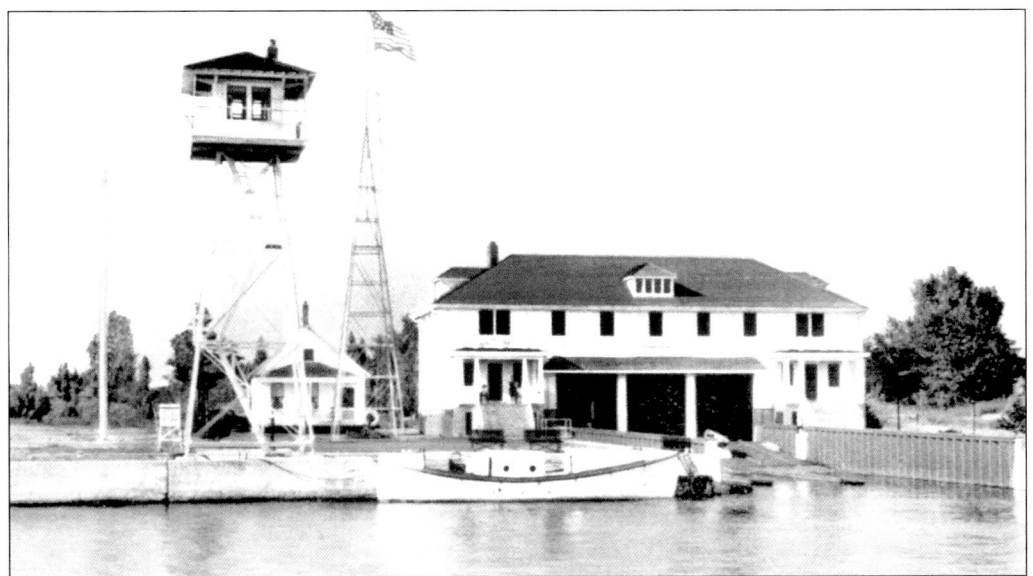

In 1934 a new Coast Guard Station was built on the north side of the channel. Four years before the completion of this station, the crew had attempted to aid in the rescue of *Our Son*. Having received the rescue call, Captain Nels Palmer and his crew left the station at 4 p.m. The water was so rough that the captain had to be lashed to the wheel to maintain control of the boat. After a horrendous night of fighting waves, struggling to keep the boat upright, and the engine quitting several times, the crew finally made it to Sheboygan, Wisconsin, at 7 a.m. the following morning. They never saw *Our Son*. After a brief rest they began their return trip home, which they completed in eight hours as opposed to the 15-hour trip the night before. Waiting for them was a huge crowd that had gathered to welcome home the crew they assumed had been drowned. Captain Palmer received a silver loving cup from the community for his bravery in attempting the rescue. (MMM)

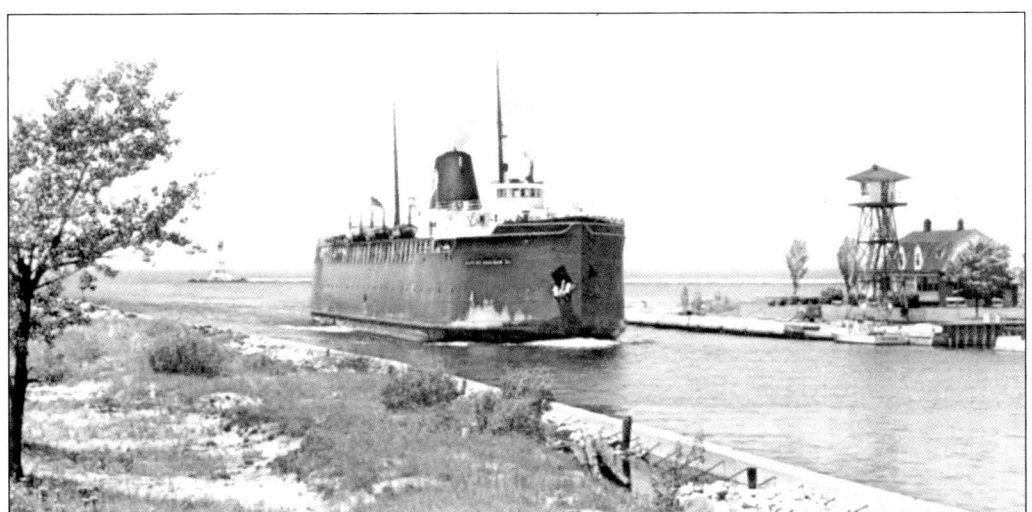

In the late 1960s, portions of the north and south breakwaters were found to be deteriorating due to wind and wave action and age. Consequently, a stone riprap was placed along the sides of both breakwaters to prevent further erosion. (MMM)

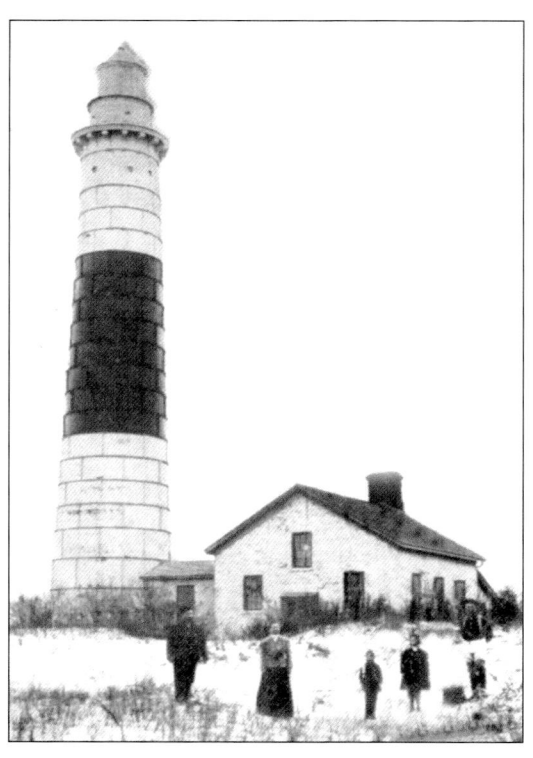

The northernmost point of the Graveyard of Ships is marked by the Big Sable Point Light. Originally named Grande Pointe Au Sable Lighthouse (Great Point of Sand), its name was changed in 1910 to avoid confusion with the Au Sable Light in Lake Superior. This coastal light was the last Michigan light seen by ships as they headed southwest to Chicago.

In its 1865 report to Congress, the Lighthouse Board recommended that a light be placed on this "most salient point on the eastern shore of Lake Michigan, between Point Betsie and Muskegon." Congress quickly responded by appropriating the necessary funds to begin construction the following year. The 112-foot-tall tower was illuminated with a fixed white Third Order Fresnel lens that began shining for the first time on November 1, 1867. (MMM)

Upon completion of the tower, a dwelling to house a keeper and an assistant was constructed and connected to the tower by an enclosed walkway. Both structures were made of buff-colored Cream City brick supplied by the Milwaukee Lighthouse Depot. The clay used in making these bricks was abundant on the western side of Lake Michigan during this time, and was believed to possess superior strength and weather resistance. However, the brick did not stand up to the elements at Big Sable, and deterioration presented a continual problem.

In 1900, after the District Inspector reported that the brick was flaking, the tower was encased with iron plates to prevent further deterioration. Concrete was poured between the bricks and the plates to give added strength. The finished tower was painted white with a wide black band around its middle to make it a better daymark. Five years later the watchroom was also encased in iron. (USCG)

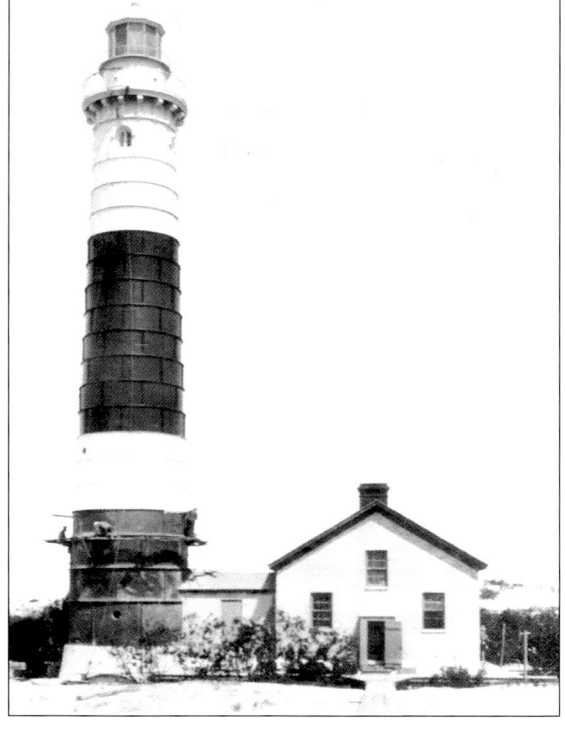

34

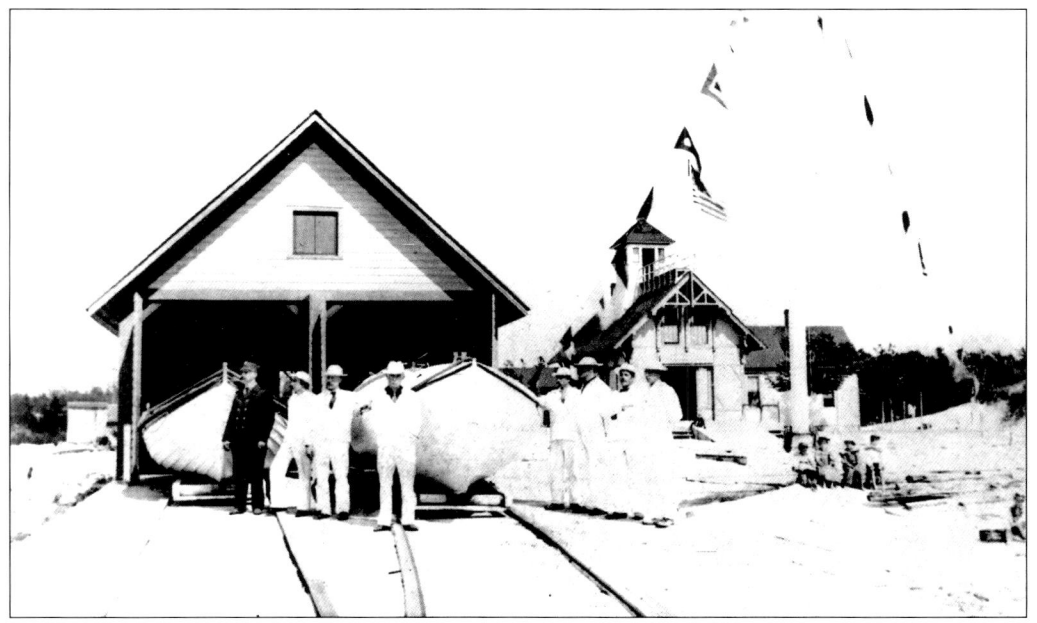

A Life-Saving Station was opened about one mile south of the lighthouse in 1877. Designed by Francis Ward Chandler, this gable-roofed style building had a double lookout on its roof. One lookout was located in the center of the roof and the other one sat directly over the boat room door. They were connected by a small walkway. Shown above are keeper John A. Nelson and his crew of 1897. (MCHS)

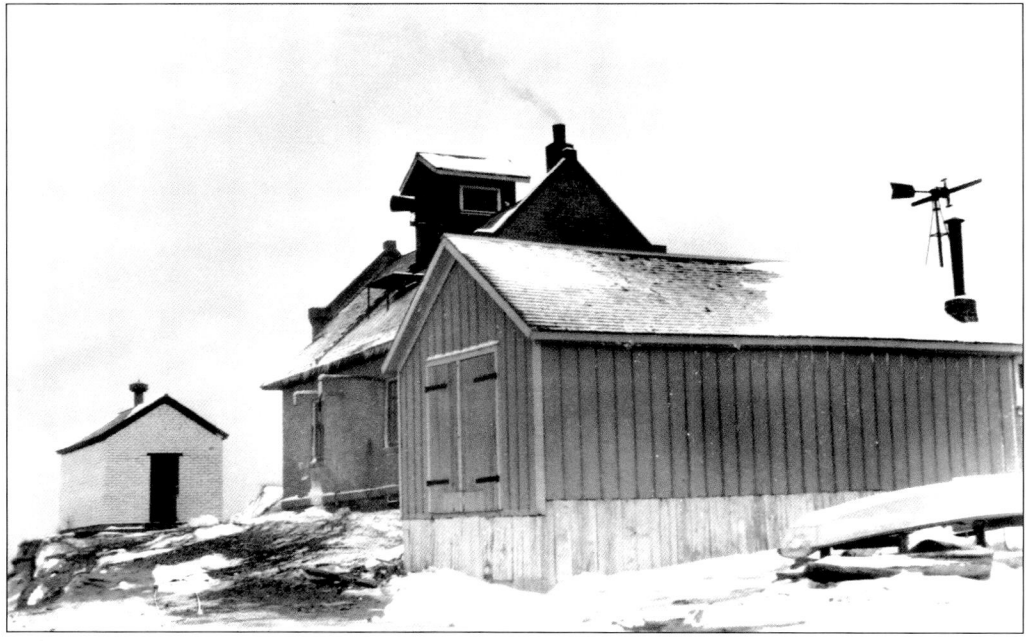

Federal government engineers constructed a brick fog signal building (center) on the Big Sable Point Lighthouse property in 1908. The fog signal was a two-tone, air-diaphone run by compressed steam and was reported to be the only one of its kind on Lake Michigan. (SAM)

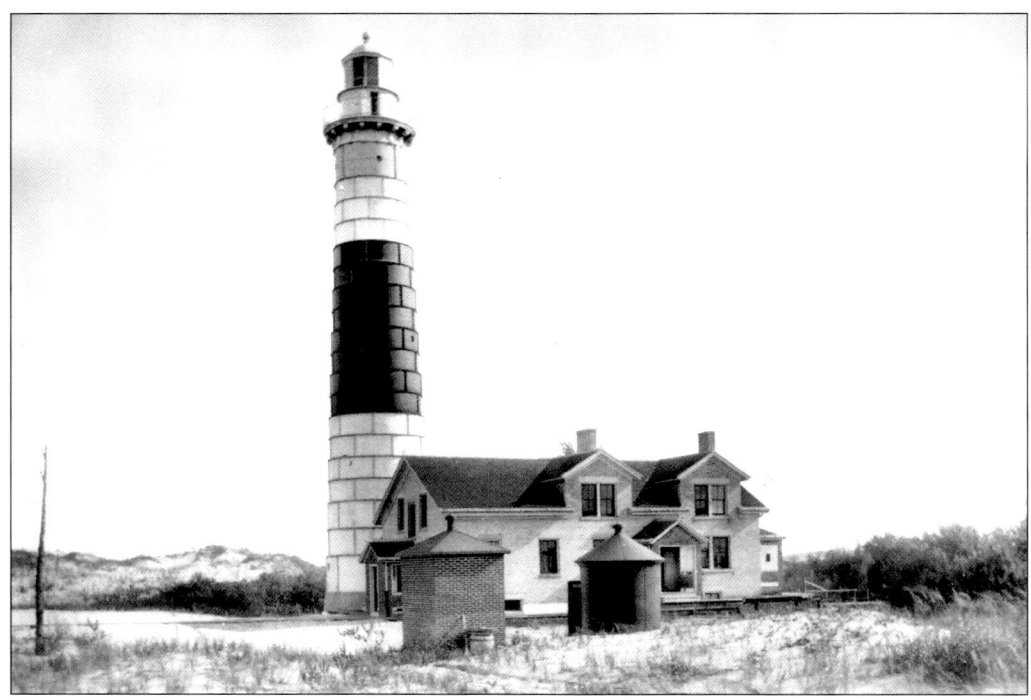

A second assistant keeper was hired to maintain the new fog signal. Rather than building a new house for the assistant's family, the decision was made to completely remodel and enlarge the existing dwelling to accommodate three families. The oil storage building was also erected near the dwelling at this time. (SAM)

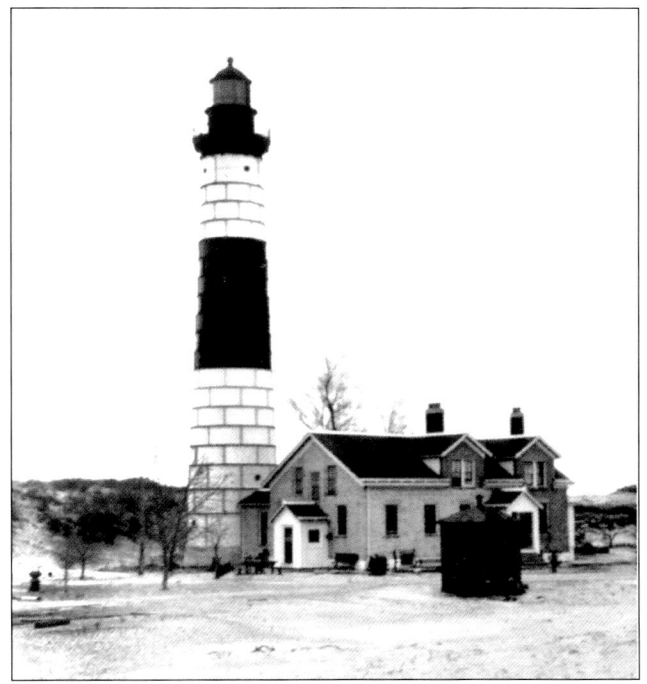

When the tower was encased in steel in the early 1900s, its top remained white in color. It proved to be difficult for mariners to see during daylight hours because it blended in with the clouds. To remedy this problem the watchroom and lantern room were painted black in 1916. (SAM)

Keeper George Rogan (left) and his assistant Ray Robinette are seen in this photograph painting the tower in the late 1930s. It was common knowledge among keepers that inspectors liked paint. A great deal of time was spent each year making sure everything was freshly painted in preparation for a surprise inspection. The brick passageway that connected the dwelling and tower can be seen on the lower left side of the picture. (MCHS)

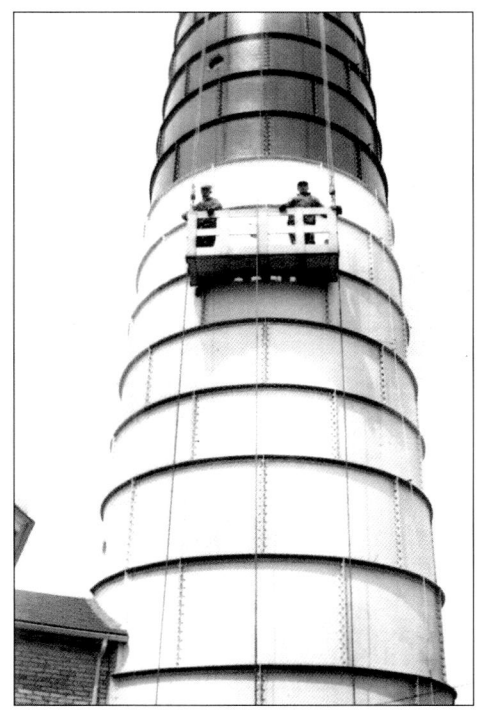

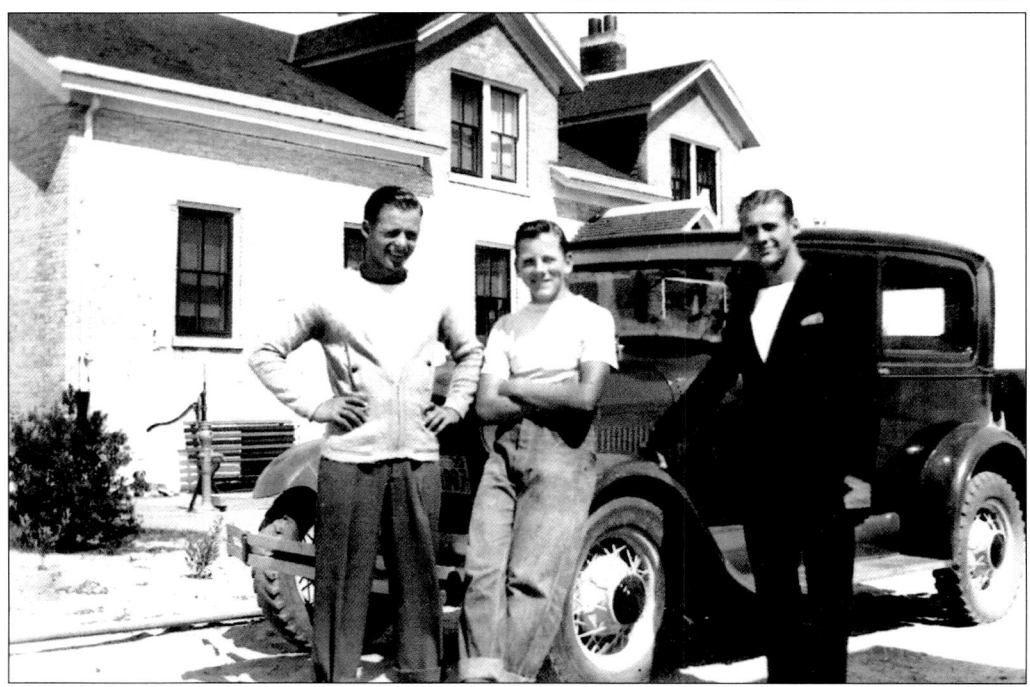

George Rogan was keeper at Big Sable Point Light from 1936–1949. Above, his sons pose for a picture on the south side of the light in the late 1930s. From left to right are Charles, Byron, and Richard Rogan. There was no road to the lighthouse until 1933, when a rough service road was extended from Ludington State Park to the light. (MCHS)

37

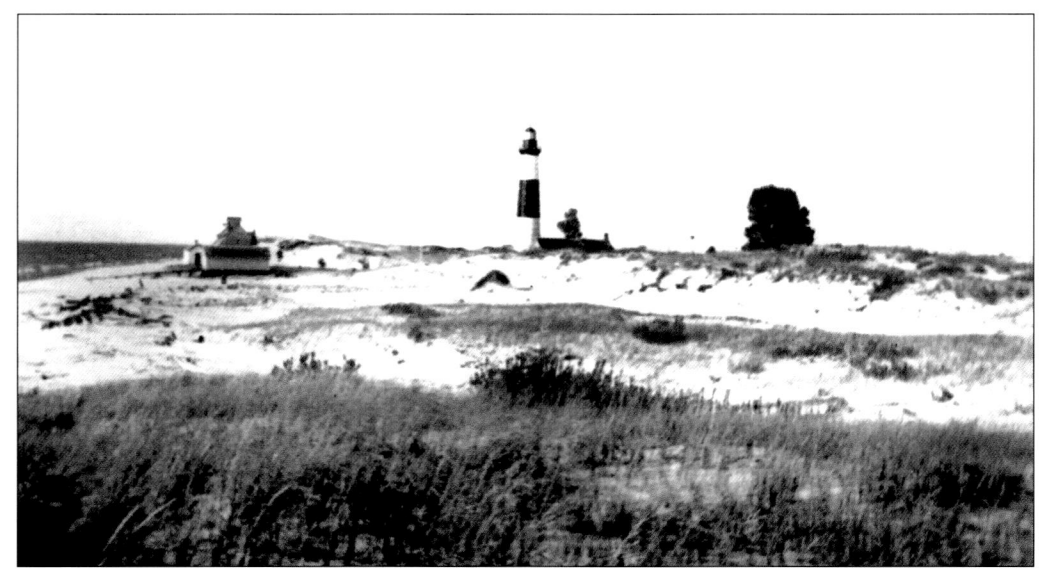

A panoramic view from the Life-Saving Station shows the lighthouse grounds with the boathouse and fog signal near the shoreline. With few trees to offer protection from the elements, the tower and buildings constantly suffered from exposure to wind-swept sand and storms. (MCHS)

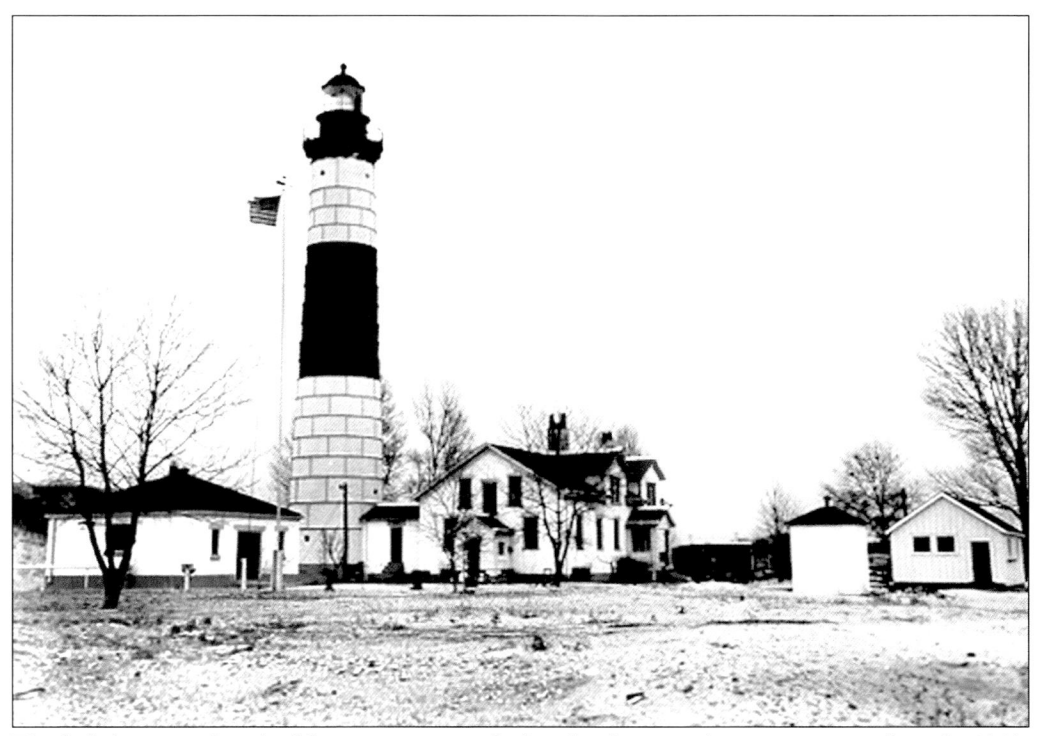

The lighthouse and outbuildings were painted white by the time this picture was taken. In 1949, Big Sable Point Light became the last light on the Great Lakes to become electrified. Power lines were extended to the dwelling about four years later. Automation eventually ended the need for a keeper and the last civilian keeper vacated the site in 1969. (USCG)

Two

The Lights of Manistee County
Manistee River and Pierhead Lights
Portage Lake North Pier Light

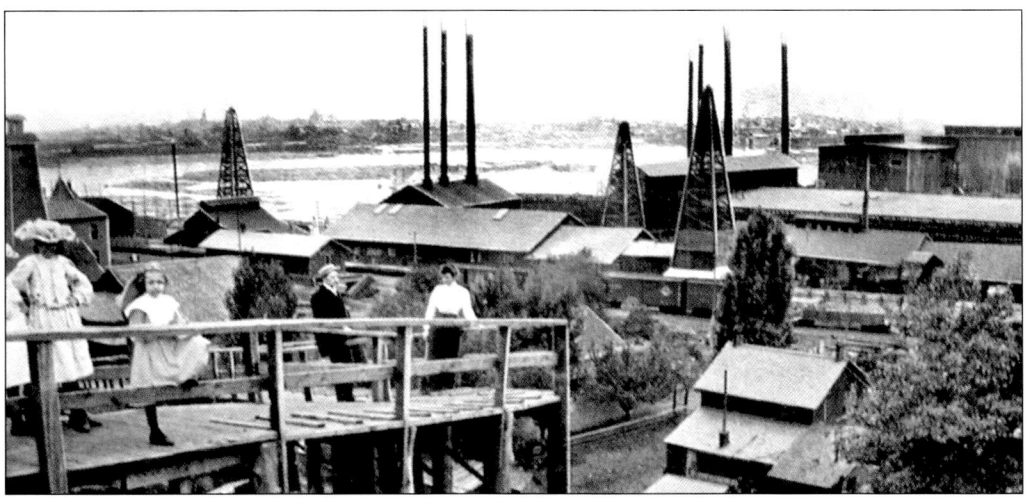

Manistee Harbor is located at the end of the Manistee River, which flows through Manistee Lake to Lake Michigan. The lure of the pine forests drew the first settlers to the area and a booming lumber industry soon followed. John Stronach and his sons James and Adam built the first saw mill in 1841 and by 1867, 21 mills were cutting lumber in the county. Many of the lumbermen became self-made millionaires and their majestic Victorian homes have since earned the city its title of "The Victorian Port City" of Lake Michigan.

In 1872 a group of surveyors visited Manistee and suggested that valuable amounts of salt could be obtained there. It wasn't until 1879, however, that local interests banded together with Charles Reitz and Brothers to begin drilling for salt. A thick vein was found around 2,000 feet deep and officially marked the beginning of Manistee's prosperous salt business. By 1898, as lumber supplies were waning, many of the lumber companies had entered the salt business. Manistee became one of the world's largest salt manufacturers, producing over 400 million pounds of salt per year. Pictured above is the Peters Salt & Lumber Co. Plant in the 1900s. Peters had one of the largest salt mills in the state in the early 1880s. (BHL)

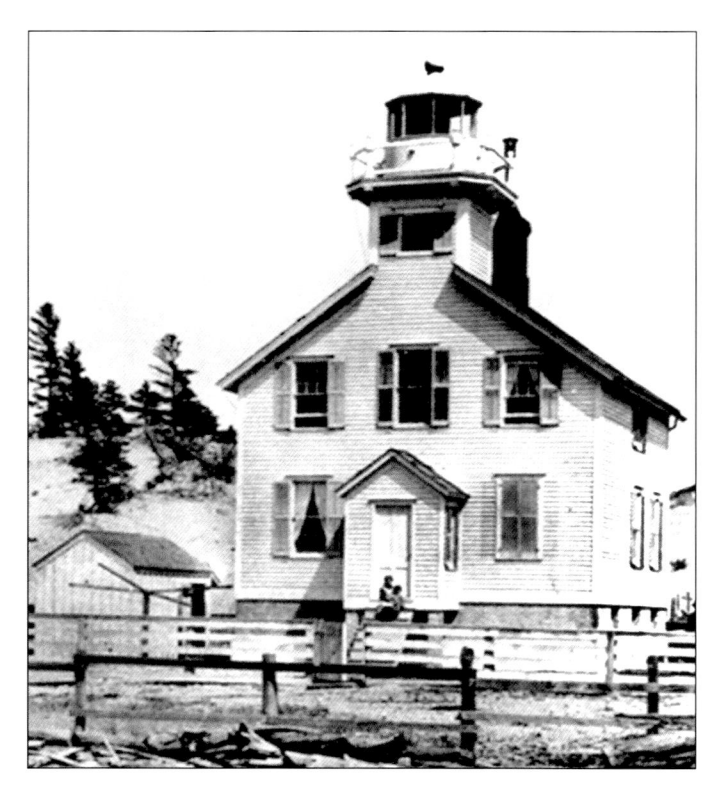

An 1861 Army Crops of Engineers report indicated the need for improvements at the river's outlet. By 1867, Congress had responded with funds for the improvements and the establishment of a lighthouse on the north side of the Manistee River. The work was completed and the lighthouse became operational in 1870. Little more than a year later, a raging forest fire swept through much of western Michigan, devastating Manistee, and burning the lighthouse to its foundation. A new lighthouse (the main light) was built in its place in 1872. The new light was thought to look much like the original light, consisting of a two-story wood-framed house with a square light tower rising from its roof. (USCG)

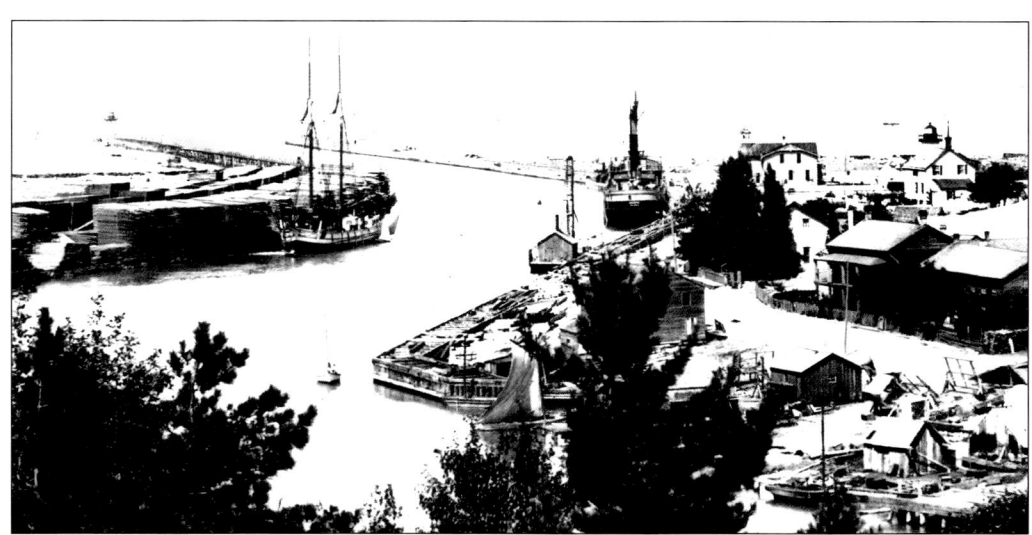

In the one-year time period between June 1874 and June 1875, 3,488 vessels entered the river. To better accommodate this traffic, the channel was dredged, both piers were extended, and a light was placed on the end of the south pier. A wooden catwalk that ran from shore was also extended to the light. With the addition of the pierhead light, the main light (on the far right of the picture) was considered unnecessary and its light was extinguished just three years after it was built. The house continued to serve as the dwelling for the keeper who rowed across the river several times each day to maintain the new Manistee Pierhead Light. (MCHM)

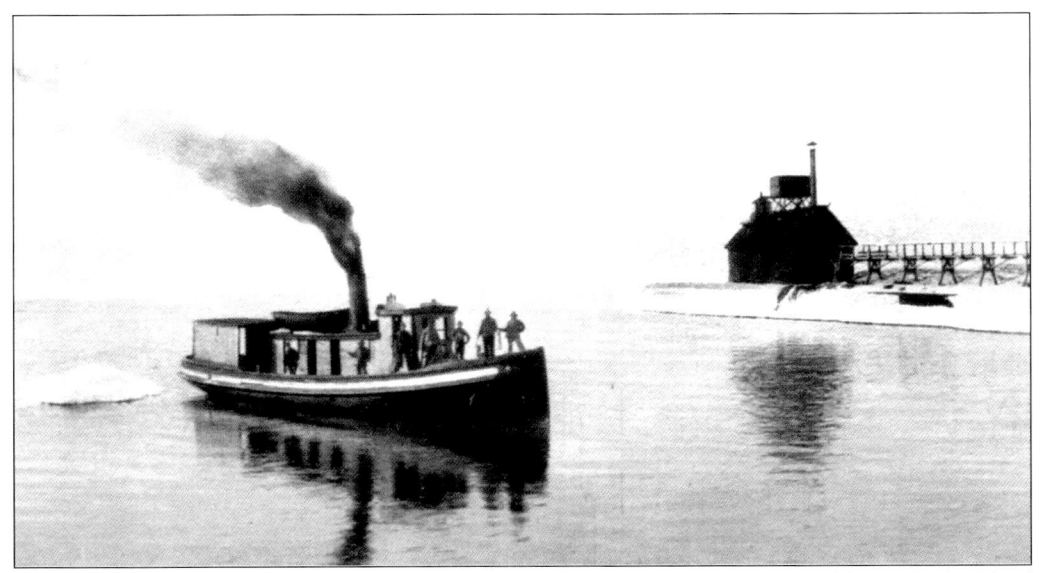

A steam-powered fog signal was added behind the pier light in 1889. The building was sheathed in cast iron and housed the apparatus used to power two 10-inch locomotive whistles. In 1894 the fog signal was relocated to the north pier and placed about 300 feet from its end. An enclosed conduit system was set up so the light could be moved back and forth between the end of the pier and the fog signal. This system did not prove to be very successful and a few years later the conduit was removed, the fog signal was moved closer to the end of the pier, and the light was placed on top of the fog signal. (MMM)

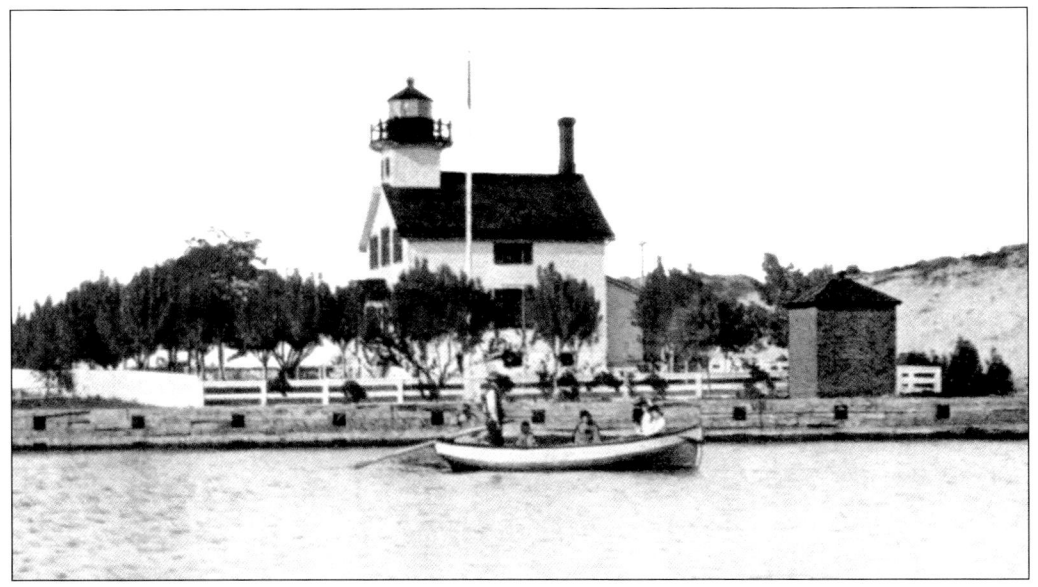

In 1894, the main light was reactivated as a shore light to aid with the high volume of shipping traffic traveling to and from the Straits. By the time this picture was taken in the early 1900s, the lantern room had been painted black and a fence had been built to surround the lighthouse property. This light remained in service until 1927 when it was permanently extinguished and decommissioned. (MMM)

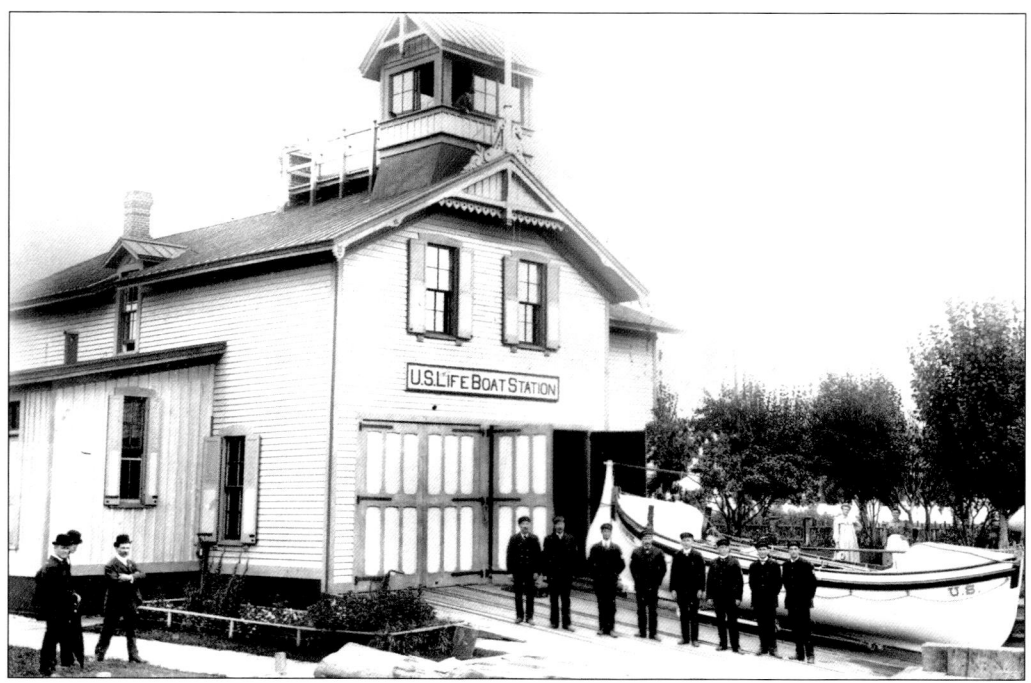

The government established a Lifeboat Station in Manistee in 1879. Lifeboat Stations, consisting of a volunteer crew and a lifeboat, were most often built on the Great Lakes. Life-Saving Stations that had a paid crew and a surfboat were usually built on the east coast. It didn't take long to realize that Lifeboat Stations were unrealistic, and they were soon changed to Life-Saving Stations, complete with a paid crew and often a surfboat and a lifeboat. By the late 1800s the Manistee station was fully equipped with self-bailing, self-righting boats and the necessary life-saving apparatus to perform rescues. (MCHM)

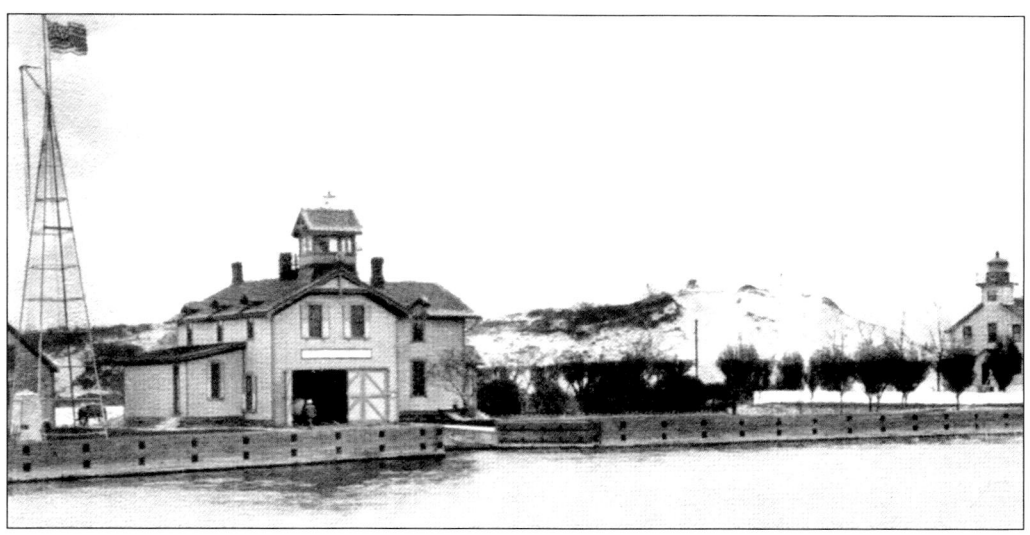

The Life-Saving Station, located at the mouth of the river on the north side, was a two-story building with a lookout on the roof that provided a good view of the lake and the harbor entrance. Members of the first crew earned wages of $45 per month. (MMM)

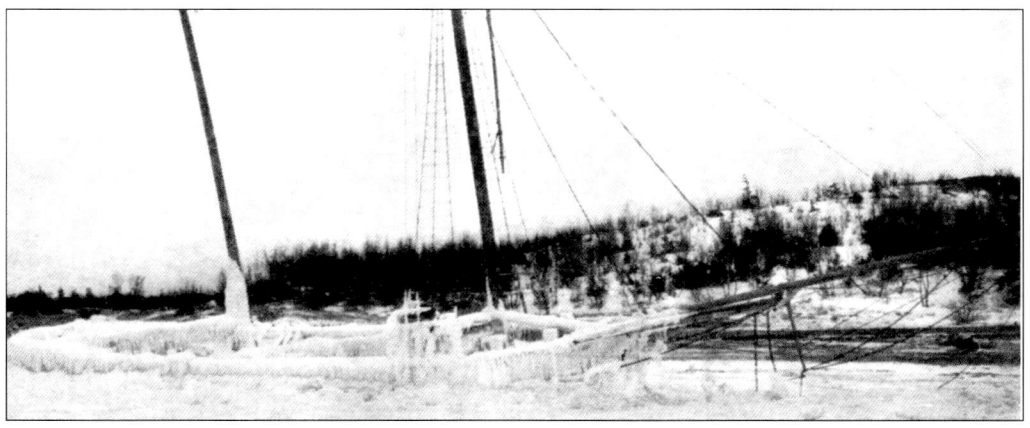

The storm of October 19–20, 1905 was one of the worst this part of the lake had seen. The schooner Lydia was bound for Manistee from Muskegon to pick up a load of lumber when she was hit by the dreadful gale. Both anchors were thrown out in an effort to stabilize her, but after six hours of battling the storm, one of the anchor chains broke and the boat was washed ashore and beached, just short of Manistee. The crew was able to evacuate safely; however, the captain did not want to spend the money to refloat the ship, so her remains lie buried on shore to this day. (MCHM)

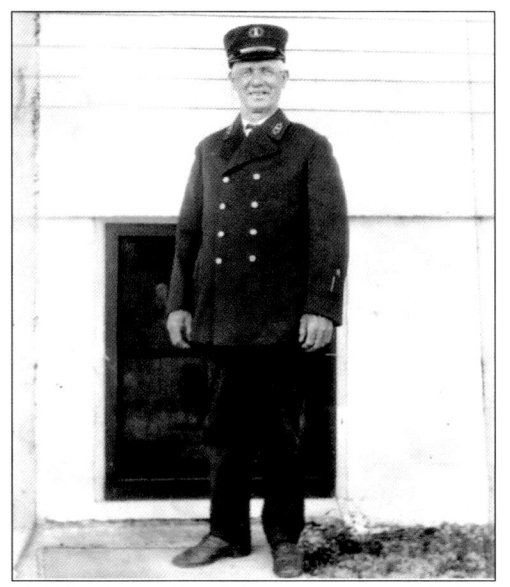

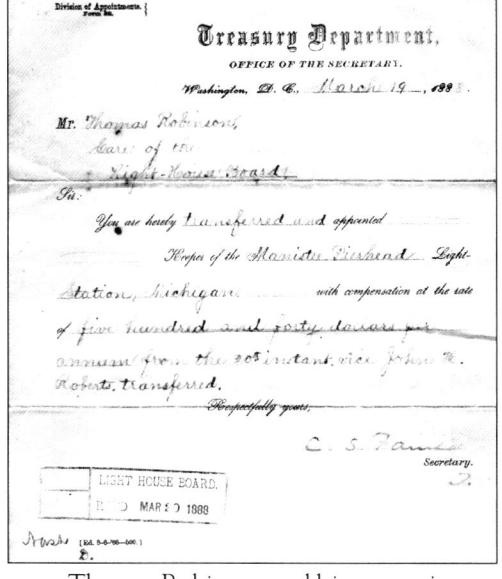

(left) In the midst of the same storm, lighthouse keeper Thomas Robinson and his two assistants removed the lens from the light/fog station and notified the lighthouse board that the station was in danger of being swept away. No sooner had he finished his work than a portion of the catwalk was ripped away, making it impossible to return to the light. Keeper Robinson later commented that he had never seen a worse storm in all of his years on the lake.

(right) According to his transfer papers, Thomas Robinson, the son of Captain William Robinson III of White River Light Station, was appointed keeper of the Manistee Pierhead Light on March 20, 1888. He received $540 per year for his services as its keeper. Thomas remained at Manistee for approximately 18 years before he was transferred to the Muskegon lights to finish out his career. (MCHM).

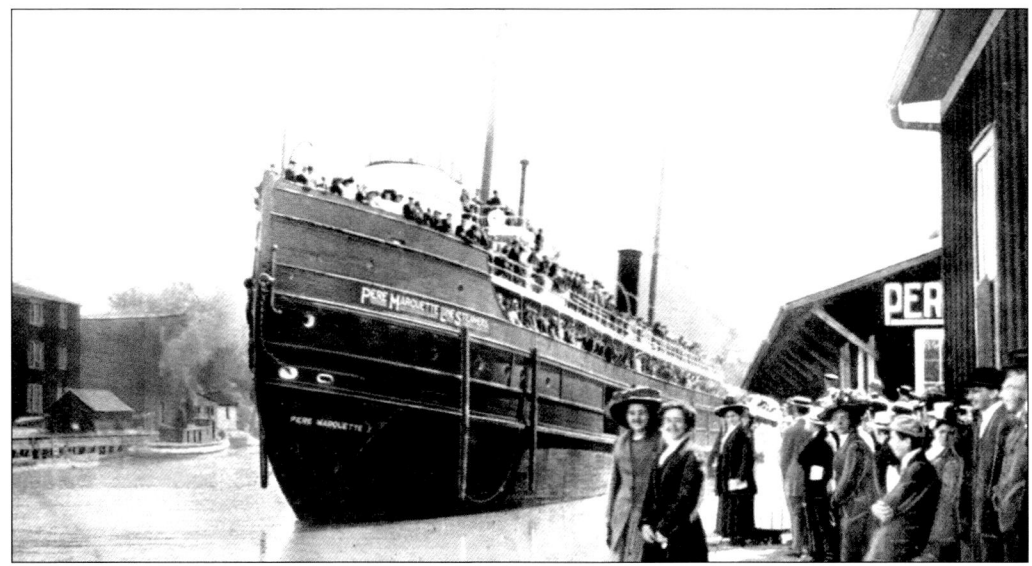

The *Flint and Pere Marquette No. 2* carferry was built in 1881. She was designed to be a passenger and freight steamer, running between Ludington and Milwaukee. In 1884 the route was extended north to Manistee, where she is seen at dock. Along with offering excursions, the *Flint and Pere Marquette No. 2* also picked up salt at Manistee and delivered it to several ports on her journey westward. In 1901 her name was changed to the *Pere Marquette 2* as can be seen in the picture above. (MMM)

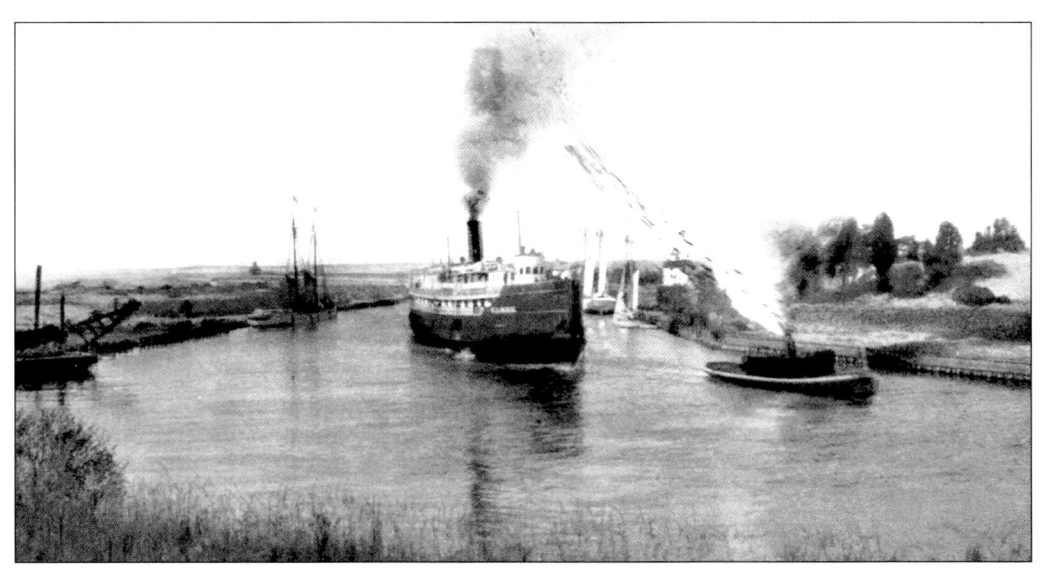

The steel steamer *Illinois* was built in 1899 by the Northern Michigan Transportation Company. Reaching a top speed of 18 miles per hour, she was touted to be the fastest passenger and freight steamer on Lake Michigan. A few months after this picture was taken in 1913, the *Illinois* was loaded with freight and headed to Chicago when she was hit by a storm near South Manitou Island. Since there was no harbor nearby for refuge, the captain ran her nose onto the shore of the island and kept her engines running to keep her from broadsiding onto the beach. He maintained this position for 29 hours until the sea calmed and it was safe to resume travel. (MMM)

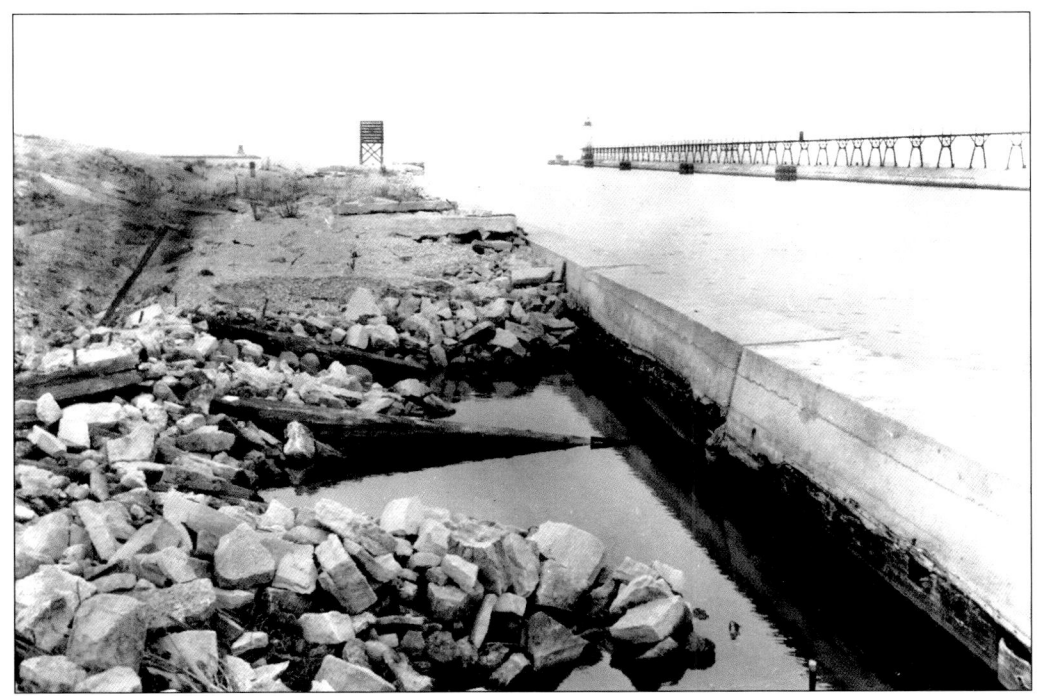

The Army Corps of Engineers returned to Manistee in 1914 to extend the south pier. Upon its completion, the north and south piers together formed a stilling basin. The stilling basin offered a wide opening from the lake to the channel, allowing waters to spread out and calm down before reaching the actual channel entrance. (MCHM)

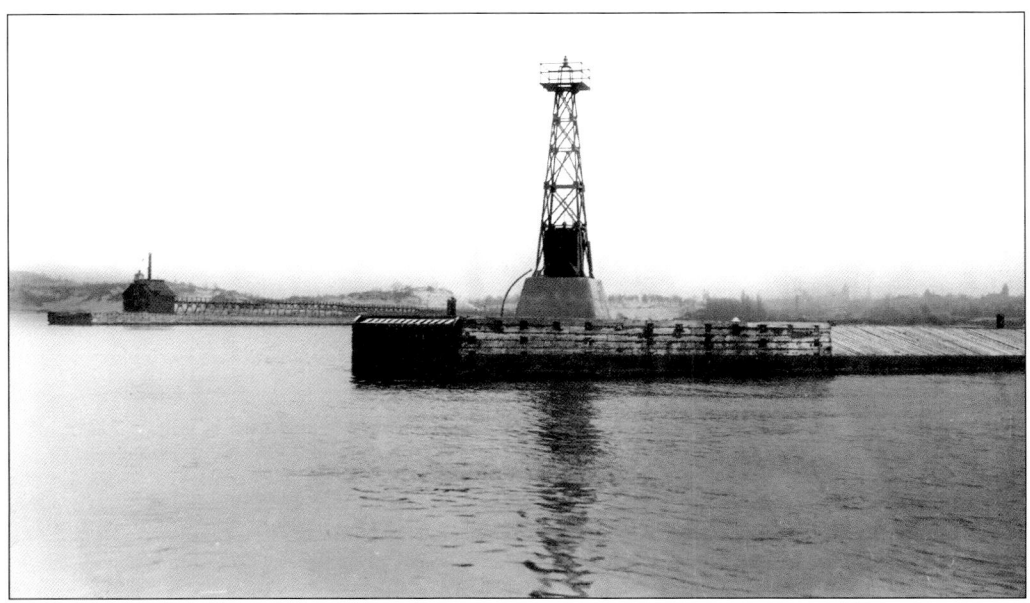

A red steel skeletal tower was placed on the new south pier, 80 feet from its outer end. The tower stood 45 feet high and was equipped with a flashing red light that was visible for seven miles. (MCHM)

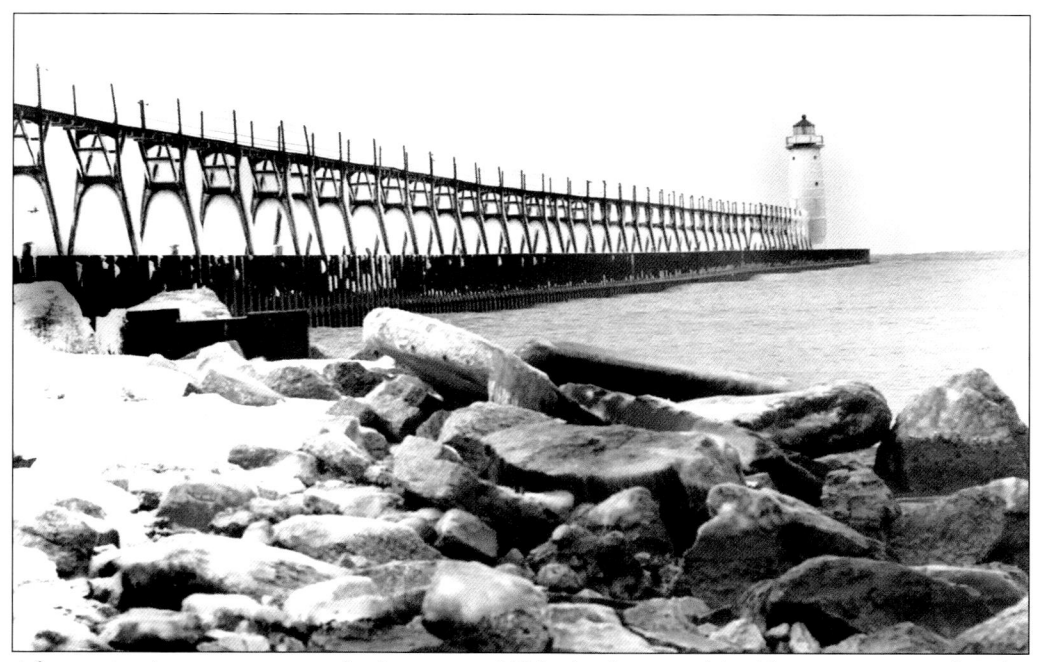

After major improvements to both piers in 1927, the fog signal building was removed and a 39-foot conical iron tower was placed on the north pier. It was topped with an octagonal steel lantern room that held a Fifth Order Fresnel lens. (SAM)

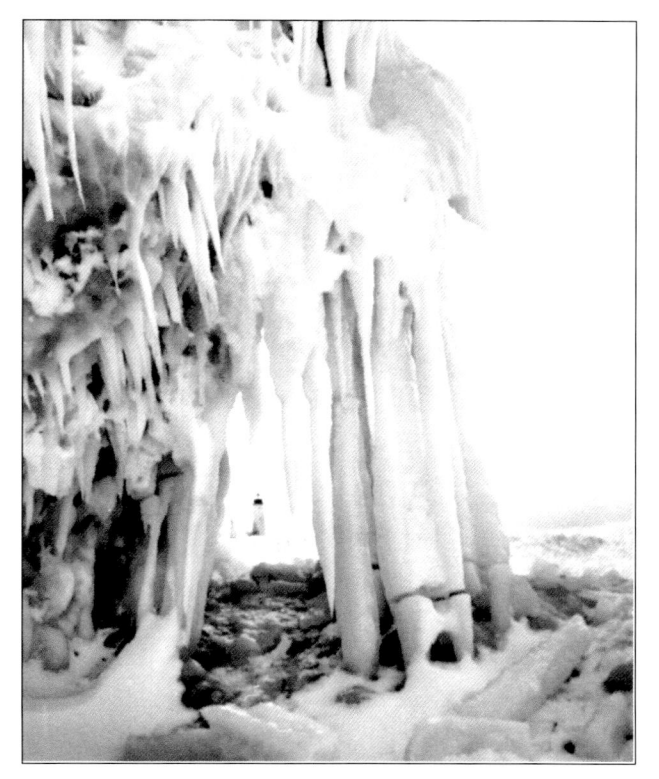

A contrasting winter shot offers a unique view of the conical and skeletal towers through the ice. Winter storms and splashing water caused many large ice formations to develop near the shoreline. (MCHM)

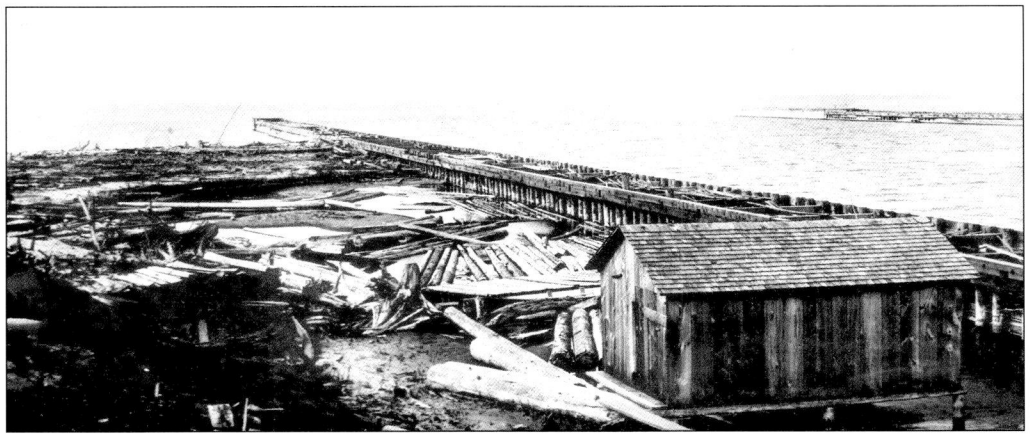

Portage Lake Harbor lies approximately eight miles north of Manistee. In 1867 Porter and Company took over operation of a water-powered mill on Portage Lake. Other than a creek that ran out to lake Michigan, the lake was landlocked. Though the creek was not big enough to handle large vessels, mill owners had, since the 1840s, maintained a dam across it to power the mill and facilitate floating logs from Portage Lake to the mill. Unfortunately, the dam caused the lake to overflow onto homesteaders' land, making it unusable for farming. Tensions that mounted for years over this issue finally came to a head in 1870 when the homesteaders took it upon themselves to dig a ditch through to Lake Michigan in hopes of eliminating the dam and their water problems.

In retaliation for this action, the mill manager had the homesteaders arrested for attempting to cut off the mill's water supply. The homesteaders prevailed, however, and when the ditch was finally finished and the dam was opened, masses of land and upright trees were washed down from Portage Lake into Lake Michigan. So much so that it appeared as though Lake Michigan contained a floating forest. The burgeoning channel ended up being several times wider and deeper than the original ditch they had dug. (MCHM)

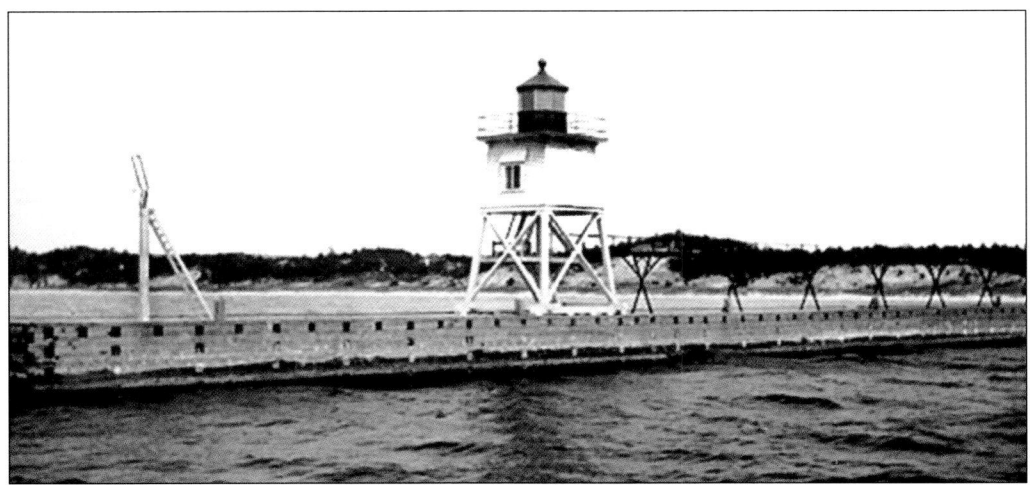

The first government pierhead lights here were placed on the north pier in 1891. The two lights of the pier together formed a range light system. When mariners saw both lights in a straight line, one behind the other, they knew it was safe to make their turn to head into the harbor. The larger rear range light, seen above, was a wooden pyramidal tower with an open frame. It was connected to shore by a raised catwalk. (USCG)

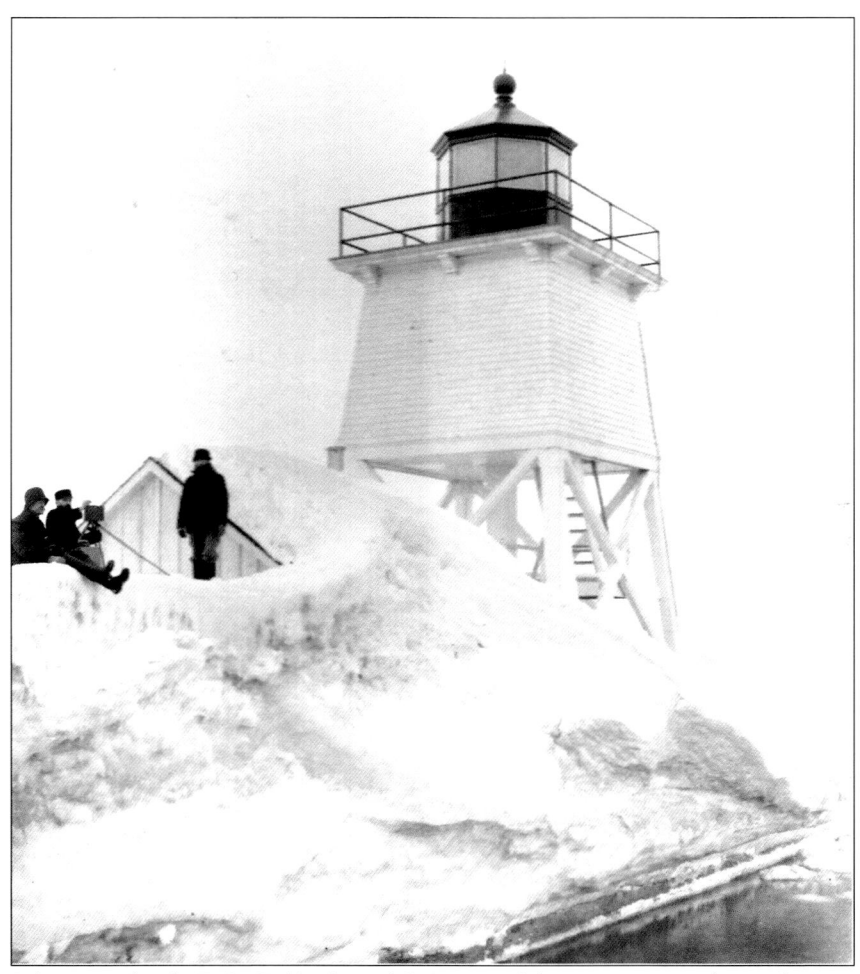

Keeper John Langland, T.O. Telford, and R.F. Wendel are seen on the icebergs near the lighthouse. Captain Langland was the first and only keeper at the Portage Lake North Pierhead Light, serving from 1891 until the light was automated in 1917.

For some unknown reason, the captain was awakened from his sleep in the early morning hours of November 8, 1905. He got dressed and went down to the beach and was surprised to find the schooner *Abbie* in trouble on the lake and unable to make the harbor. Langland sent his stepson to notify the Manistee Coast Guard of the situation, and while he was running along the beach, the crew saw his lantern and knew there must be life nearby.

Although their small dinghy had a hole in it and only a short length of line tied to it, the crew decided to let it out in hopes of reaching the shore. When captain Langland realized what they were doing, he swam out into the frigid water, dodging the sheets of tanbark that were being washed overboard and threatening to slice him in two, and tried to reach the line. After several failed attempts, one of the crewmen jumped into the water to bring Langland another line. The sailor got caught in the undertow, however, and after much struggle to reach him, Langland got him to shore unconscious. Waiting anxiously for them was Mrs. Langland, who half-dragged and half-carried the two semi-conscious men back to the light station to recover from their ordeal.

The Coast Guard eventually rescued the remaining crew, who also stayed at the station for five days while they recuperated from their near-death experience. (MCHM)

Three
BENZIE COUNTY AND THE MANITOU ISLAND LIGHTS
FRANKFORT PIERHEAD AND BREAKWATER LIGHTS, POINT BETSIE LIGHT, SOUTH MANITOU ISLAND LIGHT, NORTH MANITOU ISLAND LIGHT, NORTH MANITOU SHOAL LIGHT, AND SOUTH FOX ISLAND LIGHT

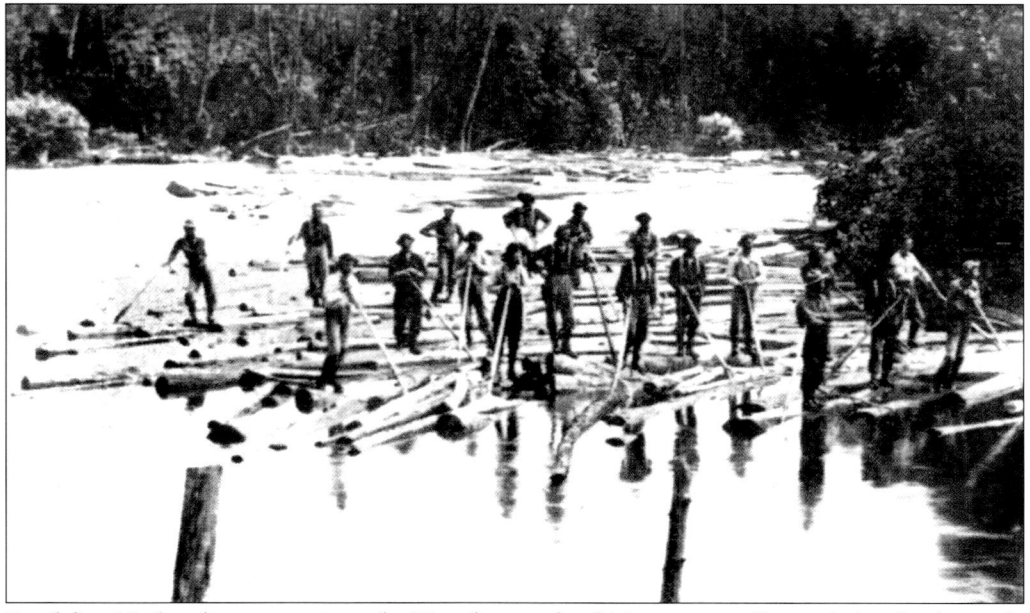

Frankfort Harbor lies approximately 27 miles north of Manistee on Betsie Lake. In the early 1830s, government surveyors suggested that the small deep lake would make a pleasant harbor for Lake Michigan vessels if the river mouth, connecting it to Lake Michigan, was improved. It took another 20 years for local interests to band together to dredge the channel and place two short piers at the mouth to form the harbor.

Early harbor traffic consisted mainly of lumbering vessels and those seeking refuge from storms on the big lake. With Betsie River flowing through the heart of the county, it proved to be ideal for transporting logs to local sawmills, and the area quickly grew to become the hub of northwestern Michigan's lumbering industry. The men pictured above are driving logs on a portion of the 50-mile-long Betsie River. (PW)

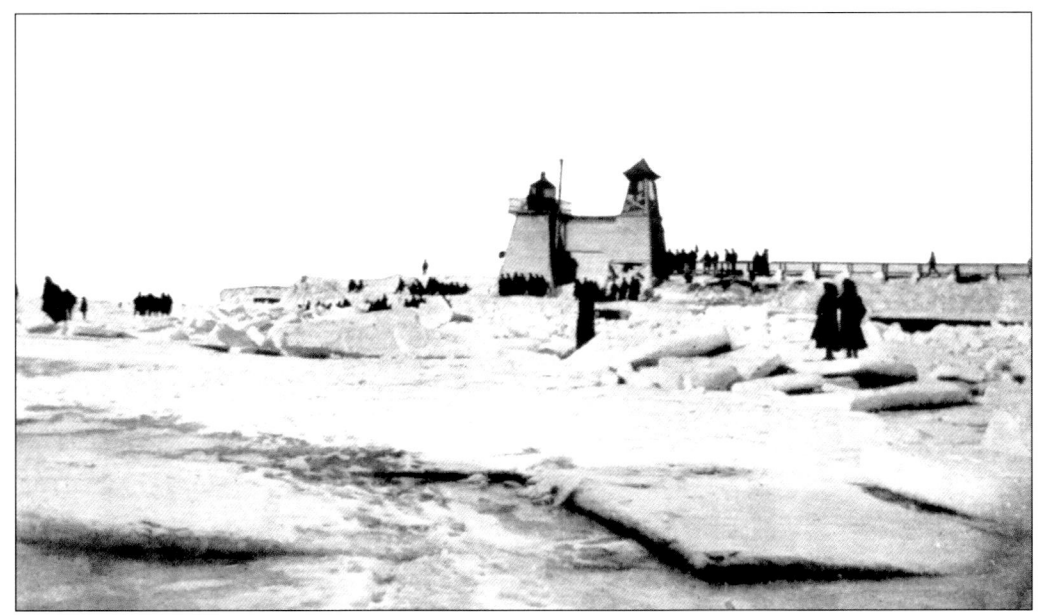

On July 1, 1867, the federal government began work on a new harbor. The new channel was opened just to the south of the natural channel. It was cleared to a depth of 12 feet and was lined on both sides with piers and revetments. When the project was completed, a lighthouse was placed on the outer end of the south pier. Its light was exhibited for the first time on October 15, 1873. (BPL)

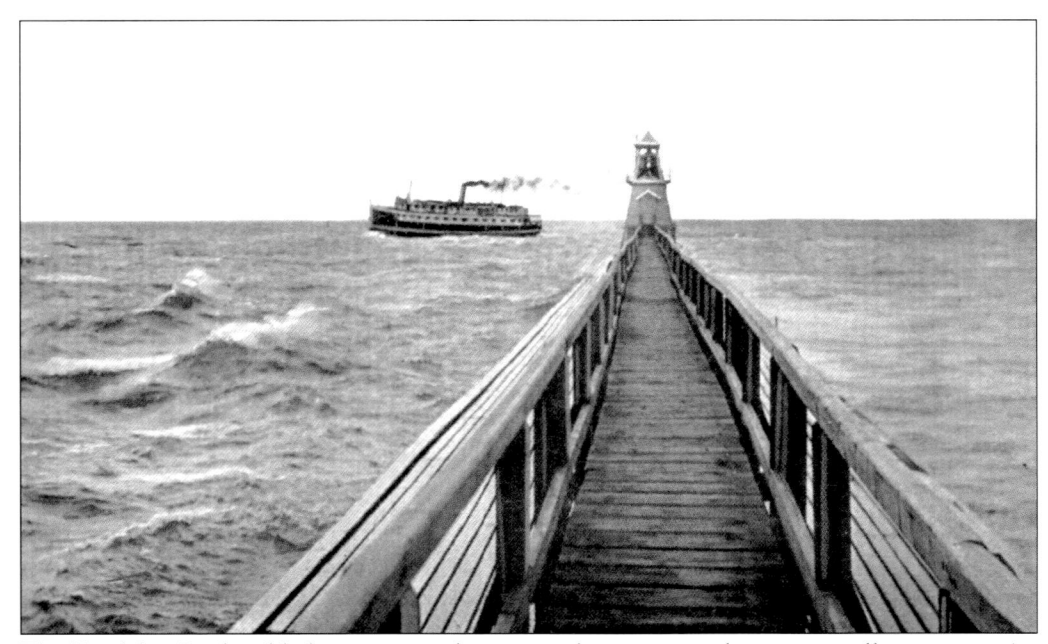

The Frankfort Pierhead light was a wooden pyramid structure with a square gallery on top. An elevated walkway ran the length of the pier, from the shore to the door of the service room. Dwelling space was never provided in this light, so keepers had to procure accommodations elsewhere. (BPL)

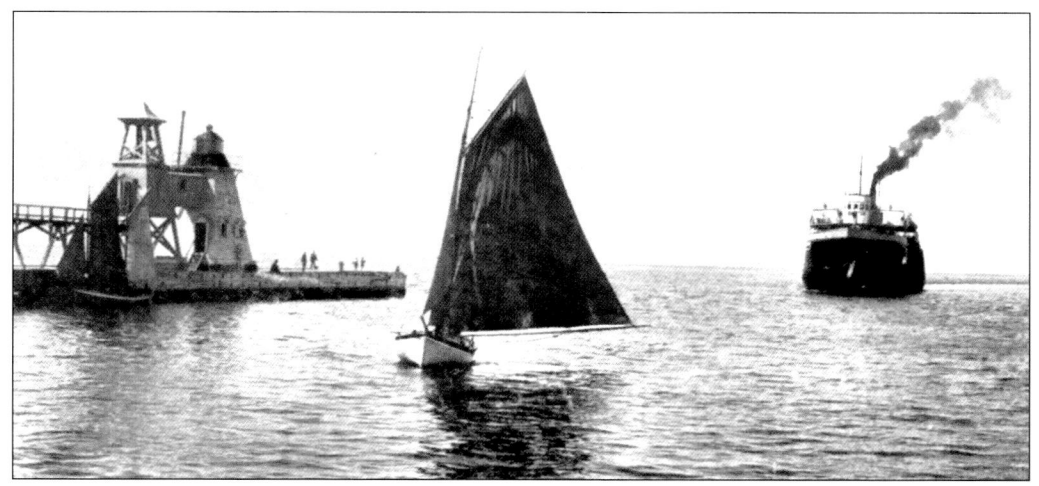

A fog signal was added behind the light in 1893. This structure was a wooden building that was similar to the light in appearance. The bell hung in the open framework on top of the tower, and the striking apparatus was housed underneath. An enclosed walkway connected the two towers. The fog bell remained in use until the early 1900s when it was replaced with a diesel-powered siren. (MMM)

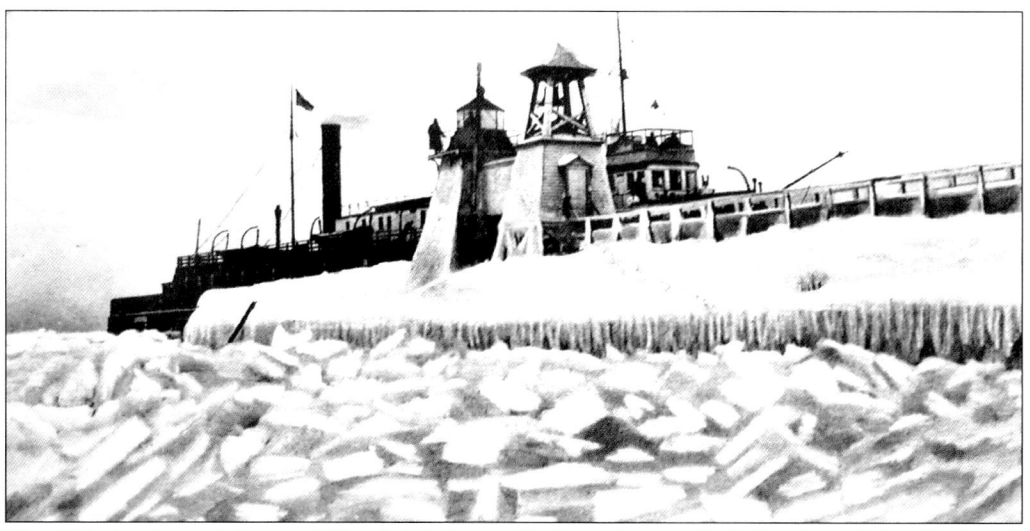

The Toledo, Ann Arbor and North Michigan Railway, later called the Ann Arbor Railroad, came to Frankfort in 1892. The builder of the line, James M. Ashley, had long dreamed of building a railroad that ran from Ohio to Michigan and across Lake Michigan to ports in Wisconsin. On the morning of November 24, 1892, his dream was fulfilled when he and his family, along with four carloads of coal, boarded the Ann Arbor #1 for the maiden voyage of the first cross-lake carferry.

Ashley's excitement was somewhat diminished, when in spite of all his planning, the ship grounded near Keewaunee, Wisconsin. She was hung up for two days before she was freed and able to continue on with her journey. This misfortune was soon forgotten, however, when foreign and domestic sources expressed interest in this new type of Great Lakes service. A picture taken several years later shows the #1 pushing through the ice as she enters the Frankfort harbor. (BHL)

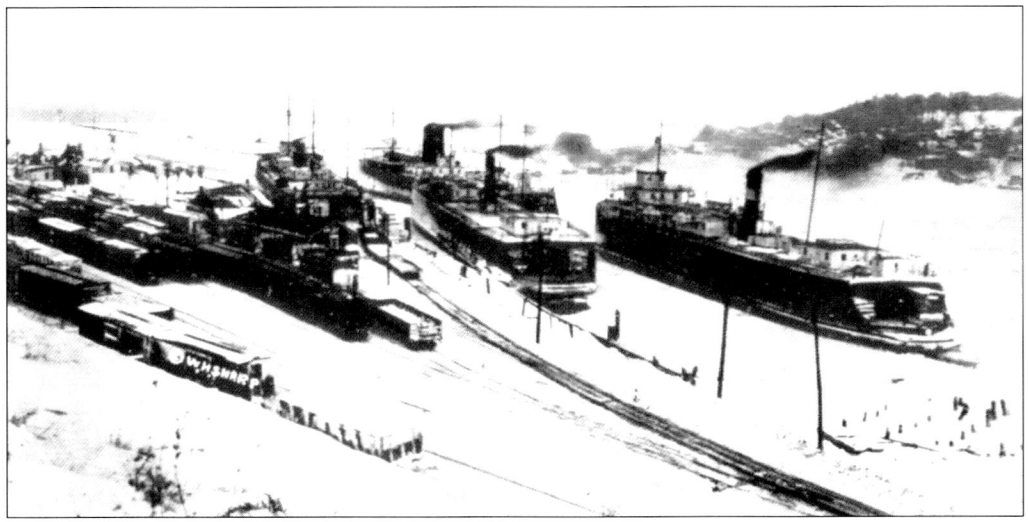

The Ann Arbor Railroad put eight carferries into commission during the years 1892–1927. The first two were wooden vessels and the remaining six were steel steamers. In 1928 the six steamers made 4,300 trips across the lake and carried nearly 100,000 freight cars. (PW)

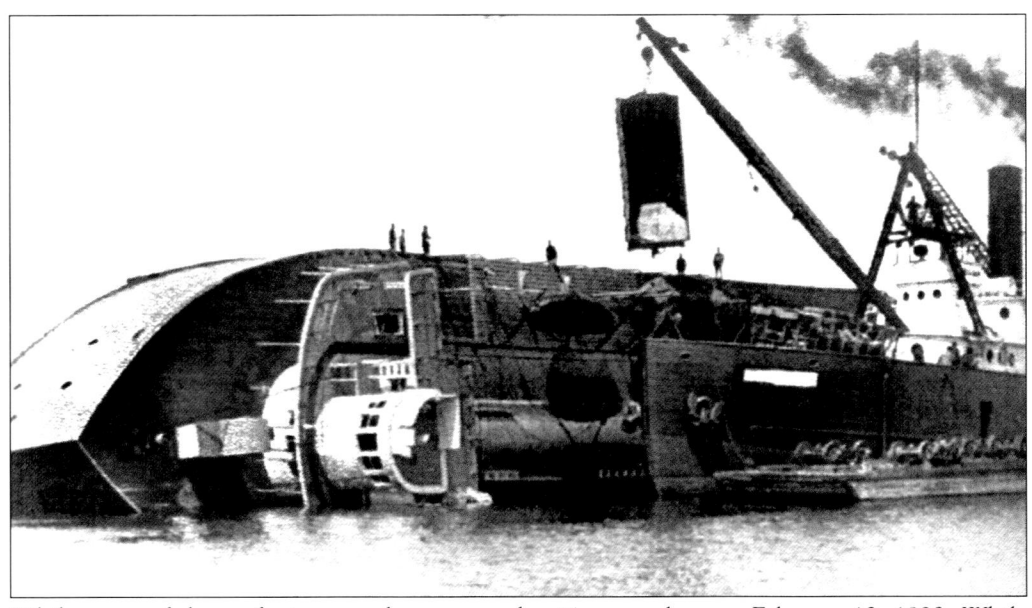

While none of the carferries were lost at sea, the #4 came close on February 13, 1923. While heading to Keewaunee, Wisconsin, she was hit head-on with a strong gale. She rocked so hard that one of the freight cars loaded with automobiles came loose, broke through the gate, and sank. Realizing he was making no headway, the captain tried to turn the ship around and return to port. With great effort he finally made the turn against the heavy seas. However, many of the freight cars had come loose in the process and there was danger of more of them being washed overboard.

The snow was so blinding that the captain didn't know where he was until he heard the fog bell and determined he was northwest of the pier. As he squared to enter the harbor, a huge wave slammed the vessel to the ground. The wind swung her around and smashed her into the south pier, where she went down. (PW)

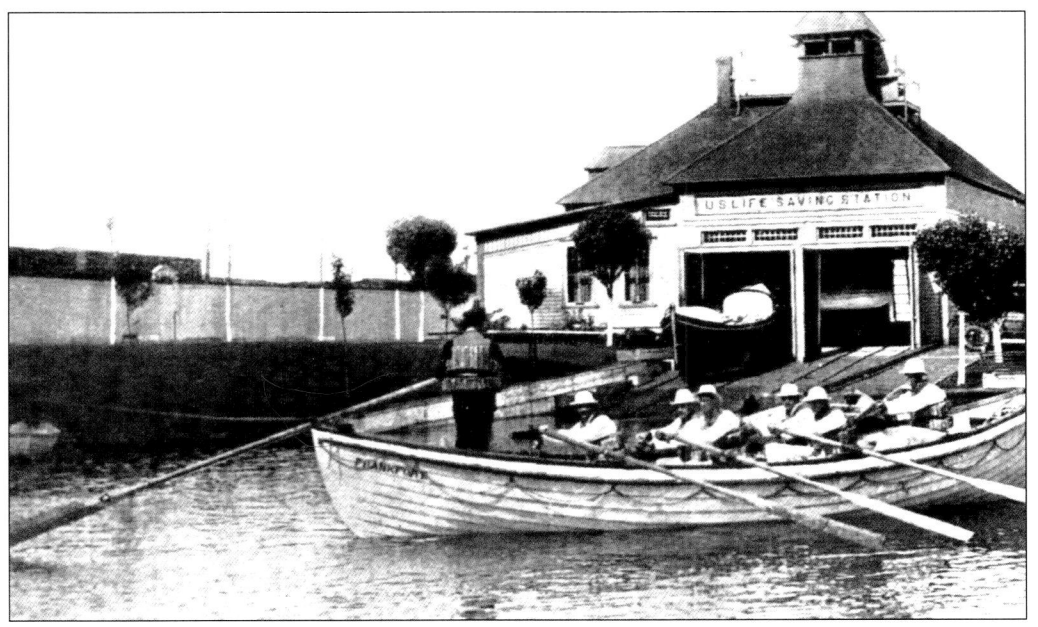

The Frankfort Life-Saving Station became operational in 1887. The station was built on the south side of the harbor, originally called South Frankfort. In 1911, its name was changed to Elberta after the Elberta peach that grew abundantly in the area. At the time this picture was taken, the station was equipped with a surfboat (in the water) and a lifeboat (on the ramp). (PW)

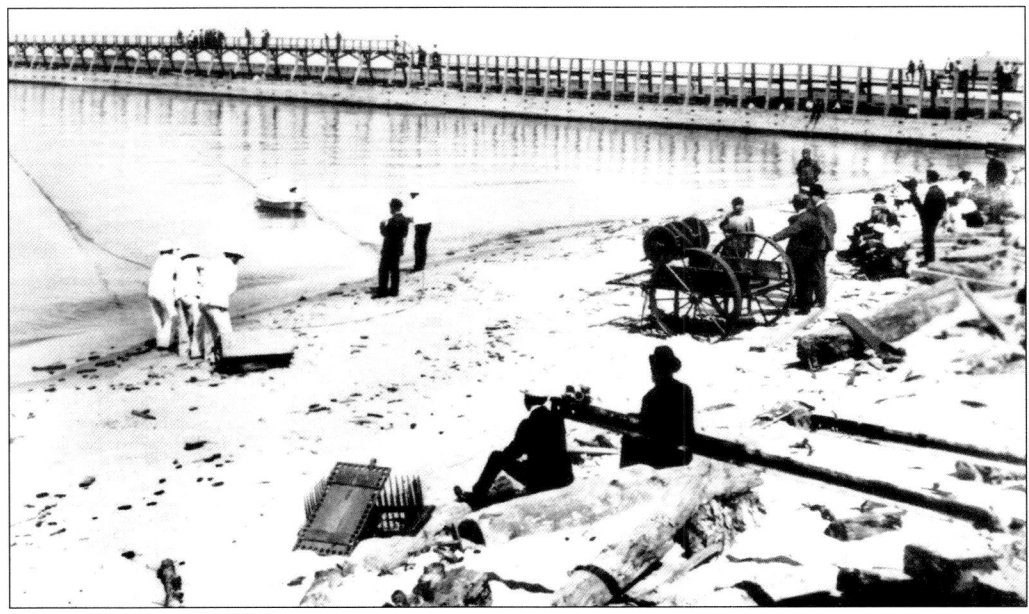

Practicing life-saving drills was a daily occurrence for the life-savers. The faking box (lower left) held the line that was shot out to the distressed boat in a rescue attempt. Faking, or coiling the shot line around the pins in the faking box, was crucial to a successful firing. It was done according to a precise method that allowed the line to come off the pins easily, without entanglement. It took one faker and two assistants 25 to 30 minutes to coil 600 yards of line. (BPL)

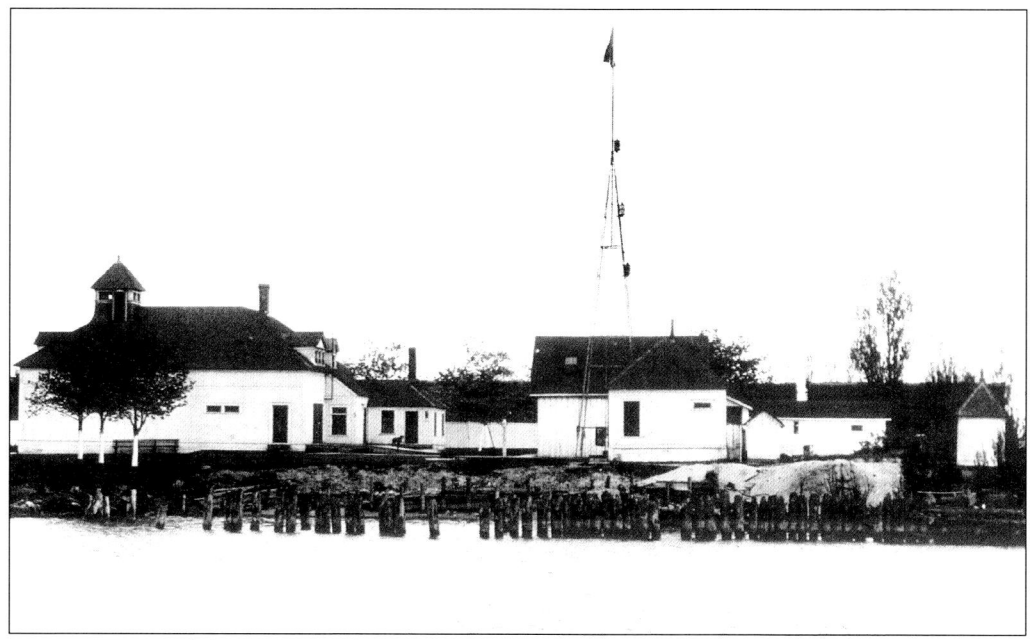

By 1915 many of the surfmen who had served for 20 to 30 years were leaving the service. The new recruits lacked experience and training and there weren't many veterans left to train them. To remedy this problem, the civilian Life-Saving Service was combined with the military Revenue Cutter Service to form the U.S. Coast Guard. The former Life-Saving Station, seen on the left, combined with the other outbuildings, formed the Elberta Coast Guard Station. (PW)

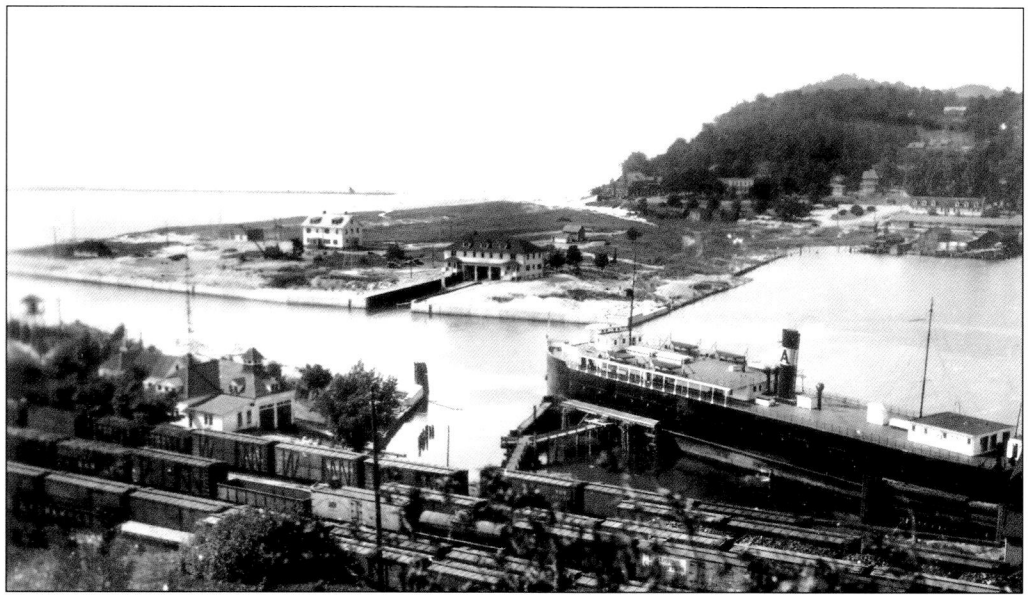

The Coast Guard Station, seen in the center of the picture, was moved to the north side of the channel in 1934–1935. The old station on the south side was given to the Ann Arbor Railroad in a trade for land to build the new station in Frankfort. The old station was then converted into an office building. (MMM)

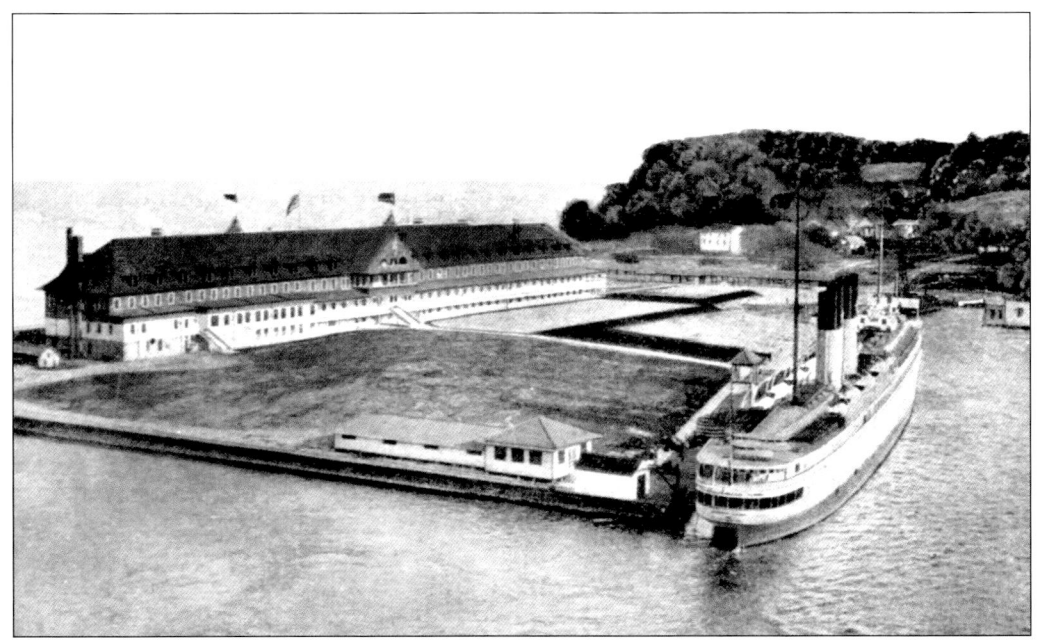

The Hotel Frontenac was built by the Ann Arbor Railroad in 1901 on a piece of land that jutted out into the channel. While under construction, a strong northwest gale blew in off the lake and caused the building to collapse. When the rubble was cleared away, the structure was rebuilt as a sturdier, fashionable hotel that became frequented by wealthy summer residents from Ohio and Illinois.

On the night of January 12, 1912, a mysterious fire destroyed the beautiful hotel. While the loss was significant, a rare off-shore wind kept the fire localized and prevented it from spreading through town and possibly destroying many other buildings. (MMM)

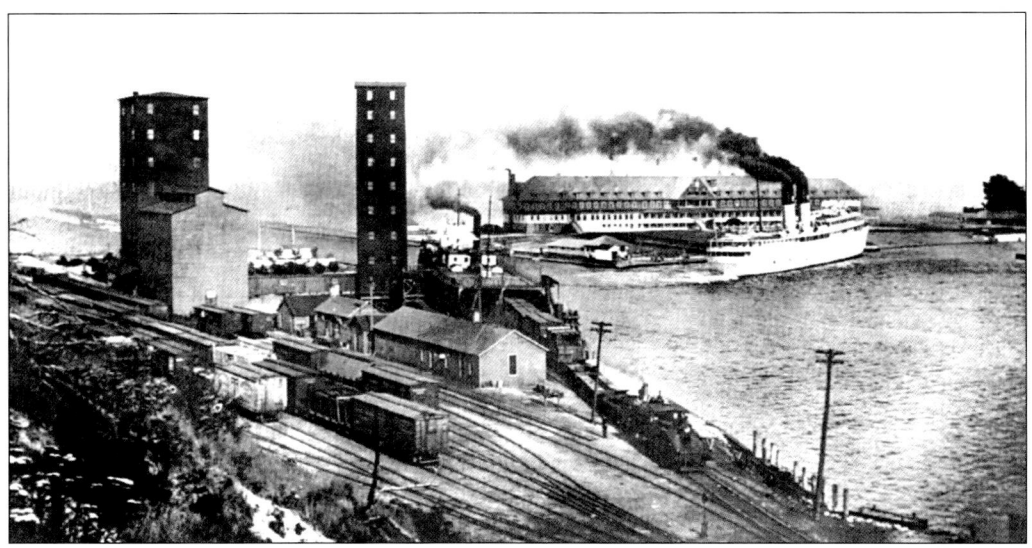

The plant on the left of the picture, across the harbor from the Frontenac, produced charcoal briquettes. Vessels often carried briquettes to Chicago to be used in fires for heating as a supplemental fuel when coal supplies were low. (PW)

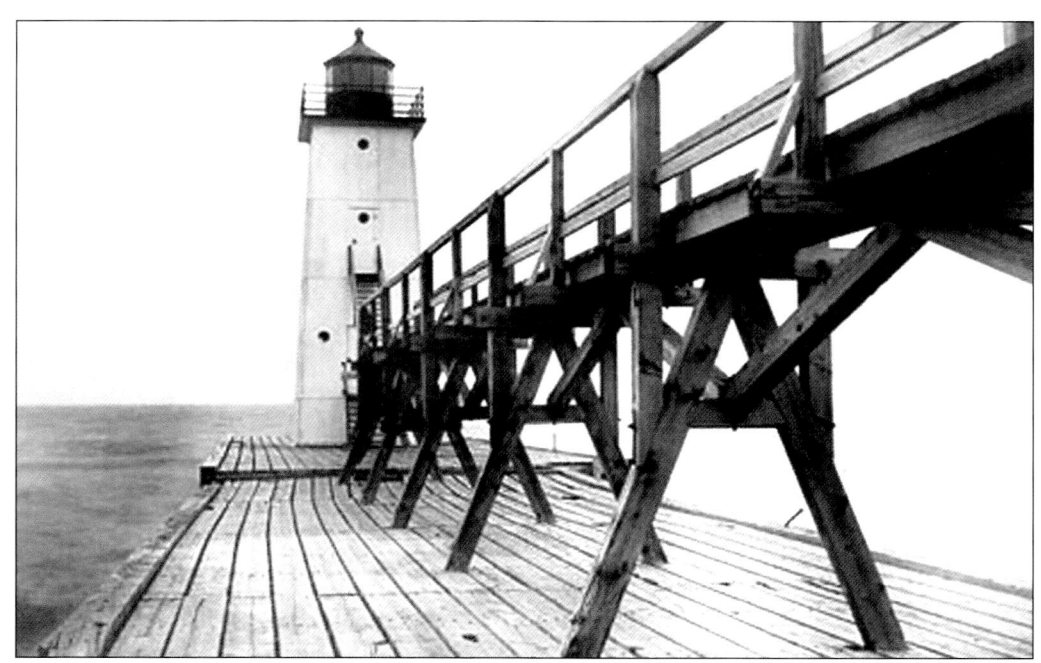

In 1912 a pyramidal light tower was built on the end of the north pier. It was plated with steel and painted white up to the lantern room. An elevated wooden walkway connected the light to the shore. The air siren was moved to the new tower, and the lens from the south pier light was placed on a post behind the new light to form a range light system. The old south pier light and fog signal were demolished. (USCG)

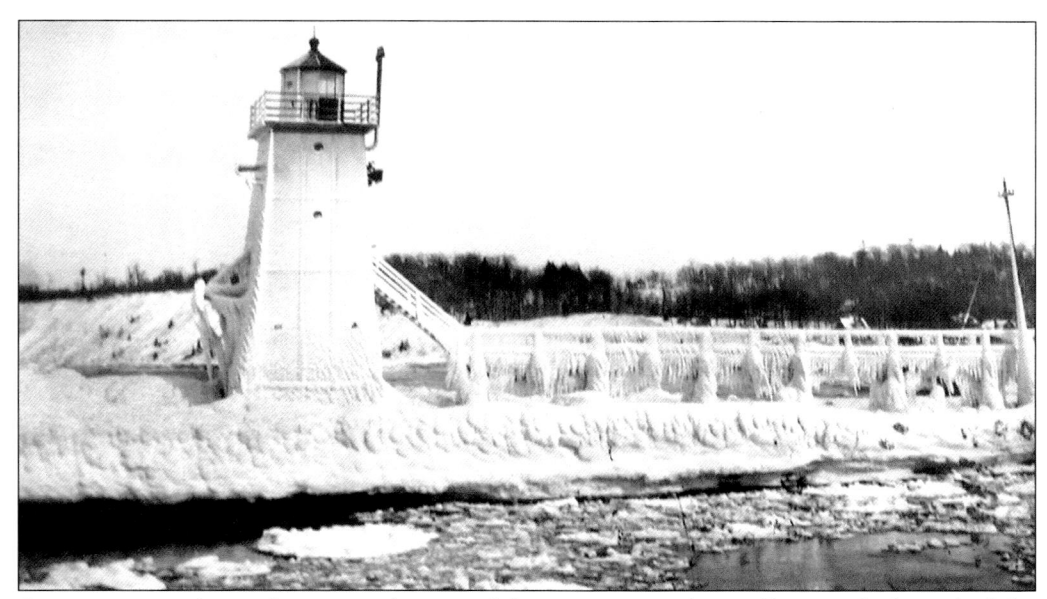

A winter view shows the unique beauty of the ice-encrusted pier. Even with the aid of the catwalk, trekking to the light several times a day could present a challenge to the keeper during winter. However, it was safer than walking directly on the pier and risking sliding into the water. (BHL)

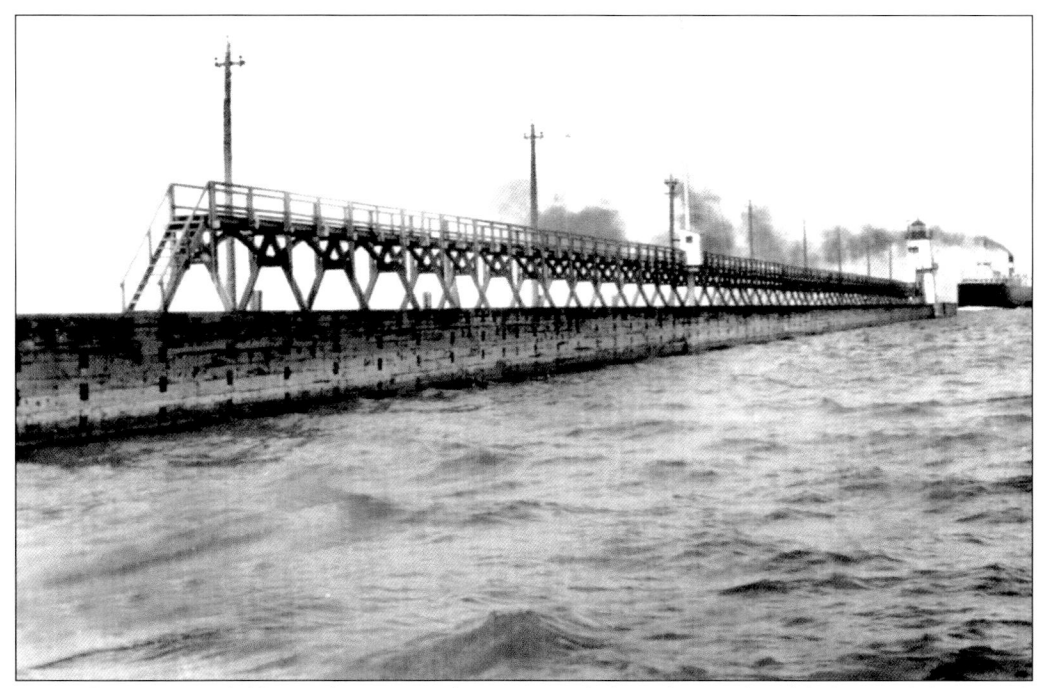

Power became available in the area and was extended to the pierhead lights and fog signal, c. 1919. This addition improved the effectiveness of the light by increasing its visible range up to fourteen miles. (PW)

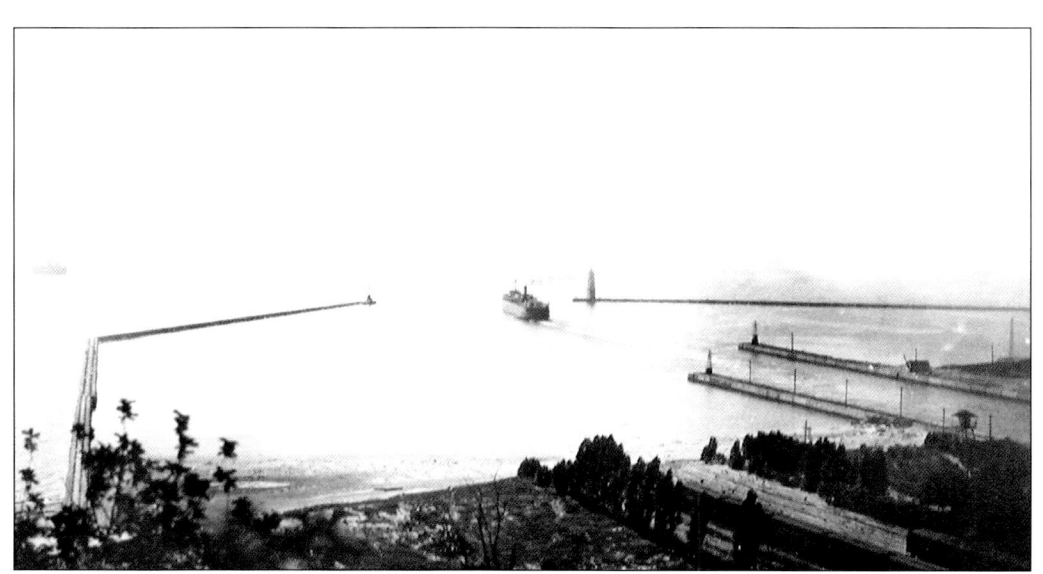

In the 1920s carferry traffic was heavy in the harbor. It was often difficult for these vessels to make the channel entrance coming off the rough waters of Lake Michigan. To facilitate their entry, the Army Corps of Engineers constructed an arrowhead harbor. Concrete breakwaters were built on either side of the entrance to form a stilling basin leading to the channel. (BHL)

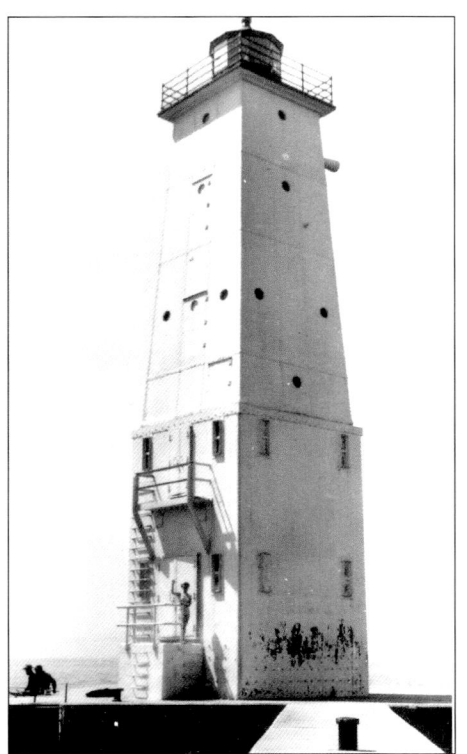

Upon completion of the breakwaters, the old piers were no longer necessary. They were shortened to stub piers and the light was removed and taken to the north breakwater. A 25-foot-tall steel base was placed on the end of the breakwater and the light was secured on top. The new Frankfort Light began shining in 1932. The entrances of the original tower can be seen directly above the stairs and current doors. (MMM)

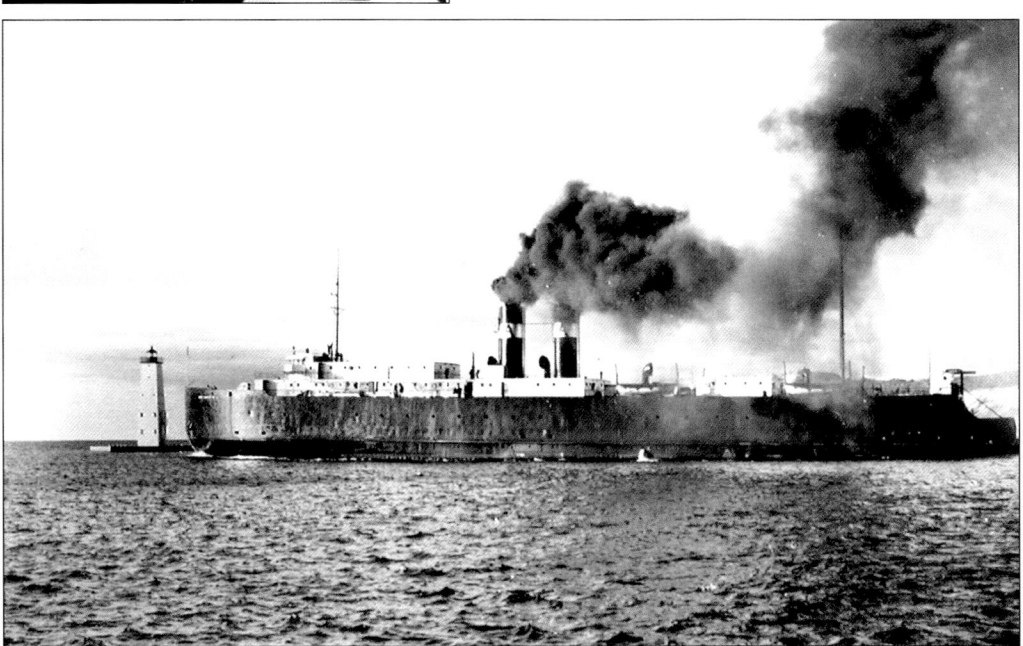

A photograph from the 1950s shows a more modern ferry leaving the harbor. The growth of the U.S. highway system and interstate trucking marked the end of the railroad heyday. The last of the Frankfort carferries lay dormant in the harbor for a few years before she was sold and towed away in 1967. (BHL)

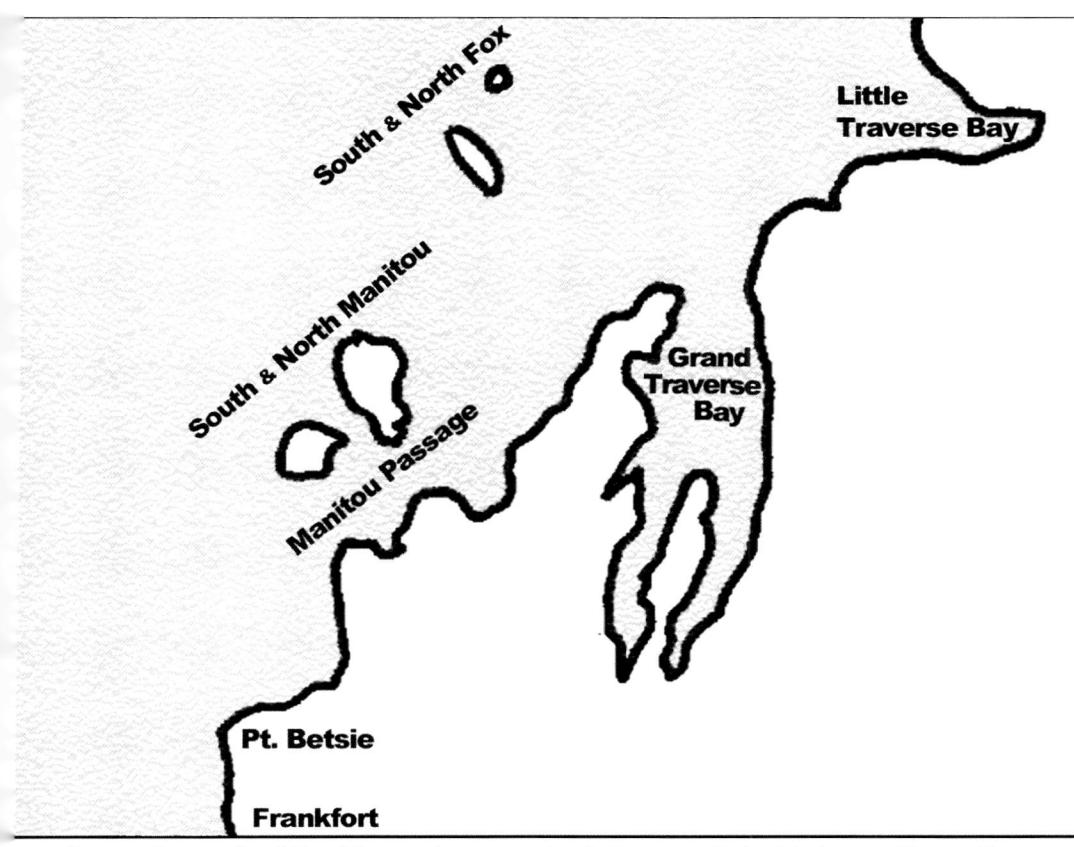

Four miles north of Frankfort, a distinct point bulges into Lake Michigan. Originally named "Pointe Aux Becs Scies" (Sawed Beak Point) by the French, the American pronunciation deteriorated to Point Betsie. The same point is also recognized with the spellings Point Betsey and Point Betsy.

The most direct and most protected route for ships heading north to the Mackinac Straits was through the Manitou Passage. This narrow shoal-lined channel ran between the mainland on the east and the Beaver Island Archipelago on the west. Although a light had been placed on South Manitou Island to mark the western side of the passage as early as 1840, no light was considered on the mainland side until the early 1850s. At that time it was determined that a light on Point Betsie was crucial since vessels used the point as a marker to indicate when they should begin their turn into the passage. On March 3, 1853, Congress appropriated the necessary funds to build a lighthouse on the point.

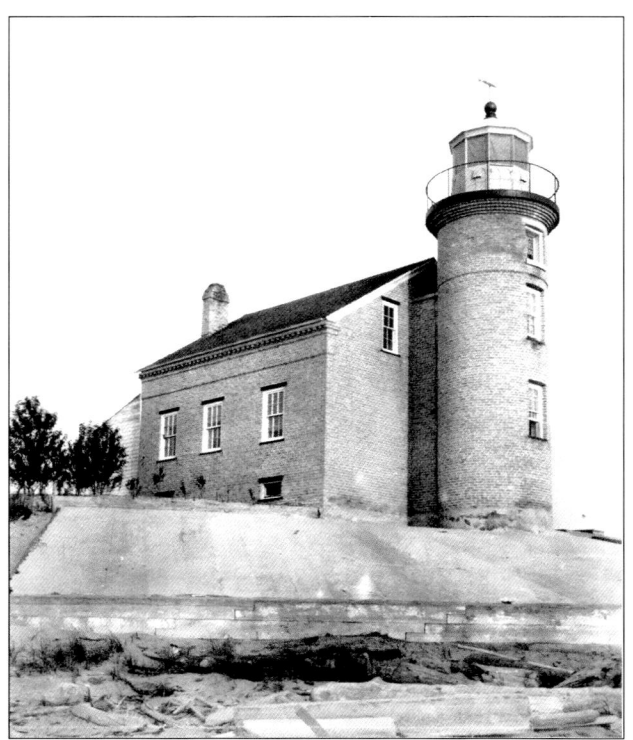

Construction began on the lighthouse in 1854 and was completed in 1858. The two-story dwelling was located directly behind the cylindrical tower and was connected to it by a short passageway. The tower had an overall height of 37 feet and held a Fourth Order Fresnel lens in its lantern room. Having been built close to the water's edge, with poor quality workmanship, it was threatened by erosion within its first year of operation. In 1890, a concrete ring 16 feet in diameter was placed beneath the tower to strengthen it, and a curved revetment was placed at the base of the dunes to help reduce the damage caused by incoming waves. (NA)

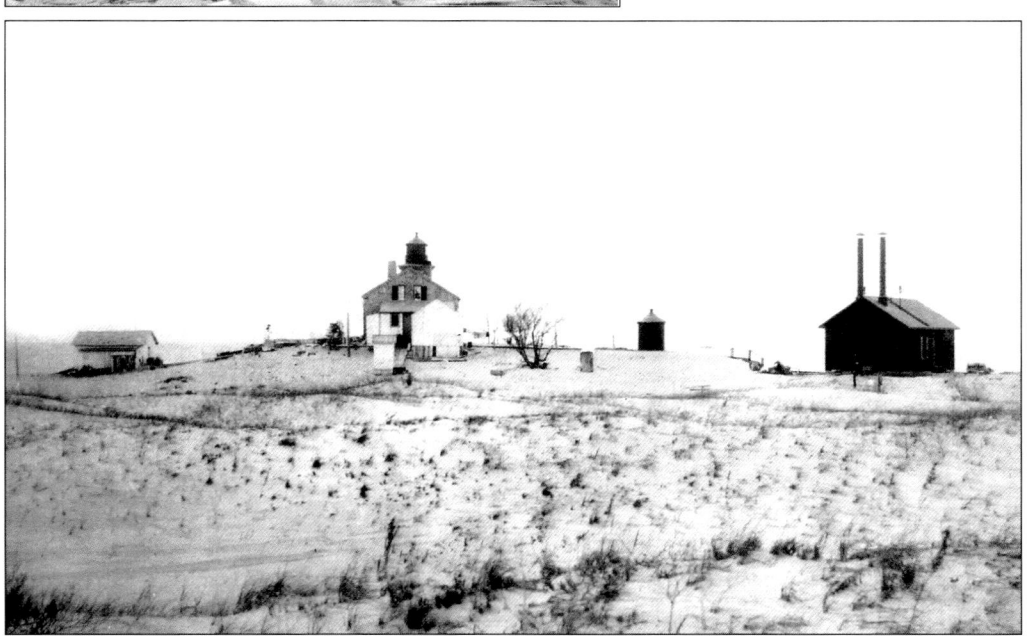

Congress approved the necessary funds to establish a fog signal building north of the lighthouse in 1890. Looking from the rear of the property toward the lake, the fog signal is seen on the right of the picture. The building was a wood-framed structure sheathed in corrugated iron. It housed two 10-inch steam whistles that began operating in December of 1891. About one year later, a circular iron oil storage building was added near the fog signal. (NA)

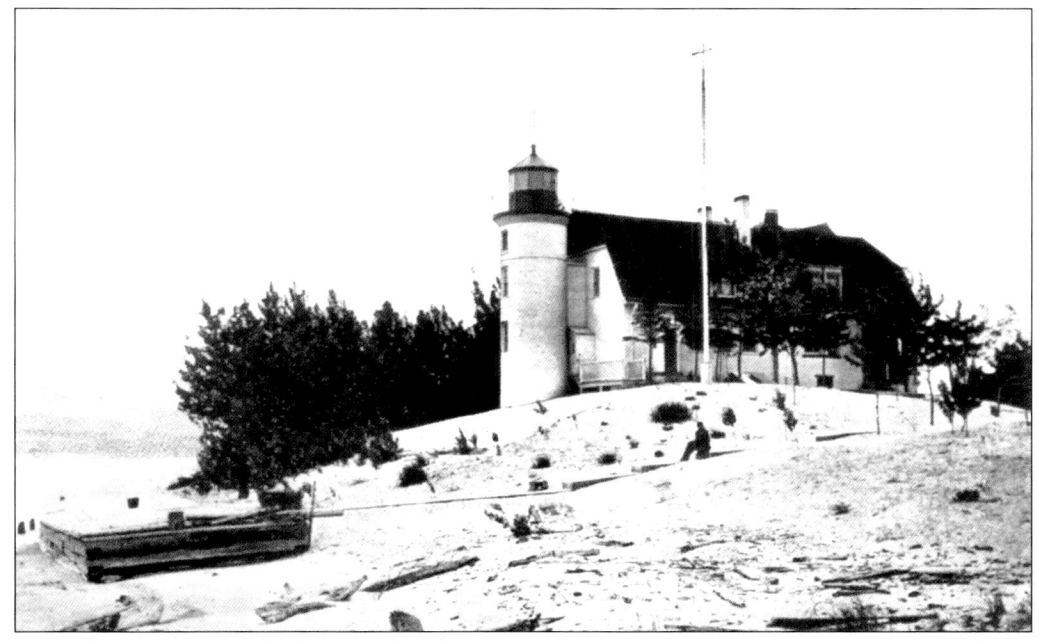

With the addition of the fog signal, it became necessary to hire an assistant to help with the increased workload. To house the assistant and his family, the original small keeper's dwelling was completely renovated and enlarged to hold two families. The new gambrel roof design of the building gave it a barn-like appearance. (MMM)

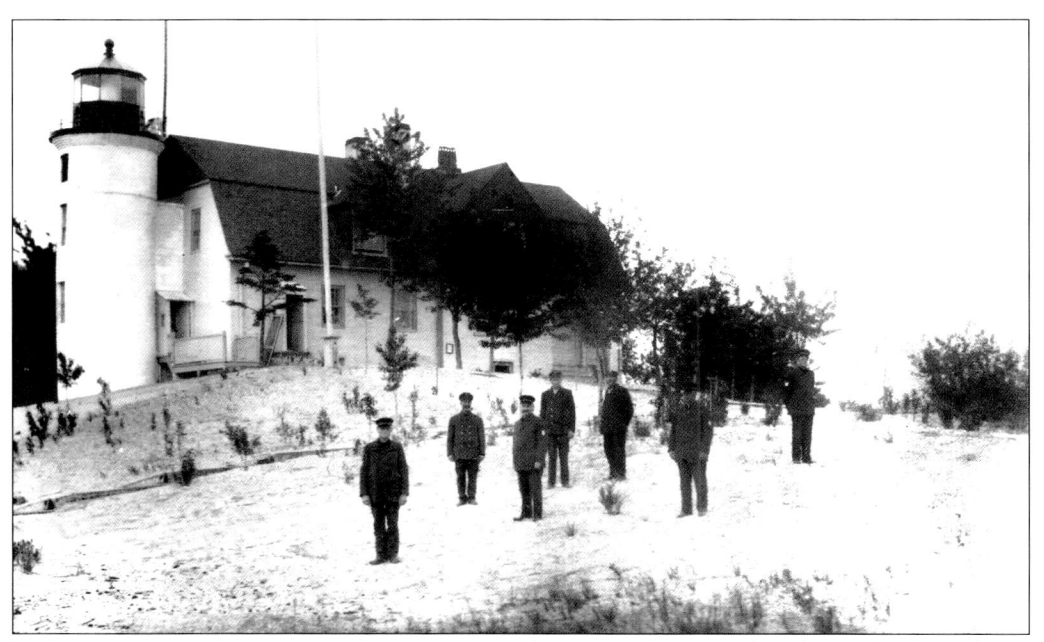

Lights were not only necessary for night travel but were also crucial as daymarks. In order to make them more visible during the daylight hours, towers were often painted white to stand out against the background. In 1900 the Point Betsie tower and dwelling were painted white and the roof and parapet were painted red. (MMM)

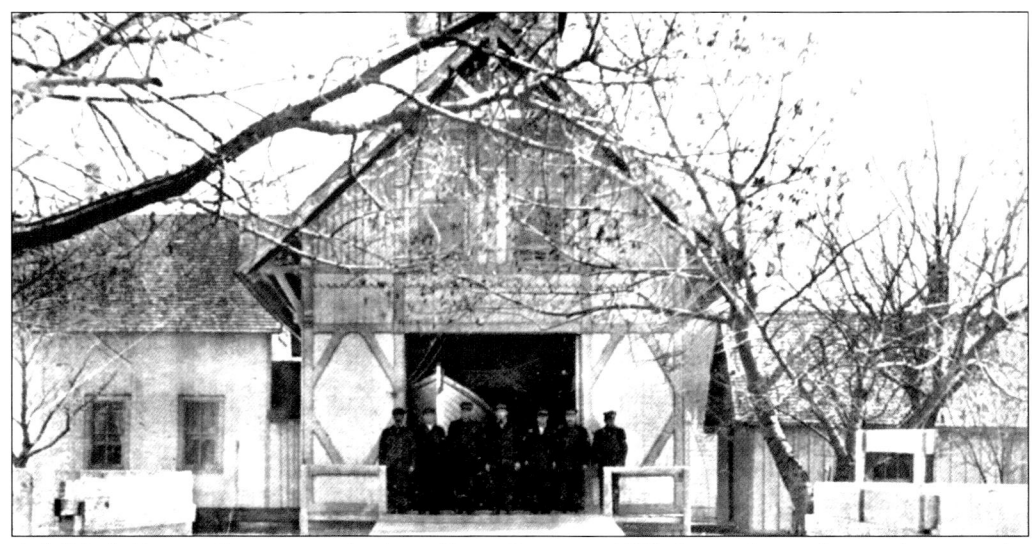

A full Life-Saving Station was built at Point Betsie in 1875. It was located near shore on the south side of the lighthouse. The station held two lookout platforms on the roof of the boat room that were connected by a walkway.

The Articles of Engagement for the life-saving crew of 1885 entitled the surfmen to a salary of $50 per month for service rendered during the active navigation season. During the "off" season they were still required to assist in rescues if called on, at an unstipulated pay rate. The 1885 crew consisted of seven surfmen and one captain, Thomas E. Matthews. Notice the discrepancy in the spelling of Point Betsie. The cover of the articles of Engagement has Point Betsey while the inside has Point Betsy. (MMM, NC, NC)

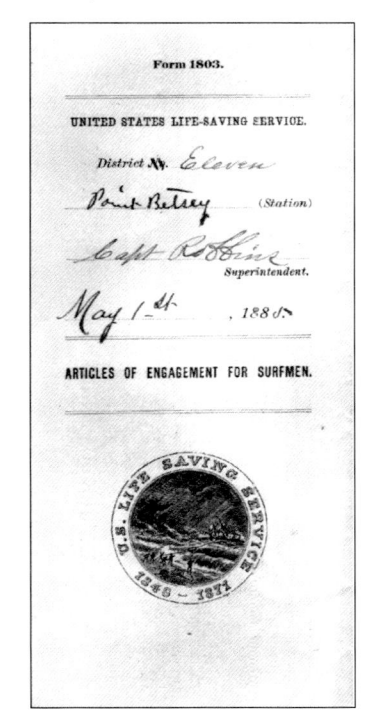

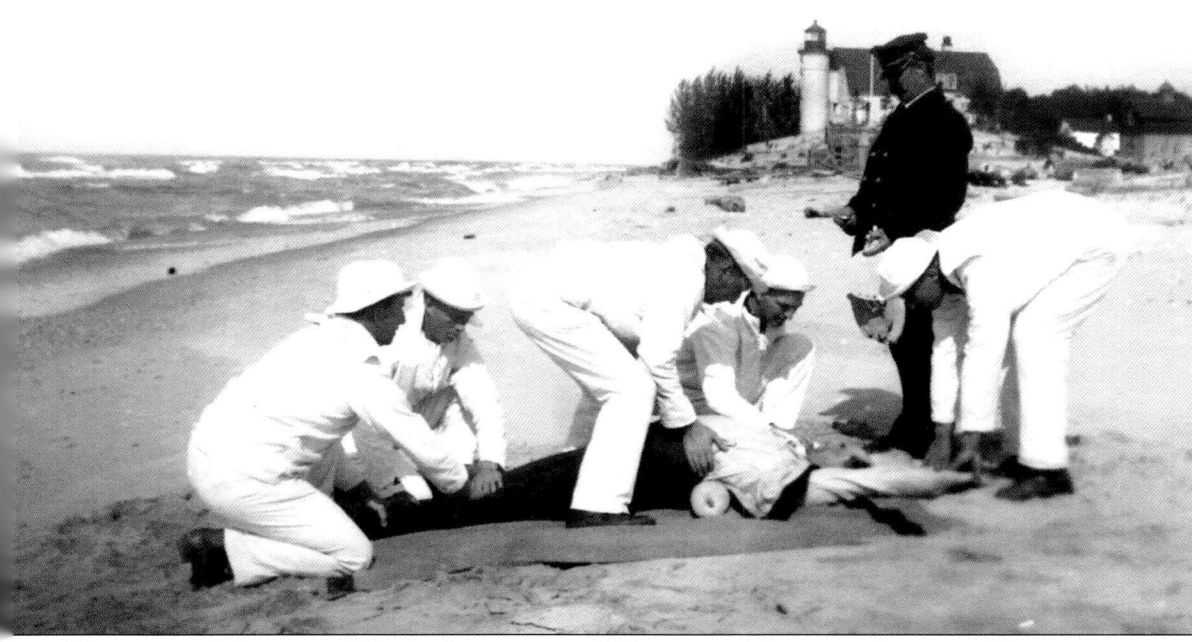

The rescue of the crew of the *St. Lawerence* in 1898 is one of the station's most well-known feats. On November 25, the steamer was heading from Chicago to Ontario when a severe snow storm with gale force winds struck and grounded her two miles south of the Point Betsie Life-Saving Station.

The surfmen, loaded with equipment, trudged through the sand and snow for nearly an hour until they neared the ship. When a rescue attempt with the surfboat failed, a lifeline was shot out to the vessel. With no response after two firings the surfmen feared the worst, when all at once they heard the whistle blowing. Apparently, the lifeline had landed across the whistle cord and each time the life-savers pulled on the line the whistle blew.

Having been alerted by the whistle, those onboard who were unaware of the lifeline's presence found it and in their haste secured it incorrectly. As a result, the surfmen were forced to pull the lifecar along the line hand-over-hand for two grueling trips to the vessel and back to rescue the crew. Only one crewman, who had attempted to make it to shore on his own, perished, in spite of attempts to resuscitate him. Above, the crew practices a resuscitation drill for use in such emergencies. (MMM)

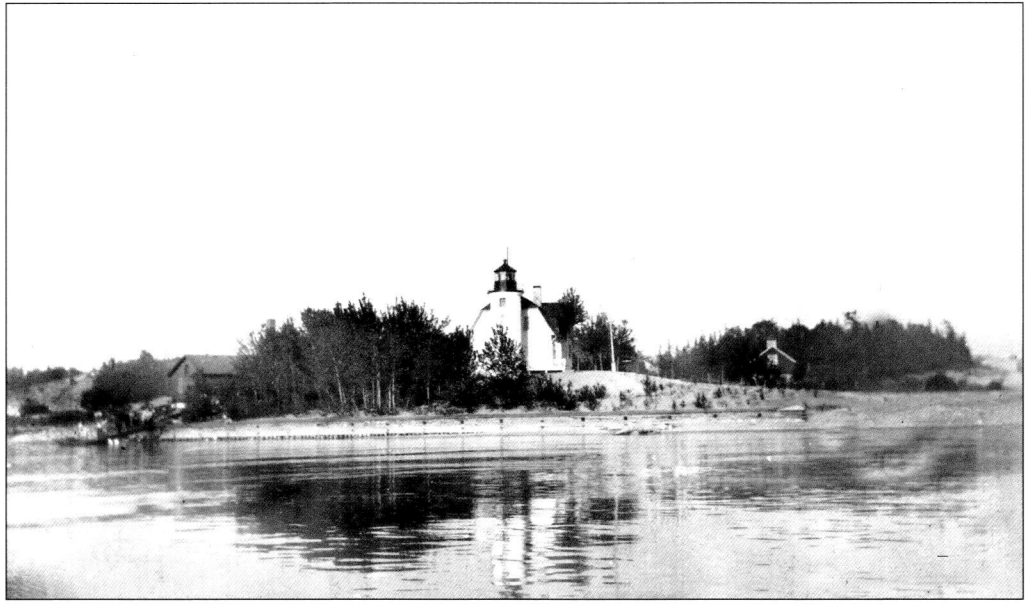

Electric power reached the light in the 1920s. An electric light bulb was placed in the lens and the fog signal was powered by electric air compressors. This greatly reduced the work the keeper and assistants had to do to keep the apparatus functioning. (MMM)

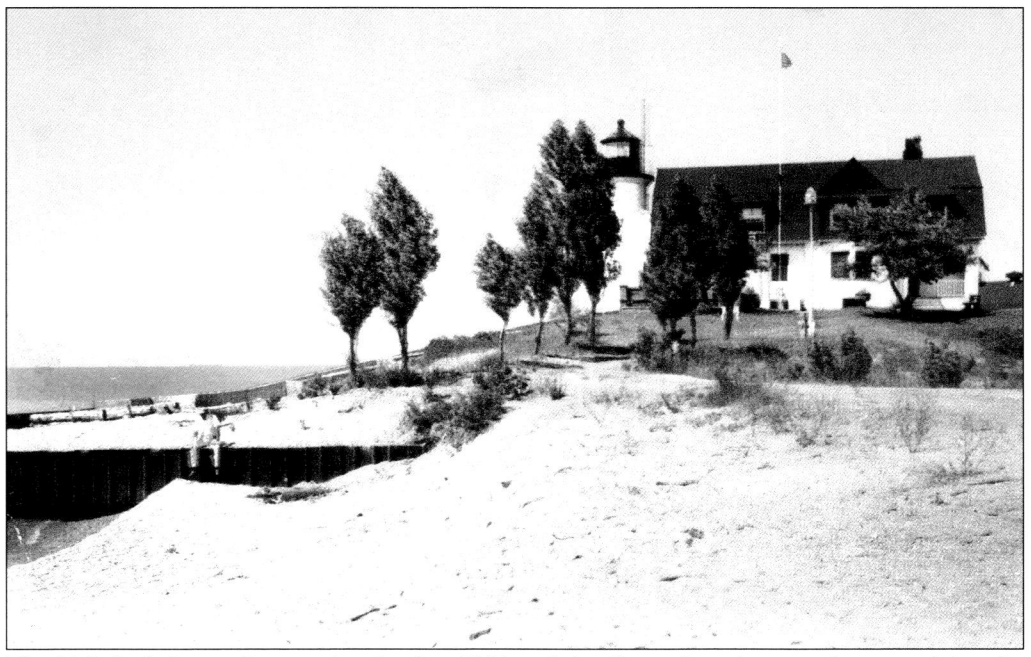

The U.S. Lighthouse Service dissolved in 1939 and the Coast Guard assumed responsibility for the maintenance of lighthouses. As automation increased, it eliminated the need for keepers. In 1940 the position of Second Assistant was eliminated. In c. 1952 the First Assistant left. The keeper remained until 1963. (NC)

Only minor changes appear in the structure in the late 1950s, such as the increase in electronic equipment on the roof, the addition of a stone railing on the porch, and a concrete skirt on the lakeward side of the tower, used to forestall erosion. (NC)

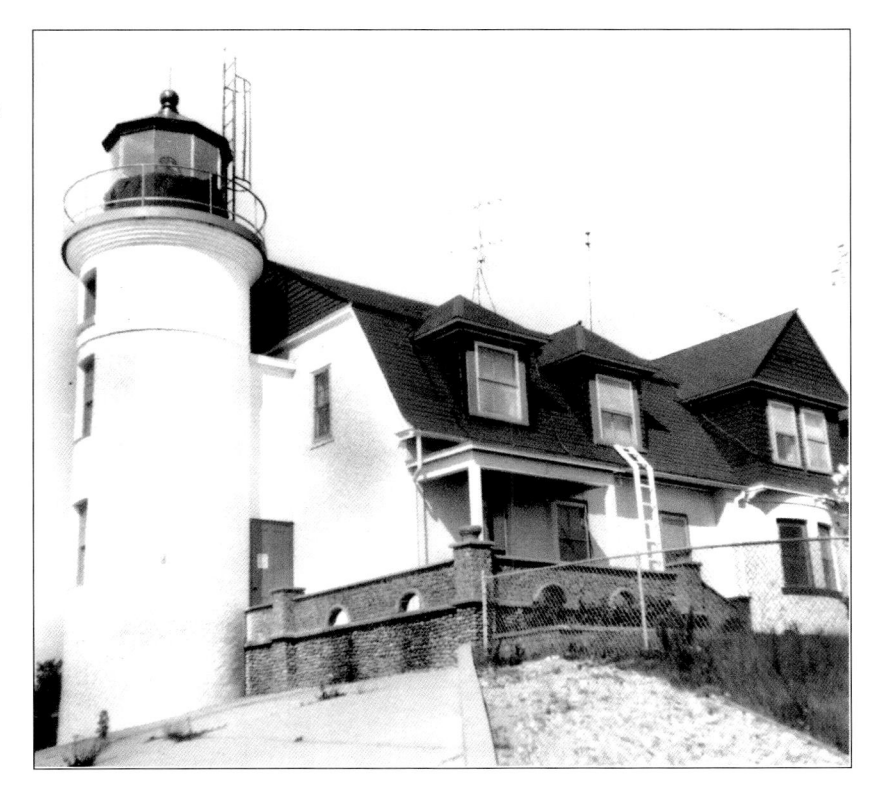

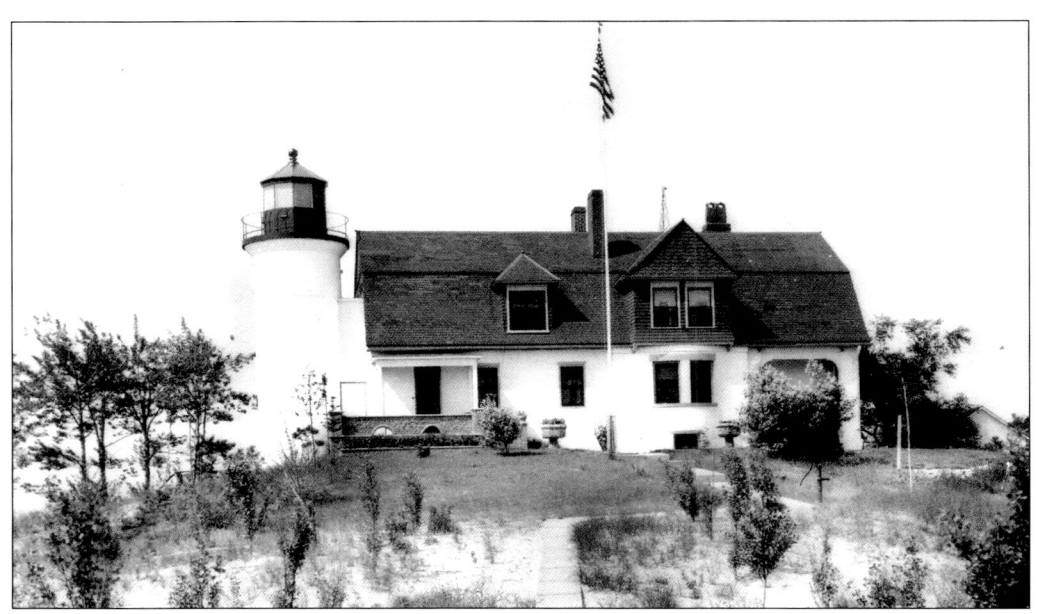

In 1983–1984 Point Betsie was automated and became the last manned lighthouse on the mainland of eastern Lake Michigan. It continued to serve as a residence for Coast Guard personnel for the next 12 years until it was finally abandoned. (MMM)

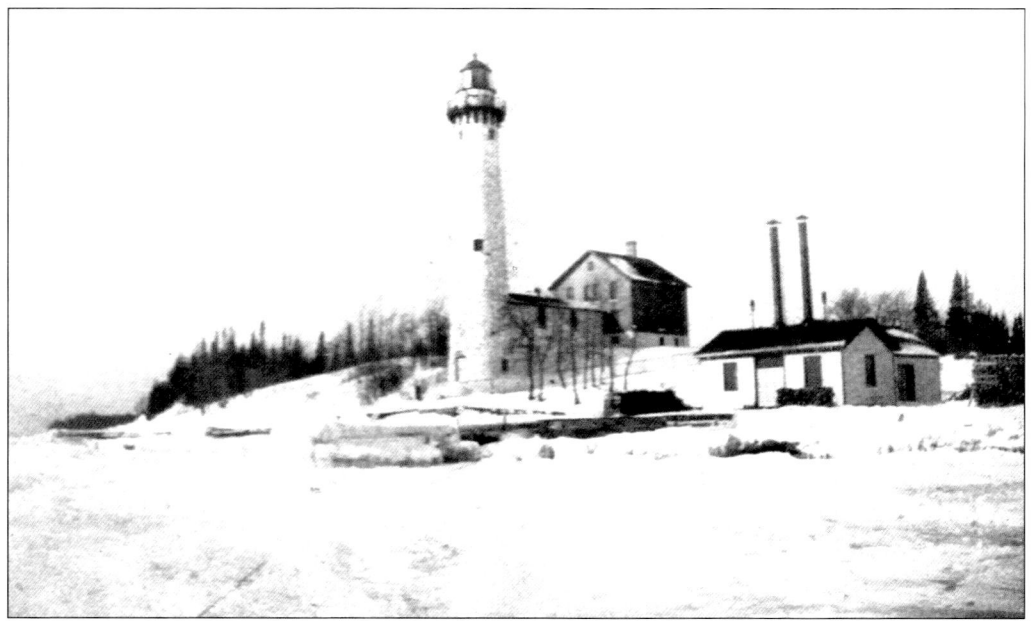

South Manitou Island marks the southern end of the Beaver Island Archipelago and the Manitou Passage. During the 1800s it offered the deepest natural harbor between Chicago and the Mackinac Straits for larger vessels seeking shelter from storms from the west and southwest; and with its abundant timber supply it was also a favorite spot for steamers to load up on wood fuel. (MCHM)

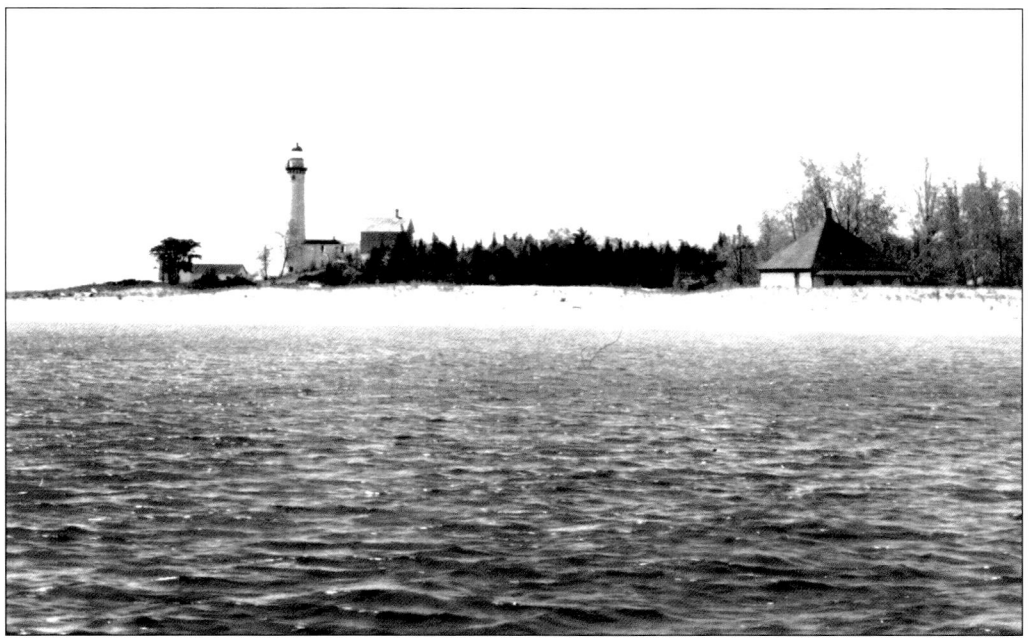

A light was built on the southeast end of the island in 1839 to aid mariners in finding the entrance to the passage during darkness and inclement weather. After 18 years of existence, for reasons that are unclear, the decision was made to build a new light. The new light station was completed on a rise near the shoreline in 1858. (SAM)

The 1858 station was a two-story cream-colored brick building with a short tower rising from the roof. Unfortunately, the light was so small that mariners often confused it with lights on vessels in the harbor. Consequently, a new 104-foot-tall conical brick tower was built and outfitted with a Third Order lens that made its light visible for up to 18 miles. (MCHS)

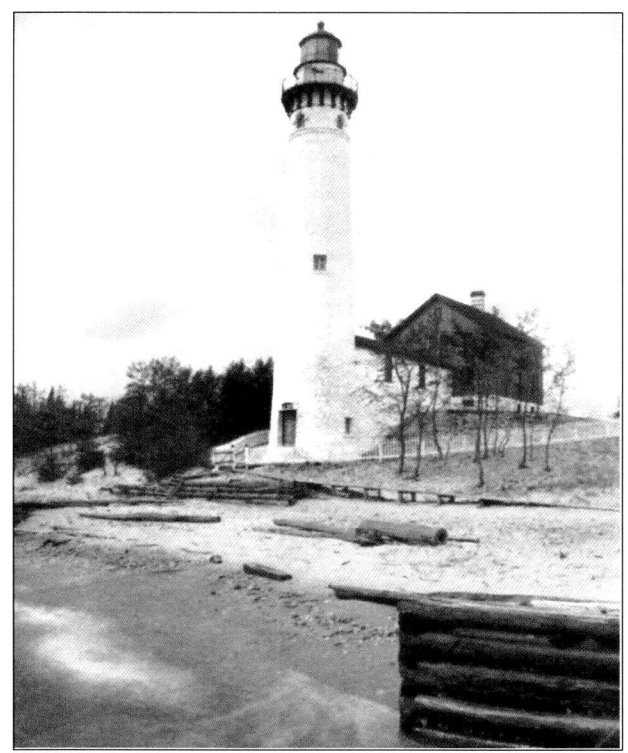

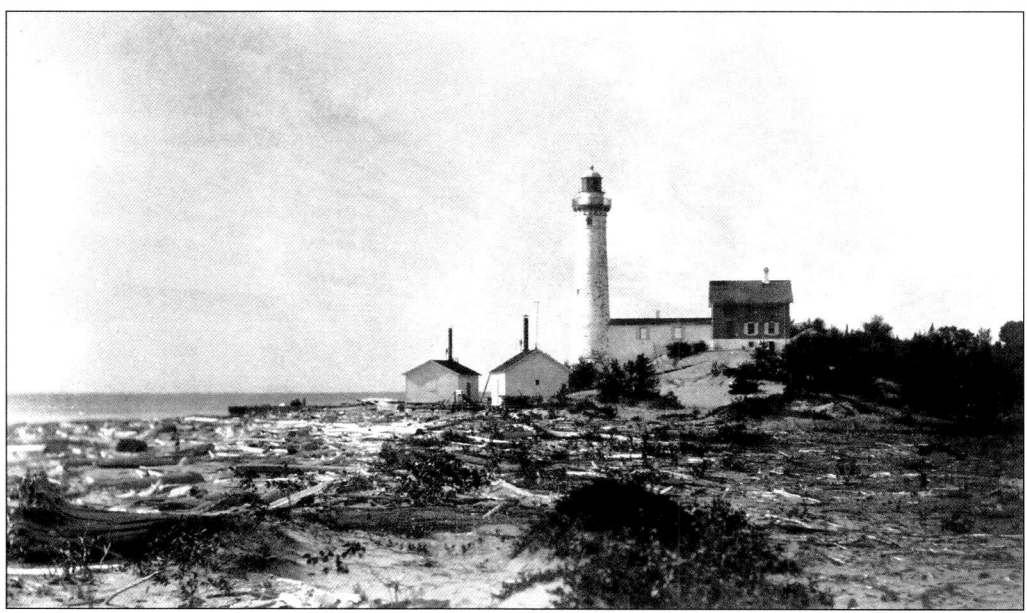

The first steam-powered fog signal on Lake Michigan was added to the grounds in 1875. It proved to be so critical to mariners' safety that a second fog signal was built next to it to act as a back up. During the shipping season of 1898, the whistles blew a record 1,085 hours. The station continued in operation until 1958 when additional markers and the use of radar made it obsolete. (NA)

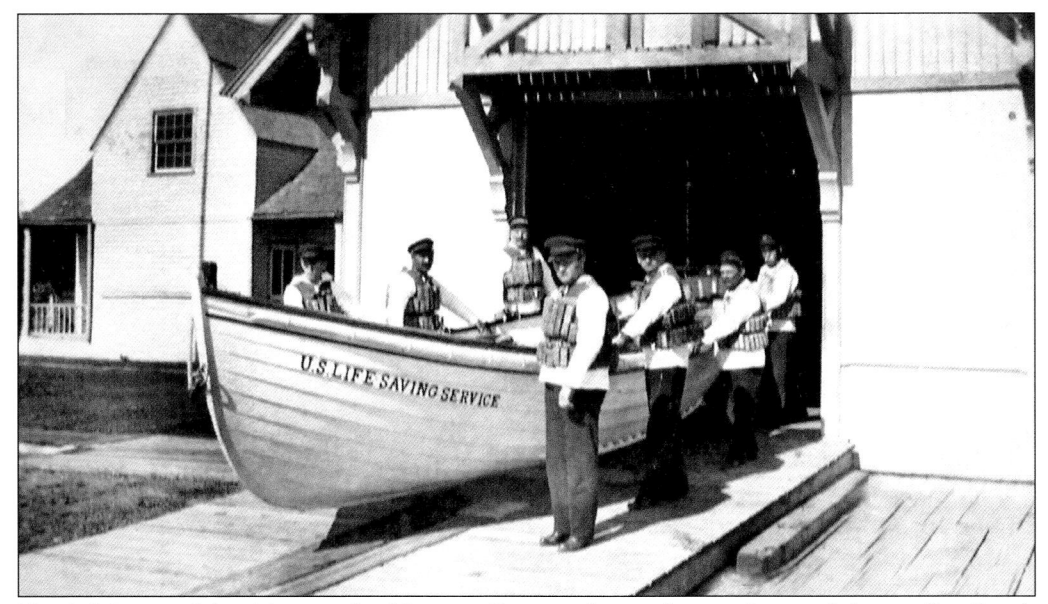

North Manitou Island lies in the Manitou Passage, four miles northeast of the smaller South Manitou Island. The volume of shipping traffic was heavy through this narrow passage and resulted in many shipping casualties. A volunteer life-saving service was established to aid the victims of these vessels in 1854. It was taken over by the U.S. Life-Saving Service in 1874 and a Lifeboat Station was added in 1877. The station continued in existence as the Coast Guard until 1938. (BHL)

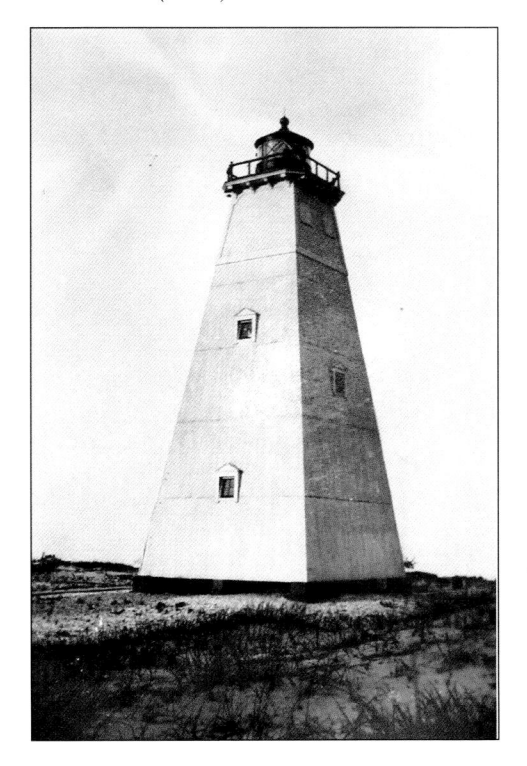

A light was established on the southern end of the island in 1898 to mark the three-mile-long North Manitou Shoal. The unusual looking tower was a clapboard clad wooden structure that flared out near its base. It stood about 50 feet tall and housed a Fourth Order Fresnel lens. (BHL)

68

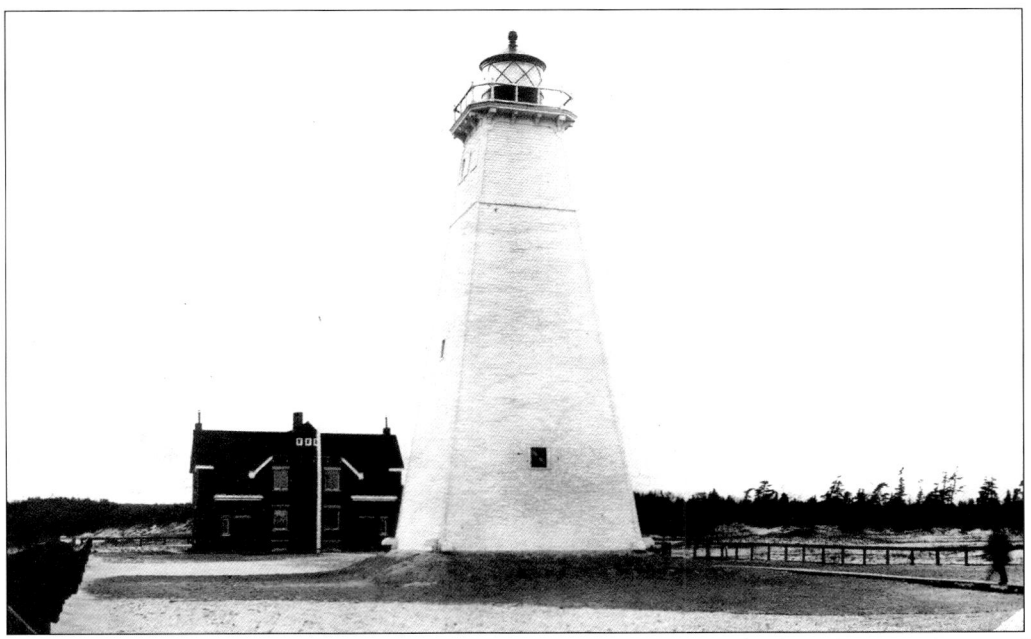

Delay in making a decision regarding the shape of the tower resulted in the completion of the red brick keeper's dwelling and a few outbuildings prior to the tower's construction. These buildings were established in 1896, two years before the light became operational. (MCHS)

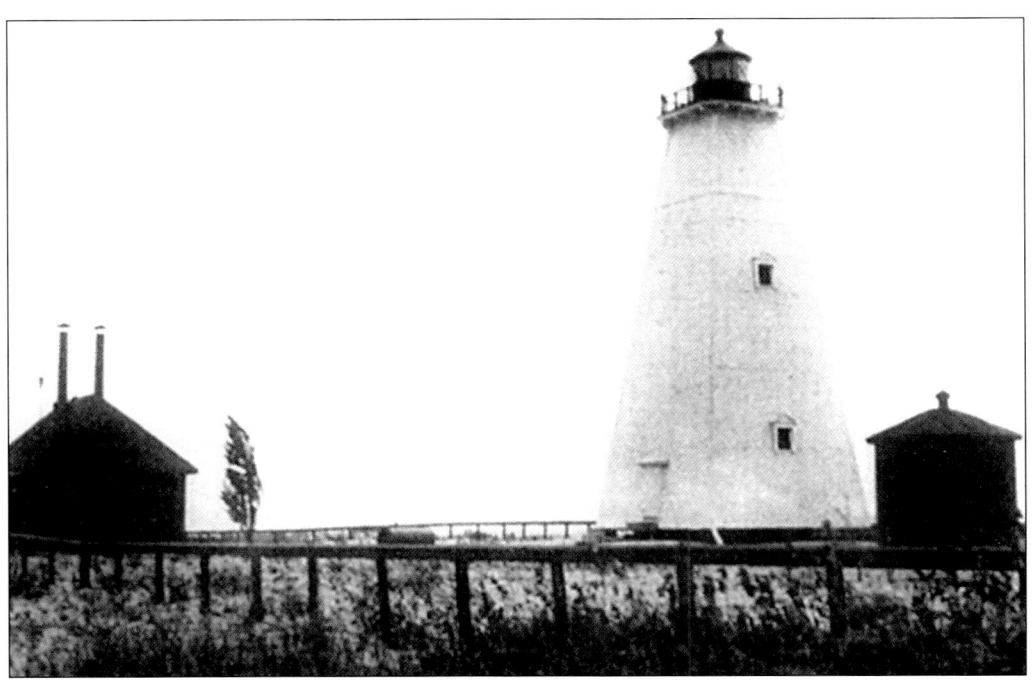

Included among the seven buildings of the complex were a steam-powered fog signal and an oil storage house. Having been built on a sand spit only a few feet above water level, this light was constantly plagued by erosion which ultimately caused it to fall into the lake in 1942. (USCG)

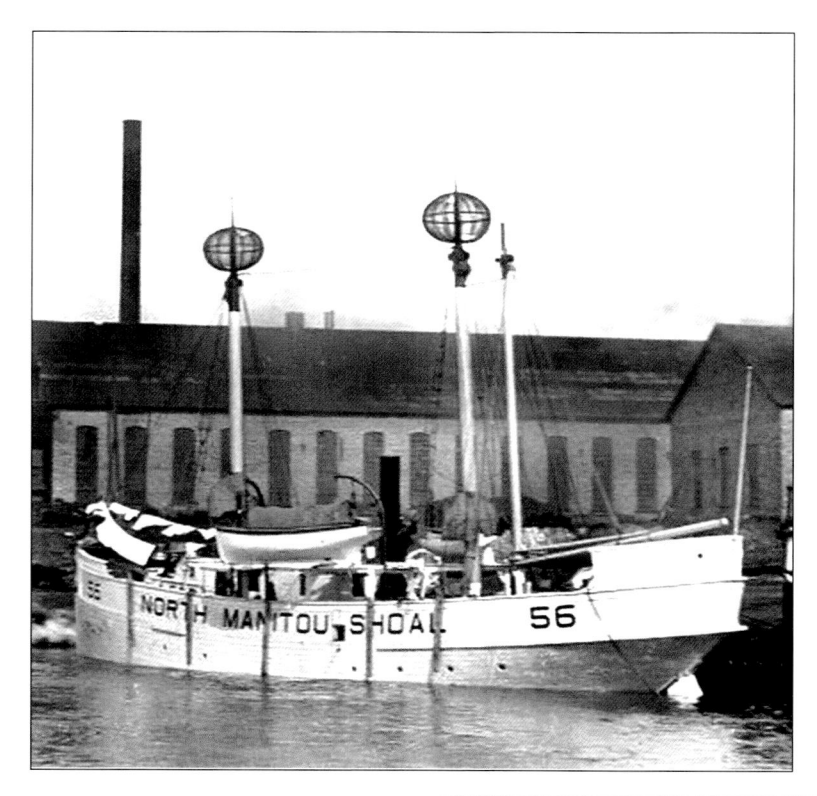

The North Manitou Island Light proved to be inadequate by itself and was supplemented with a lightship, placed offshore on the edge of the shoal, in 1910. A lightship was chosen to help avoid the costs of building and maintaining a permanent lighthouse on the shoal. Lightship *LV 56* was a wooden vessel that was equipped with lights, a hand operated fog bell, and a daymark on the foremast. She housed a full crew during the shipping season. (MMM)

After several lightships had served on the shoal, a permanent light was constructed on the site in 1935. North Manitou Shoal Light was a steel-framed, steel-plated structure that stood in a diamond configuration on its square concrete crib. Upon completion of the new light, the North Manitou Island Light was deactivated and its Fourth Order lens was placed in the new light tower. (USCG)

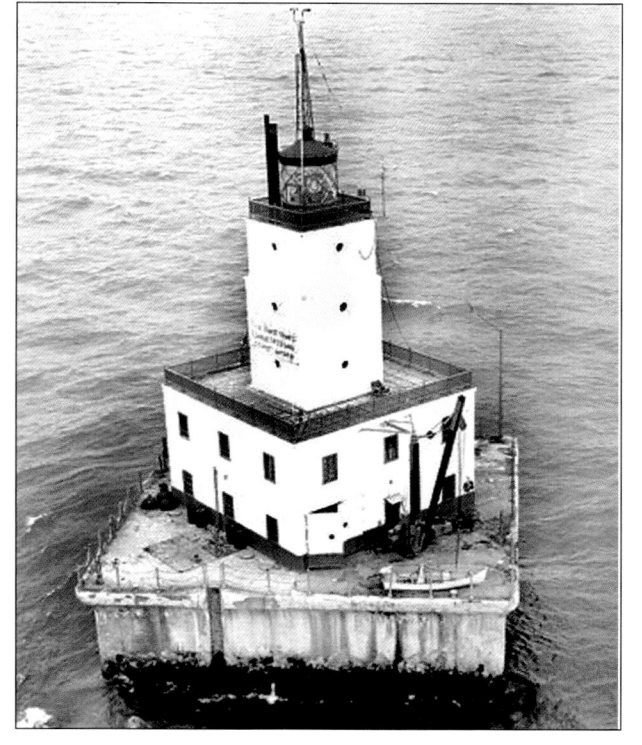

South Fox Island marks the northern end of the Manitou passage on its western side. In 1867 the federal government set aside $18,000 to build a lighthouse to mark the nine miles of shoals extending south of the island. The floor plan of the light shows the main floor living area that held an oil storage room and access to the tower. (SAM)

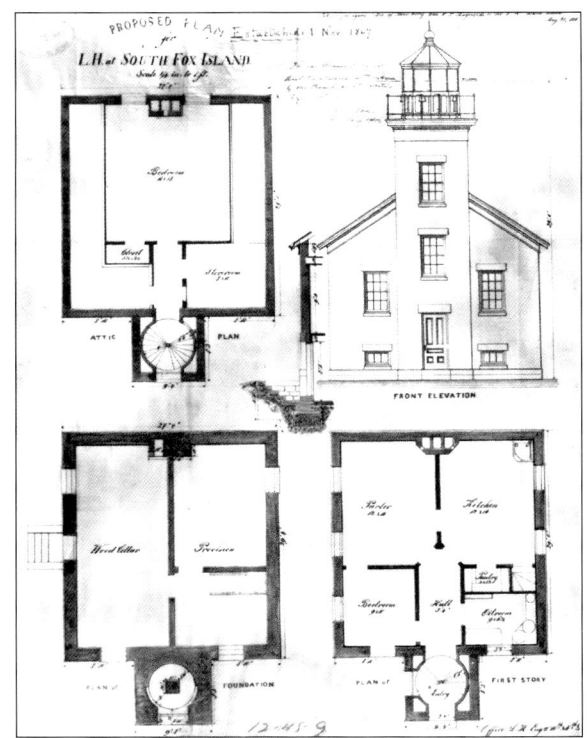

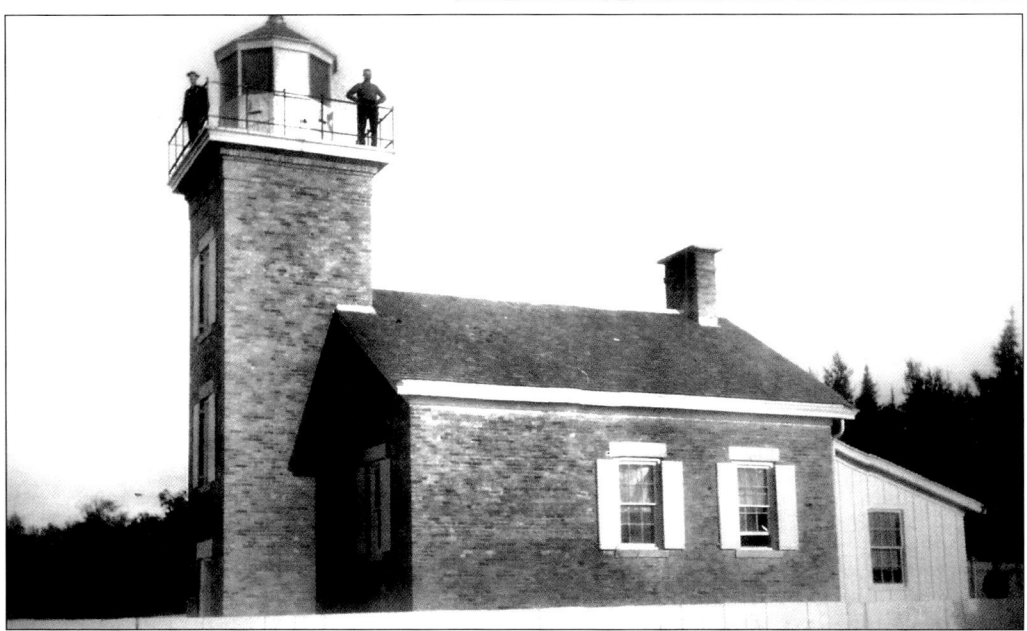

The lighthouse consisted of a one-and-one-half story brick dwelling with an attached square light tower rising to 45 feet. This building served as the keeper's dwelling while a duplex housed the assistants and their families who arrived when the fog signal was established. A five-foot-tall wooden fence was constructed around the property in 1880 to keep blowing sand and snow from battering the house. (NA)

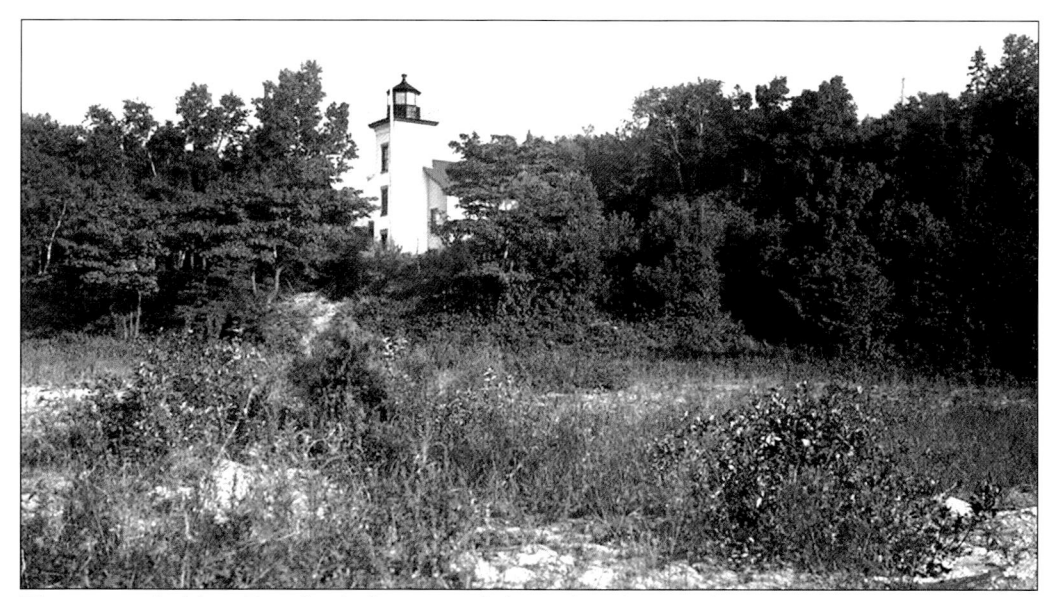

The tower held a Fourth Order Fresnel lens that began shining for the first time on November 1, 1867. Its unique flash indicated to mariners which light they were near so they could more accurately calculate their location within the channel. At some later point the tower was painted white to make it more visible during daylight hours.

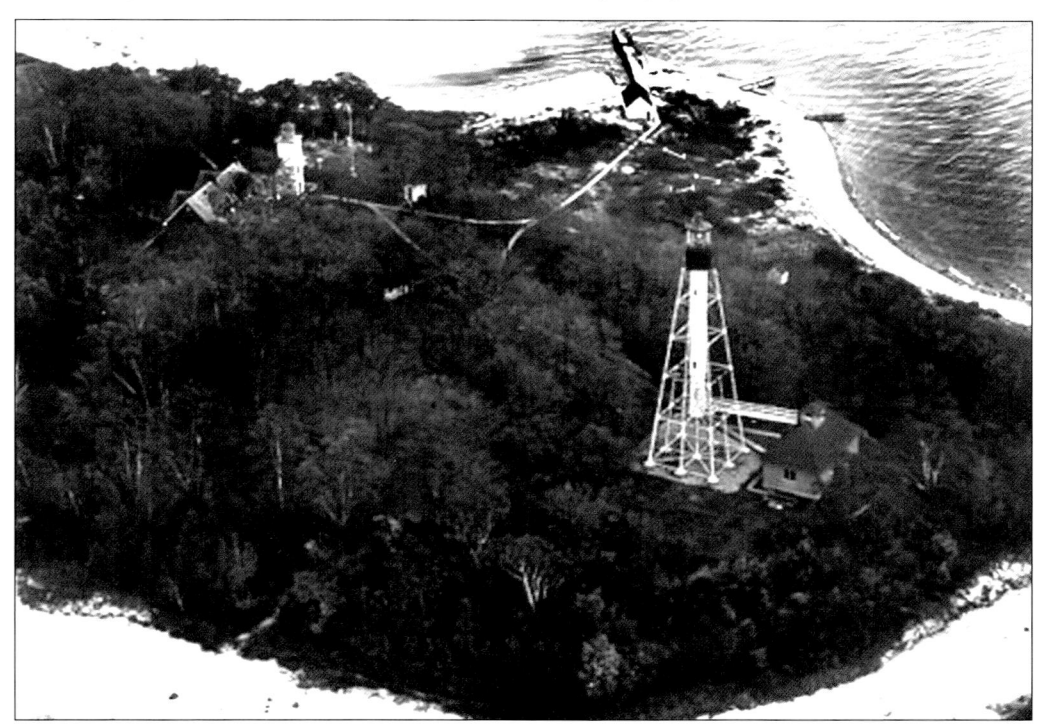

In 1934 a taller skeletal steel structure was constructed near the shoreline. The new tower had a 105-step spiral stairway inside the cylindrical tube that led from the ground to the lantern room. This light was automated in 1958 and discontinued in 1976. (USCG)

Four

THE LIGHTS OF GRAND TRAVERSE BAY
GRAND TRAVERSE LIGHT AND OLD MISSION POINT LIGHT

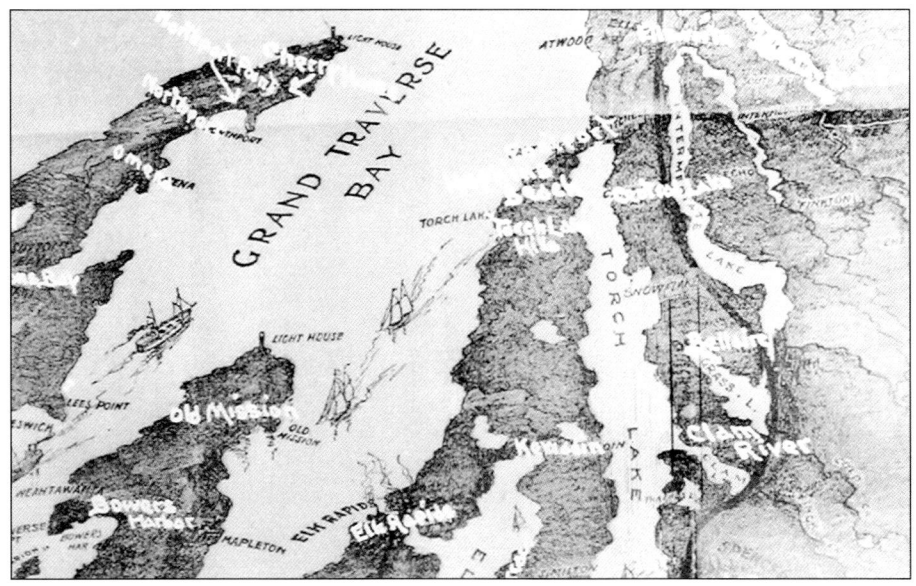

Located on the tip of the Leelanau Peninsula, the Grand Traverse Light marks the entrance into Grand Traverse Bay. Although no known photographs exist of the first light, erected in 1853, it presumably consisted of a small tower with a detached keeper's dwelling placed near the shore.

Second keeper Philo Beers reportedly warded off an attempt to steal the light's Fresnel lens during the early years of its existence. It seems that King Strang, self-proclaimed Mormon King of Beaver Island, along with his band of renegades, found it an acceptable practice to steal from others in order to build his kingdom. Apparently, he wanted this lens for use in the lighthouse on the Island. However, Beers former experience as a U.S. Deputy paid off and he was able to thwart Strang's efforts and save the lens.

The height and location of the light tower proved to be inadequate so the structures were razed and a new lighthouse was built in 1858. (BHL)

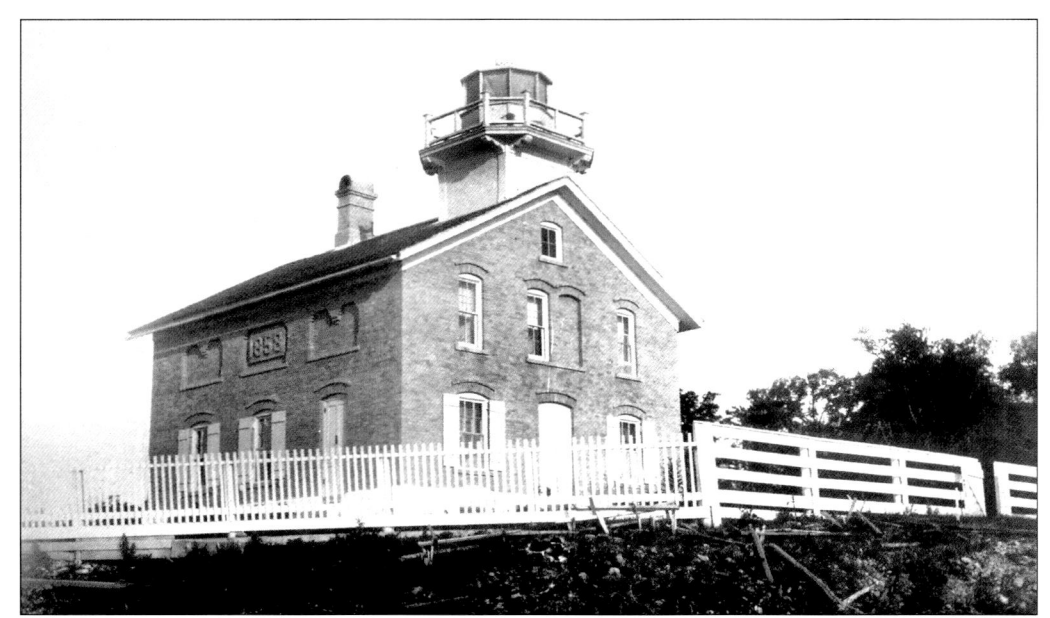

The new lighthouse was called the Grand Traverse Light Station. It was erected on the end of the peninsula, on higher ground than the original light had been. The structure, made of the popular Cream City brick, was a two-story building with a short nine-sided light tower on the roof. A stairway leading from the second floor allowed access to the light, which held a Fifth Order Fresnel lens. (NA)

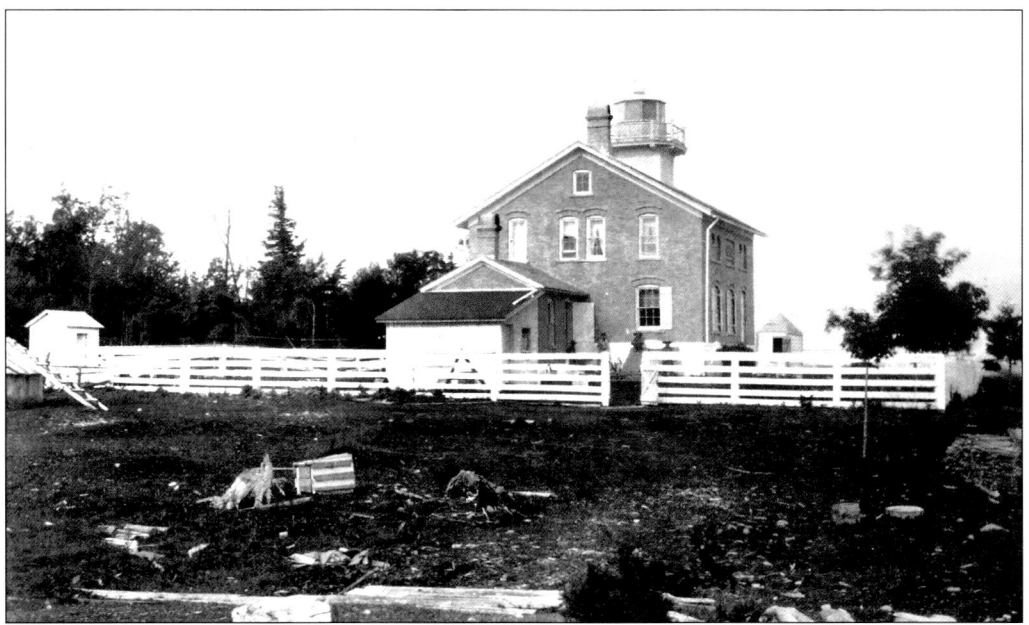

Recognizing how vital the light was to shipping traffic, the decision was made in 1870 to upgrade the lens to a larger Fourth Order Fresnel. Over the next few years a wood storage shed and a barn were added to the property and a boat landing was built. Concrete was also poured over the original dirt floor of the cellar. (NA)

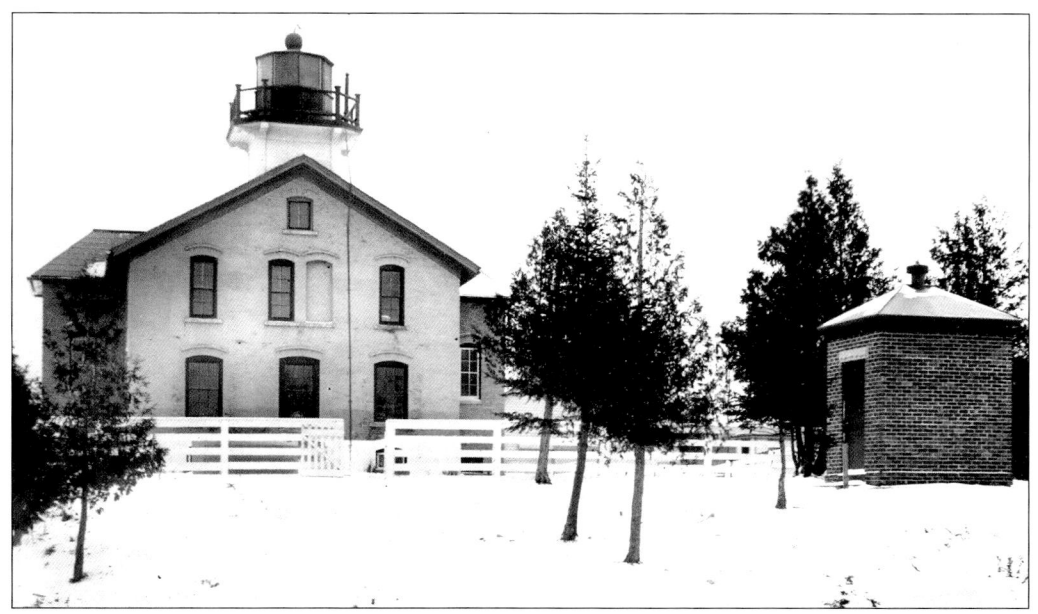

In the mid-1800s, many U.S. lights were being fueled with non-volatile sperm whale oil or lard oil. By the 1870s, kerosene was recognized as an effective illuminant and became the fuel of choice. However, many fires resulted from the volatile kerosene being stored in lighthouse cellars. Consequently, the lighthouse service began erecting separate buildings to hold this dangerous fuel. The oil storage building, on the right, was added to the Grand Traverse property in 1896. (MCHS)

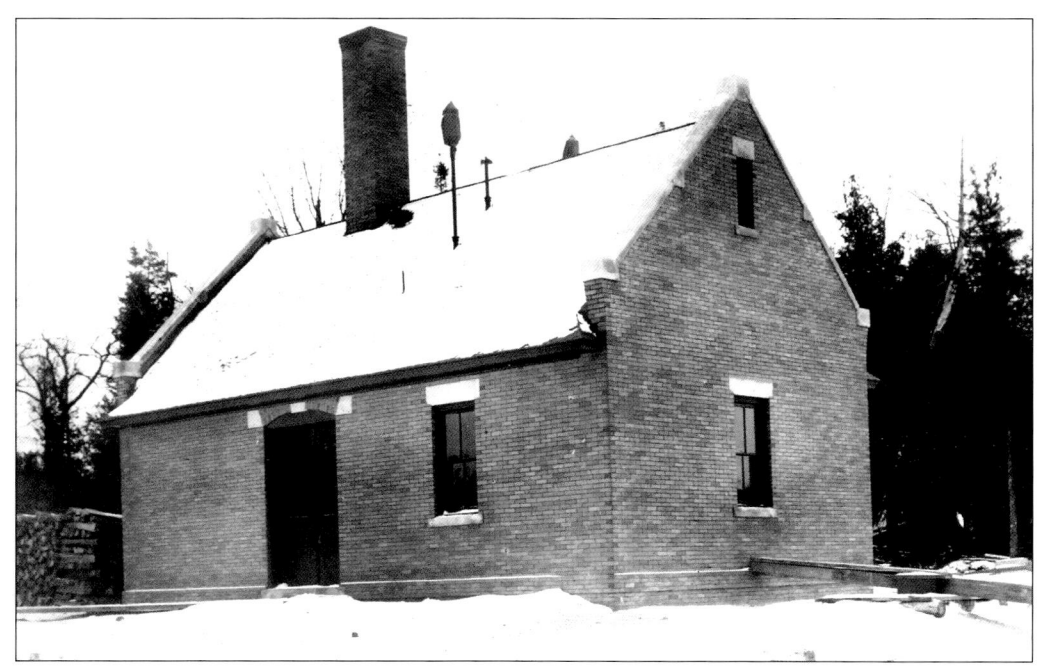

Thick fog often blanketed the area and prevented mariners from seeing the light as they headed to the Straits or into the Bay. On July 1, 1898, Congress appropriated the necessary funds to establish a fog signal that was built and became operational the following year. (MCHS)

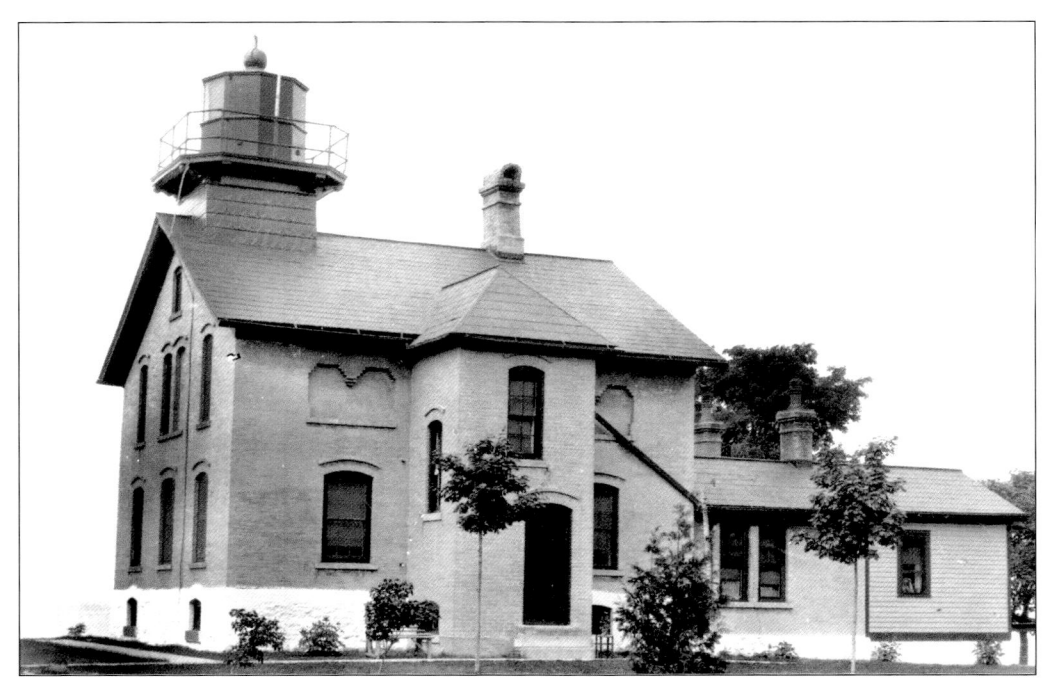

With the establishment of the fog signal, it was decided that an assistant keeper was needed to share the increased work load. In 1901 the house was enlarged and converted into a duplex to accommodate the assistant and his family. Wings that held separate stairways and entrances were added to both sides of the building. (SAM)

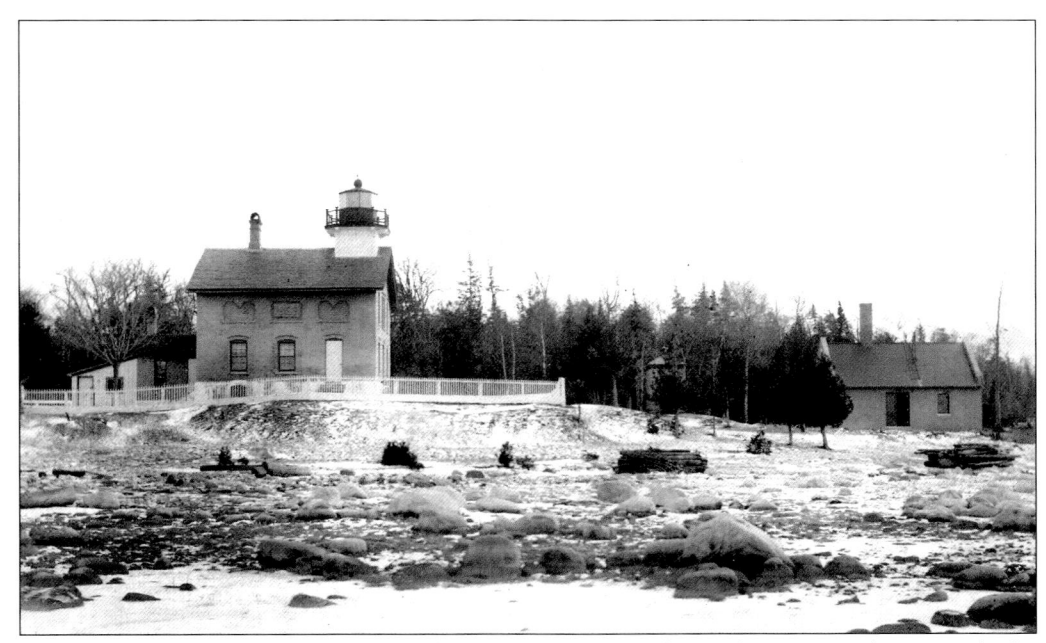

A view of the lighthouse grounds in the summer of 1905 shows the property layout with the fog signal building, the oil storage building (between the light and the fog signal) and the remodeled lighthouse. (MCHS)

James McCormick, reportedly the first white man born in Emmet County just north of Traverse City, was the lighthouse keeper from 1922–1938. He and his wife Mary had 12 children, eight of whom lived with them at the lighthouse. Known as an industrious man, in addition to maintaining his regular duties, McCormick also raised a large vegetable garden and did quite a bit of stonework on the grounds, including building this bird feeder.

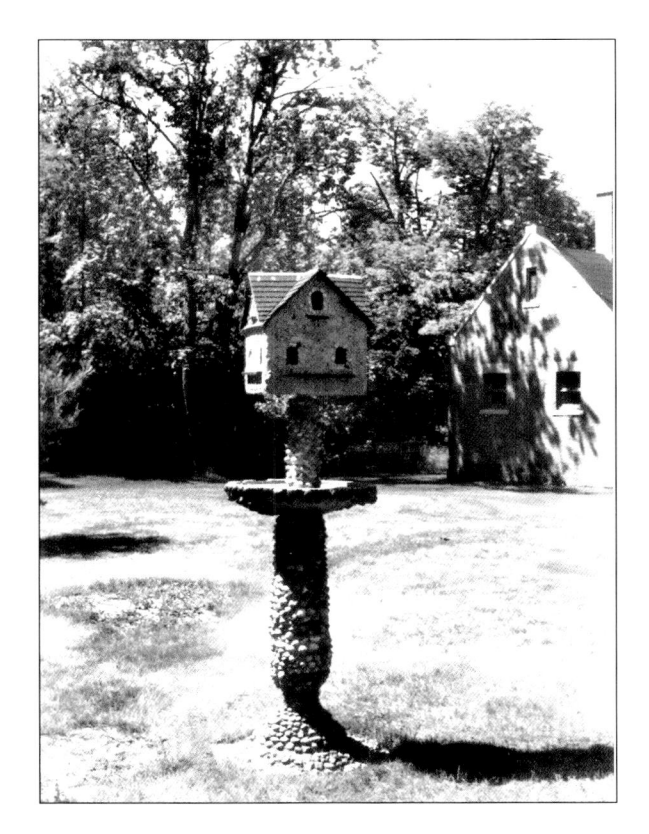

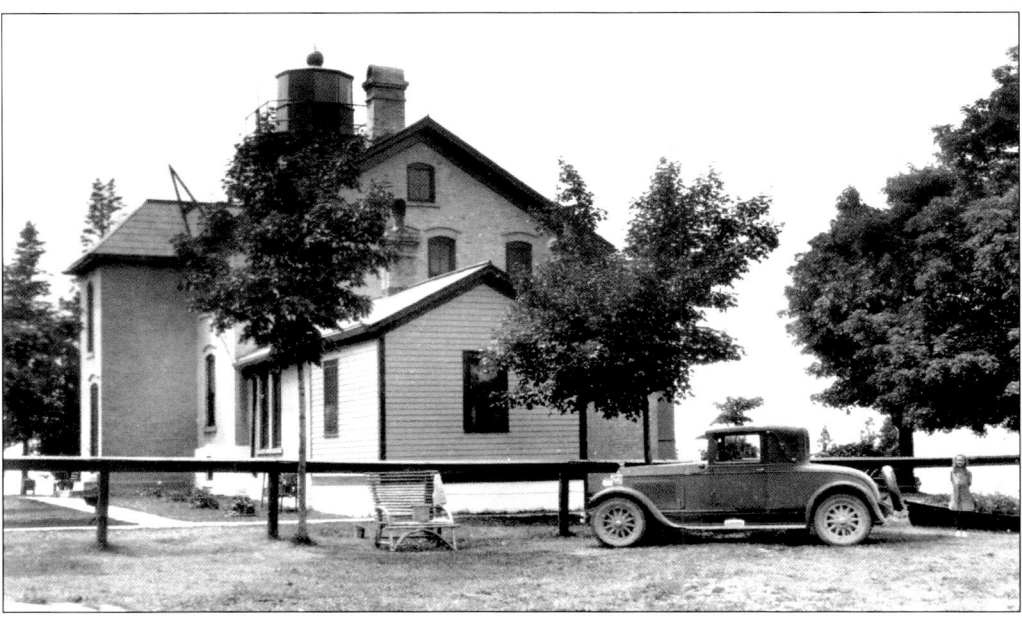

An unidentified girl stands near the kitchen that was added to the southern end of the station in 1916. Between 1948 and the early 1950s, wooden back porch wings were added to the kitchen and a cast iron spiral stairway was installed in the tower. (SAM)

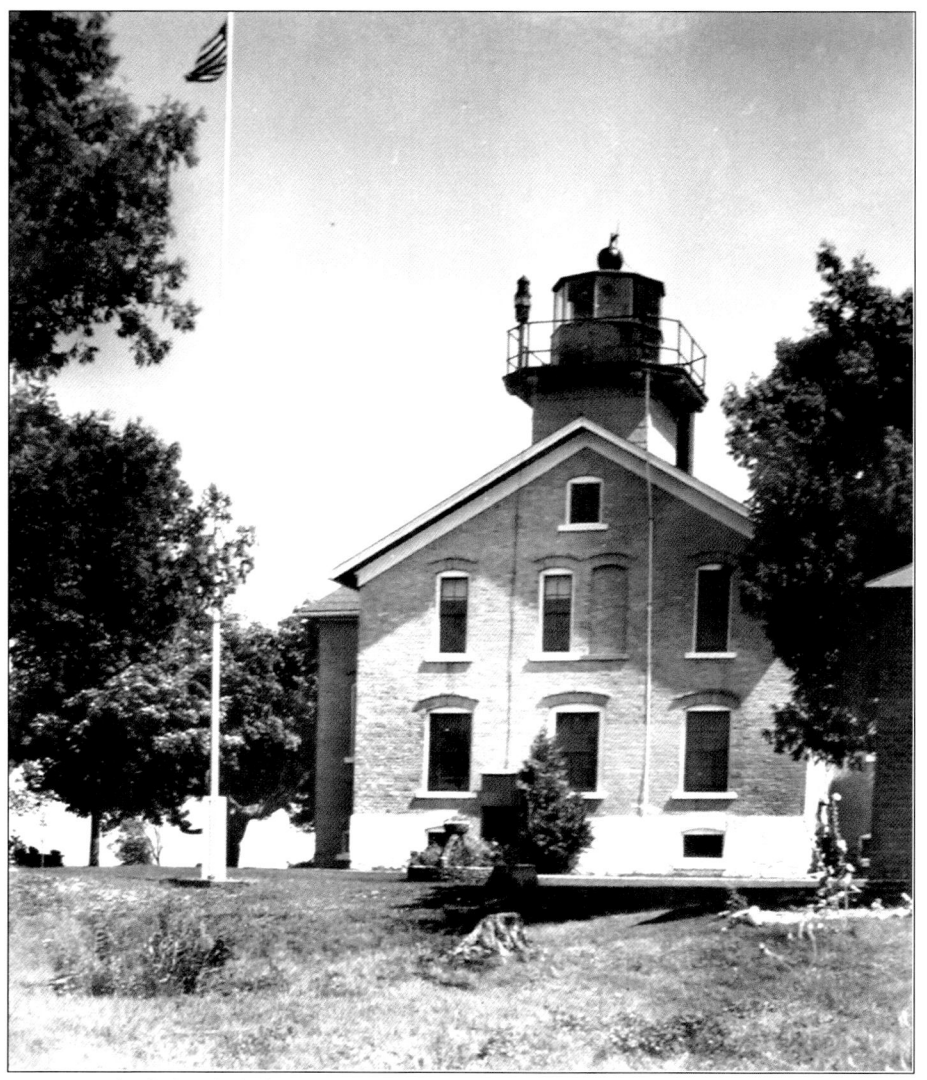

Electricity reached the lighthouse c. 1950. All buildings were wired at that time; however, a diesel generator was kept for emergency backup. In 1972, the light was replaced with an automated light on a steel tower. The lighthouse was then closed and the fog signal was discontinued. (BHL)

Many years later, the lighthouse reopened as a museum and Doug McCormick, son of keeper James McCormick, returned to act as its caretaker. He recalls that during his childhood at the lighthouse, the food supplies were kept in the cellar. His parents borrowed a truck in the fall of the year and made the long trip to the store to stock up on a year's worth of food products that weren't grown in the family garden. Sixty bushels of potatoes, barrels of apples, and cases of peanut butter lined the cellar floor along with the shelves of canned goods put up by his mother. It wasn't uncommon for some of the children to sneak down to the cellar during the night and raid the peanut butter supply. On one such occasion, Doug ate so much that he got sick and couldn't look at peanut butter again for a number of years.

The lighthouse remains open today as a museum with many of the McCormick family's personal items on display.

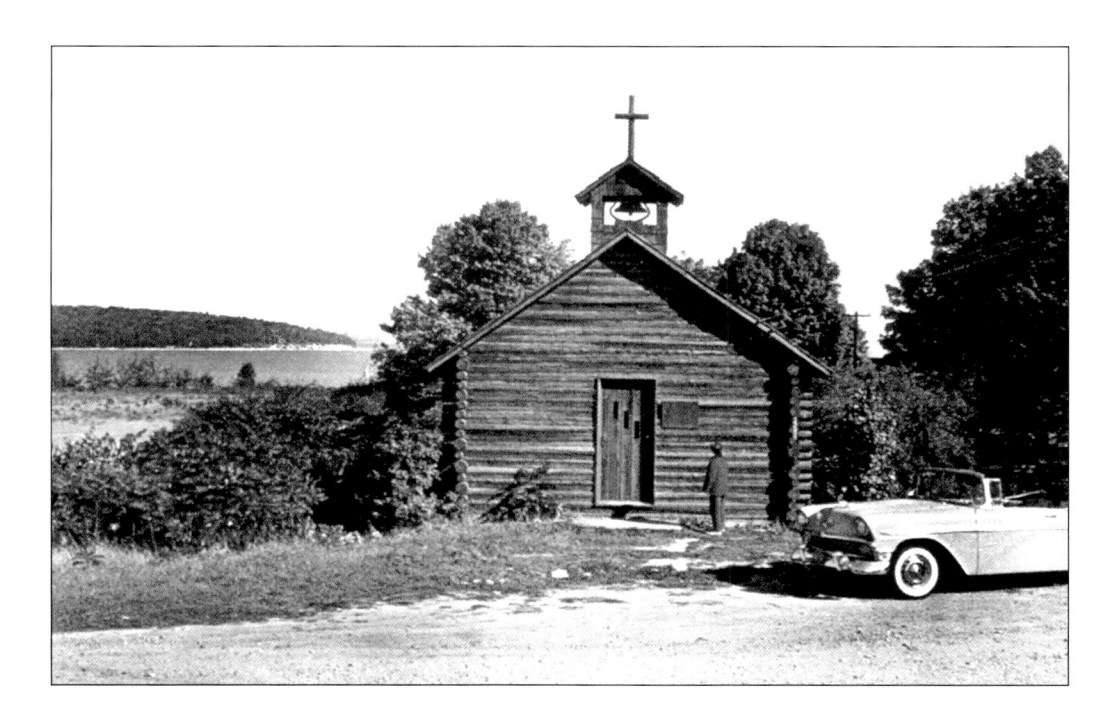

Old Mission Peninsula reaches approximately 17 miles north from the mainland into Grand Traverse Bay, separating the east and west arms of the bay. In 1836 the government made a treaty with the Native Americans to provide them with a school and a mission on this peninsula. Two years later Rev. Peter Dougherty arrived and established the mission from which the peninsula received its name. (CHL)

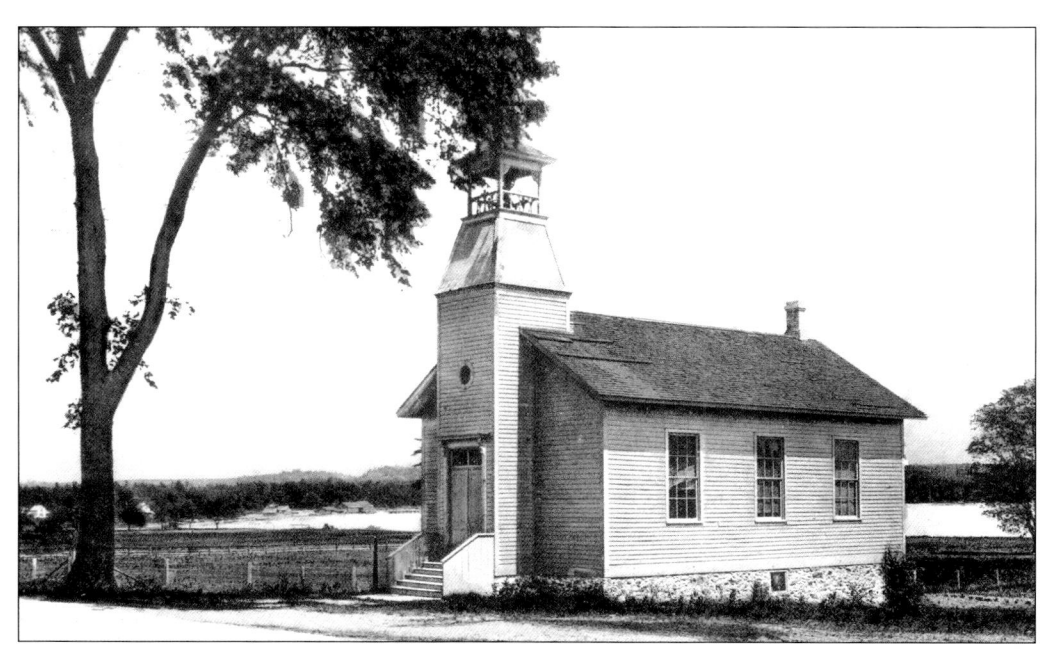

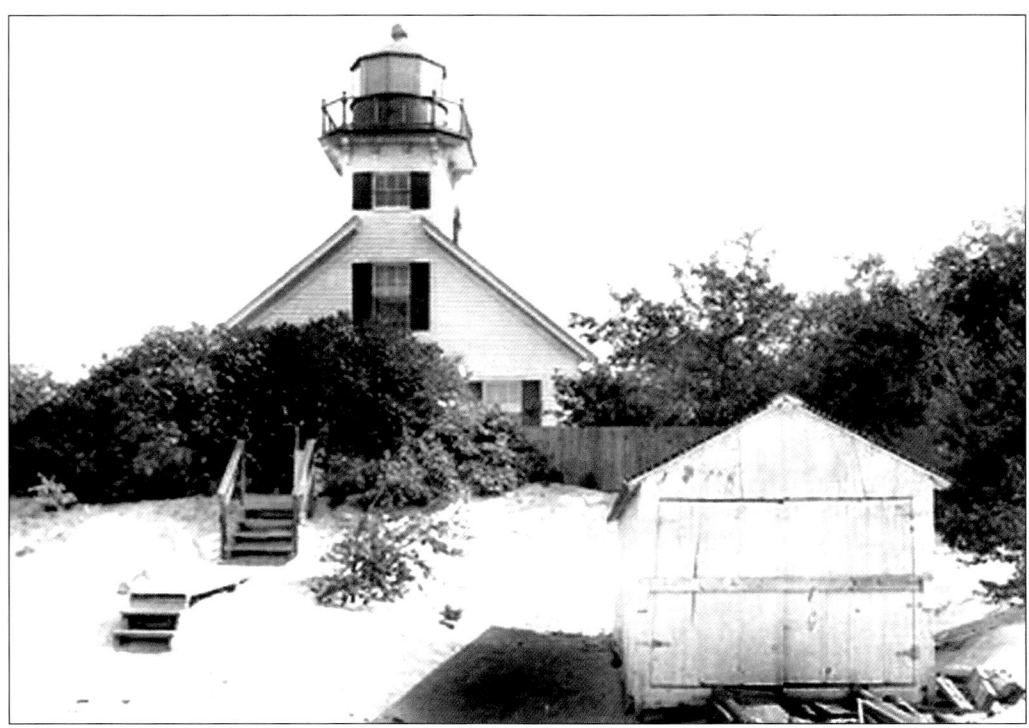

Increasing numbers of settlers came to the area as word of its excellent growing conditions spread. As more crops were produced, more ships entered the bay to carry these goods to various ports on the lake. In 1859, Congress appropriated $6,000 to establish a light on the end of the peninsula to mark the two miles of shoals that lined the entrance to either arm of the bay. However, with the onset of the Civil War, the actual construction was delayed until 1870. (USCG)

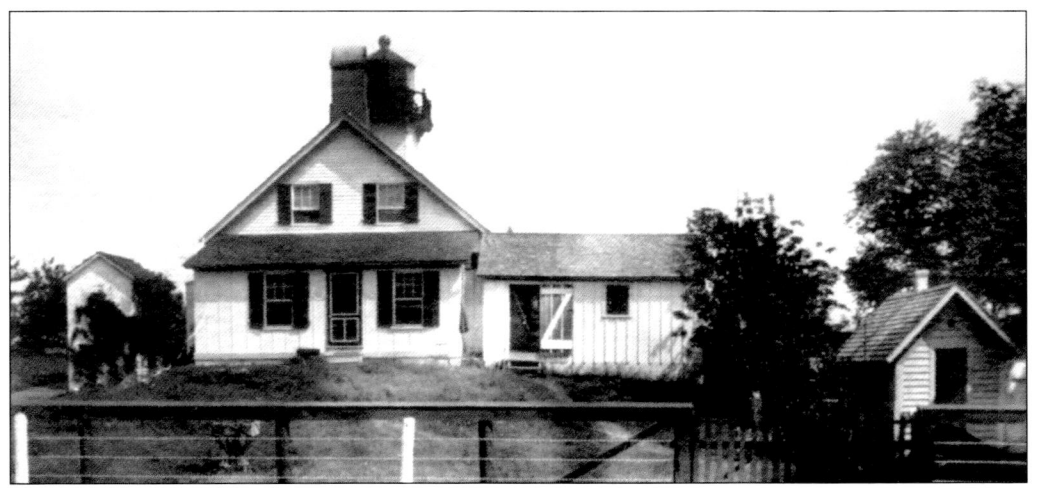

Old Mission Point Light was built on the 45th parallel, halfway between the Equator and the North Pole. It was a one-and-one-half-story wood-framed building with a square tower rising from the lakeward end. Its black cast iron parapet held a Fifth Order Fresnel lens that was first exhibited on September 10, 1870. (MCHS)

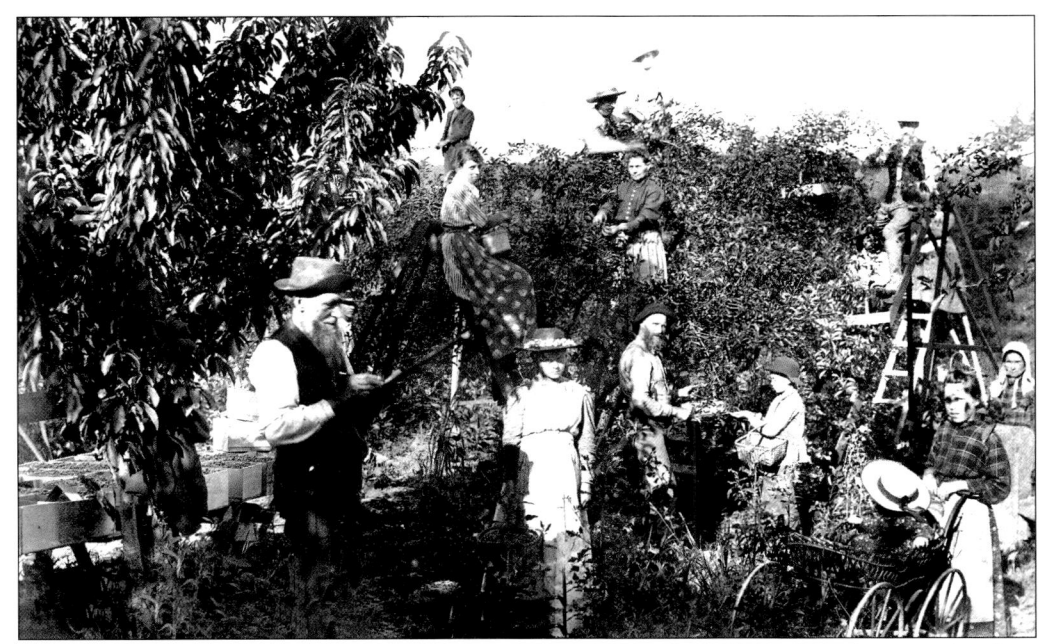

Against the advice of local farmers, Rev. Peter Dougherty planted the first cherry orchard on the peninsula in 1852. The sandy soil and moderate temperatures near the lake proved to be excellent for growing fruit, and the entire bay area eventually grew to become the producers of three-quarters of the nation's tart cherry supply. The family pictured above is picking cherries on one of the many orchards in the Mission Peninsula area. (CHL)

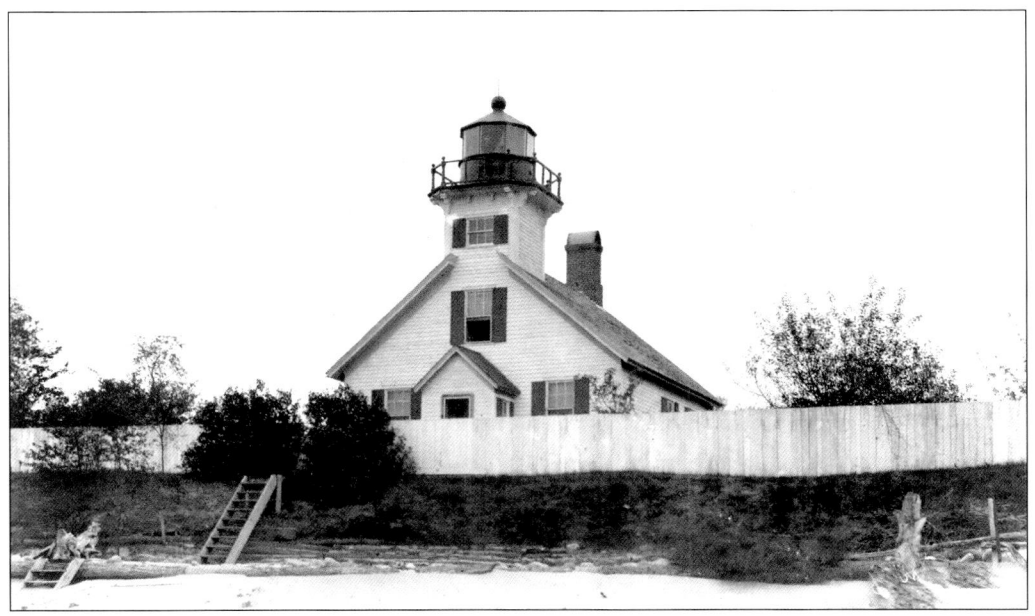

In the late 1800s, a cellar was excavated under the lighthouse and an oil storage building was placed on the property. By the turn of the century, a fence was placed around the station and wooden walkways were built, connecting the light and the outbuildings. (CHL)

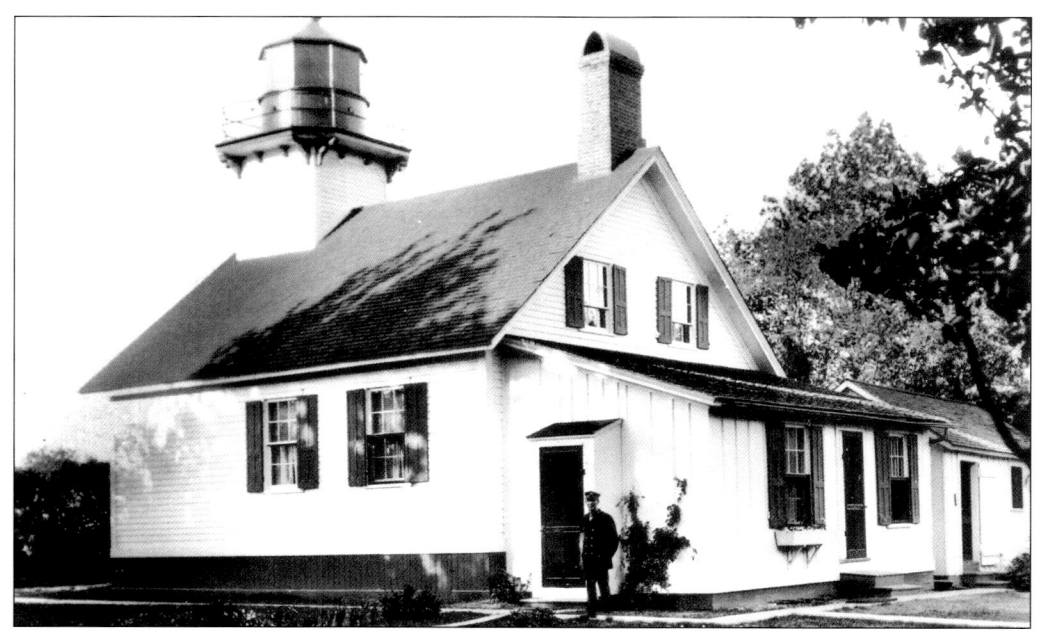

When McGulpin's Point Light closed in 1906, keeper James Davenport, seen above, was transferred to the Old Mission Point Light. He served as its keeper until 1919 when he retired from service and returned to Mackinaw City to live out the remainder of his life. (MMM)

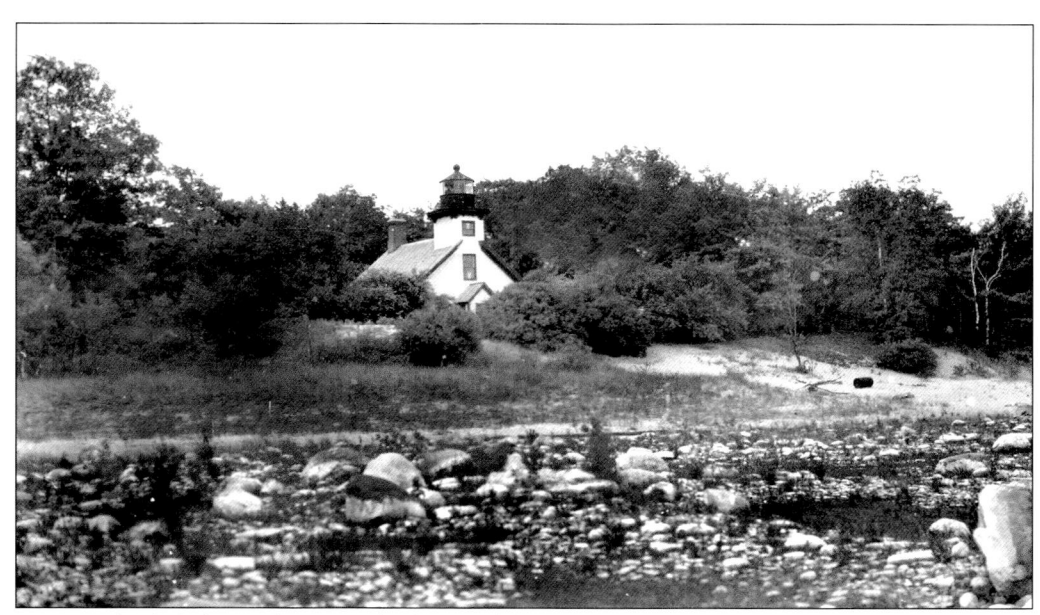

In 1933 the lighthouse became obsolete and the lens was removed when a light on a skeletal steel tower was placed directly on the shoal. After World War II, the State of Michigan purchased the old lighthouse site which has since been maintained within a park. (MMM)

Five

CHARLEVOIX COUNTY AND LITTLE TRAVERSE BAY LIGHTS

CHARLEVOIX PIERHEAD LIGHTS, BEAVER ISLAND LIGHT, ST. JAMES LIGHT, PETOSKEY BREAKWATER LIGHT, AND LITTLE TRAVERSE LIGHT

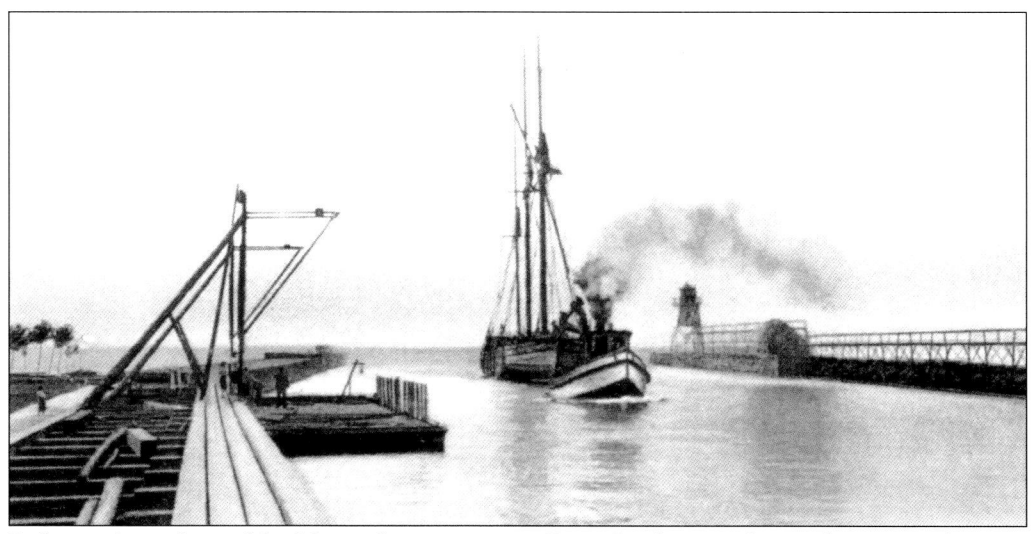

Before a deep channel had been dug connecting Round Lake to Lake Michigan via the Pine River, Amos Fox and Hiram Rose built a 900-foot dock from the shoreline into the big lake. Large, deep draft vessels tied up to the dock while horse-drawn carts delivered loads of lumber and other goods to them. This method of loading freight proved to be economically beneficial for a while, but it soon became apparent that a better, more permanent solution needed to be made.

In 1873 work began to dredge the river in order to accommodate larger vessels. By 1882 the channel was lined with piers and dredged to a depth of 12 feet and a width of 35 feet. A decision was then made to place a light on the end of the north pier to act as a guide to incoming vessels. (CHL)

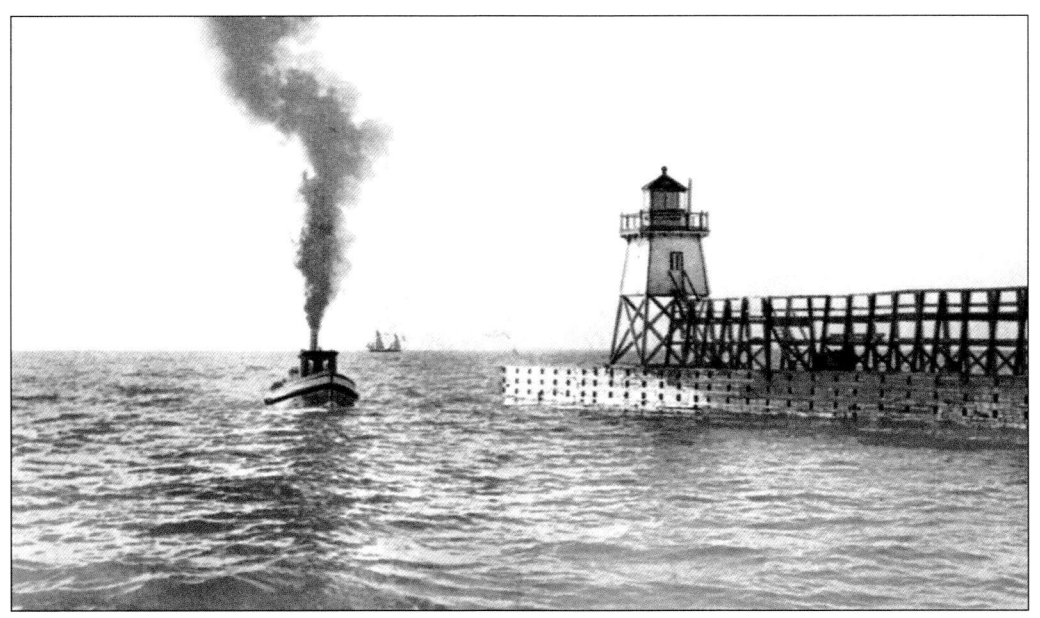

The new Charlevoix Pierhead Light was exhibited for the first time on September 1, 1885. It consisted of a wooden white pyramidal tower with an open framework base. The enclosed portion of the tower was used as a service room. Since there was no dwelling attached to the light, a catwalk was connected to the shore to allow the keeper safe access to the tower. (CHL)

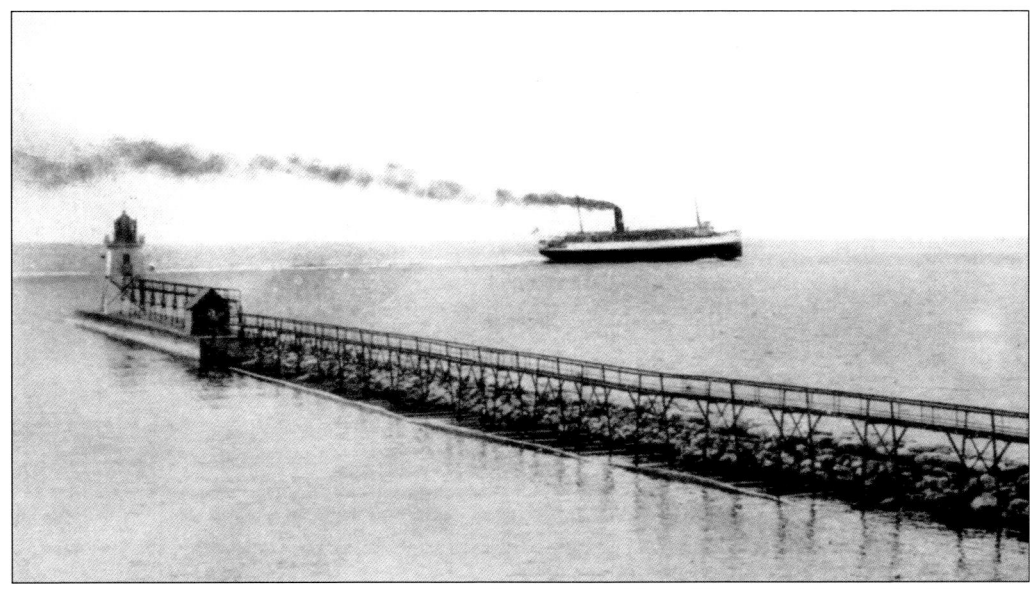

In 1890 a crew arrived on site to erect an oil storage building. The wood-framed building was placed a short distance behind the light near the raised portion of the catwalk. (MMM)

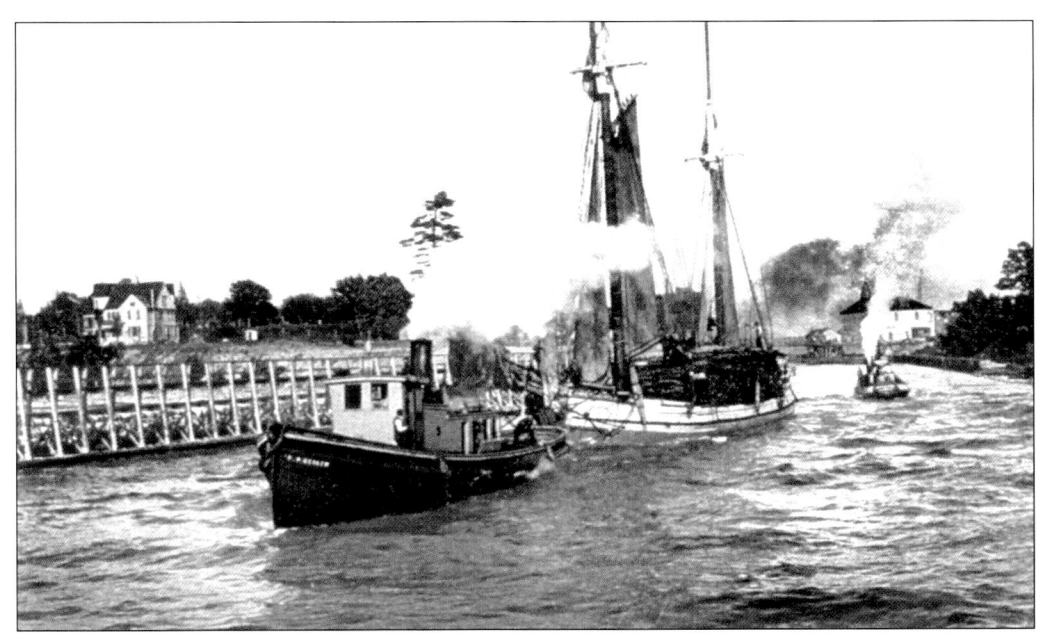

It is said that the Pine River is the shortest navigable river in the world and the only river where the currents flow both ways at the same time. Above, a tugboat assists a lumber schooner through the swirling waters of the river in the late 1890s. (MMM)

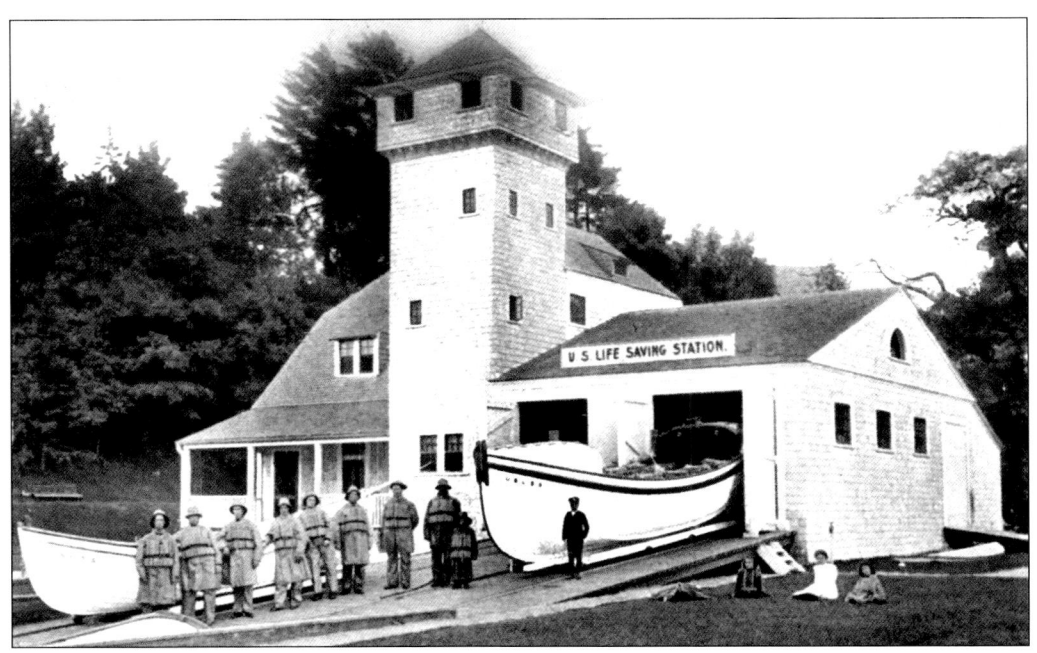

A United States Life-Saving Station became operational in Charlevoix in 1900. It was located on the south pier about one-eighth mile east of the light. The station was designed by Life-Saving Service Architect George Russell Tolman. Typical of this design was a shingle-covered building with a clipped gable roof over the living quarters and a four-story tower rising from the center of the building. The opposite end of the station contained a two-bay boat room. (CHL)

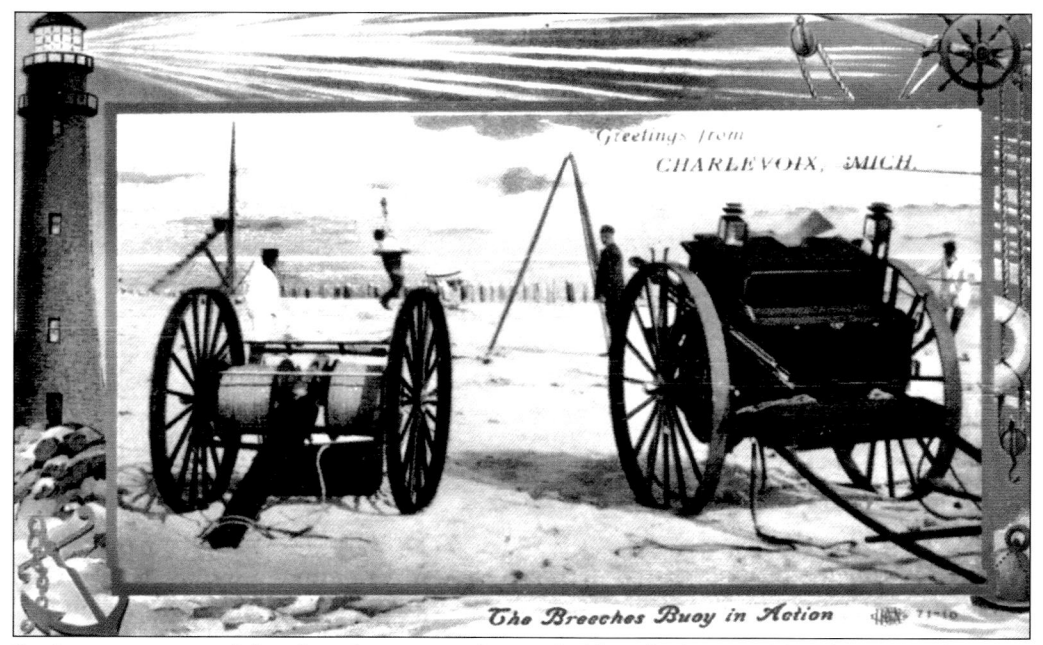

Surfmen were noted for their bravery and were held in high regard by the general public. Postcards depicting their drills were popular during the service's existence. This postcard shows a practice rescue using the breeches buoy. In order to simulate rescuing a victim from a vessel a wreck pole was set up on the beach to represent the ship's mast. The victim, who rode in the breeches buoy, was pulled along a line that ran from the wreck pole, across a portion of the beach, to the ground. (MMM)

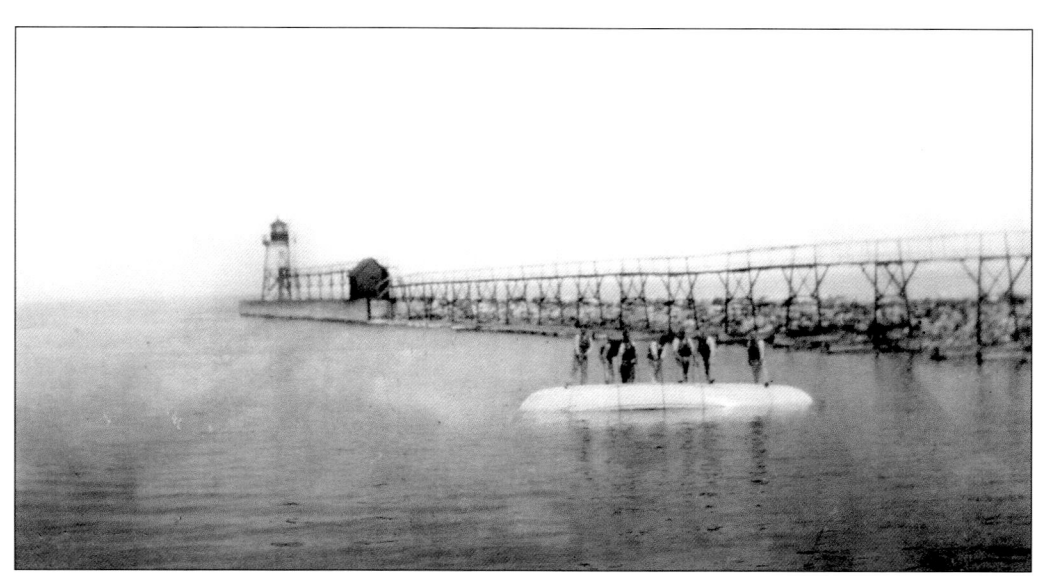

The capsize drill was the most dangerous of the drills. Surfmen were known to have been injured or killed when struck by an overturned boat while practicing in heavy seas. Whenever possible, this drill was performed in channels or rivers on calm days. (MMM)

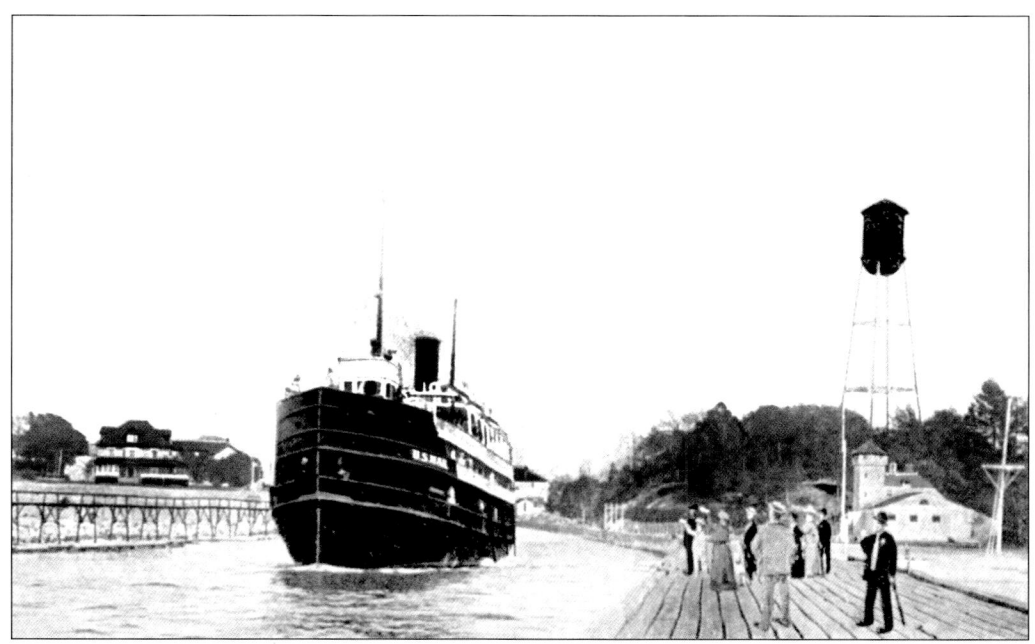

A view looking in from Lake Michigan shows the *Missouri* leaving the channel. The *Missouri* and her near sister ship the *Illinois* were the main mail and freight carriers from Chicago to ports along the eastern shoreline during this time. Notice the Life-Saving Station on the right with the wreck pole standing near it. (MMM)

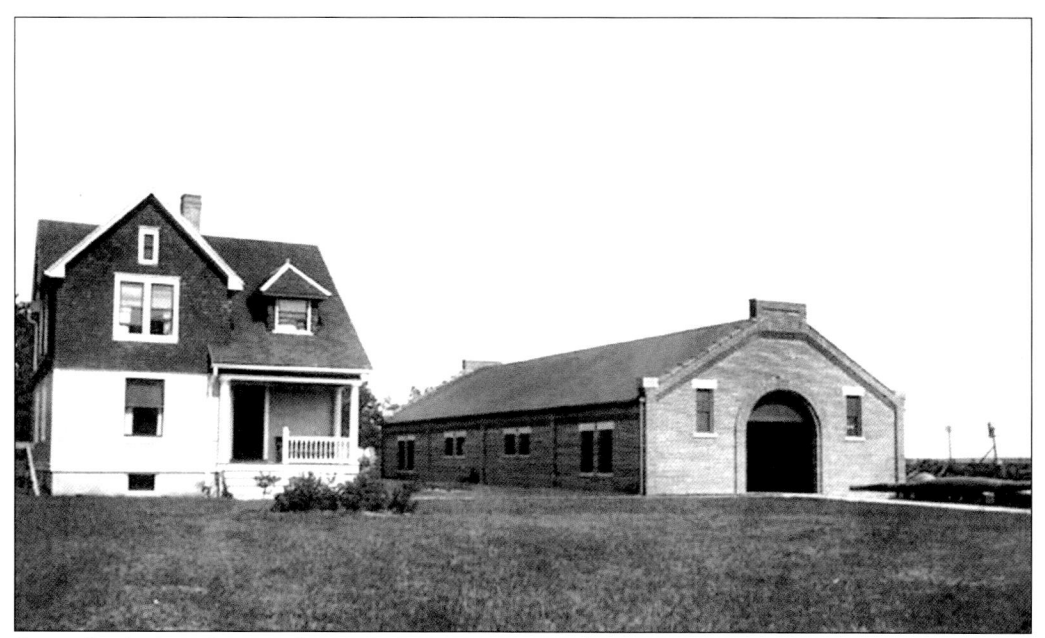

One of only five Great Lakes Lighthouse Depots (right) was built in Charlevoix in 1900. The depot stored lamps, lenses, chains, buoys, and other supplies for the lights in its area. It was also responsible for repairing damaged items returned from the lighthouses by lighthouse tenders. The Charlevoix Depot had an on-site keeper whose house can be seen on the left.

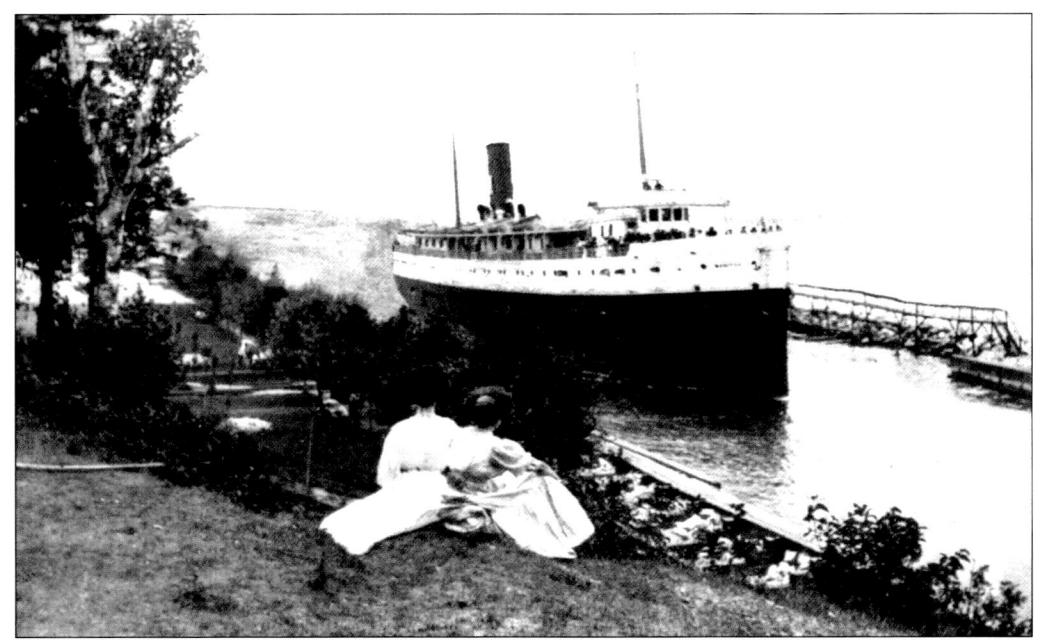

The propellor *Manitou* was a passenger ship that was very popular with Chicago's socially elite during the turn of the century. It ran the Chicago-Mackinac Island run for forty years before it was destroyed by fire in 1936. Seen above, the *Manitou* passes the lighthouse on its way to Round Lake. (MMM)

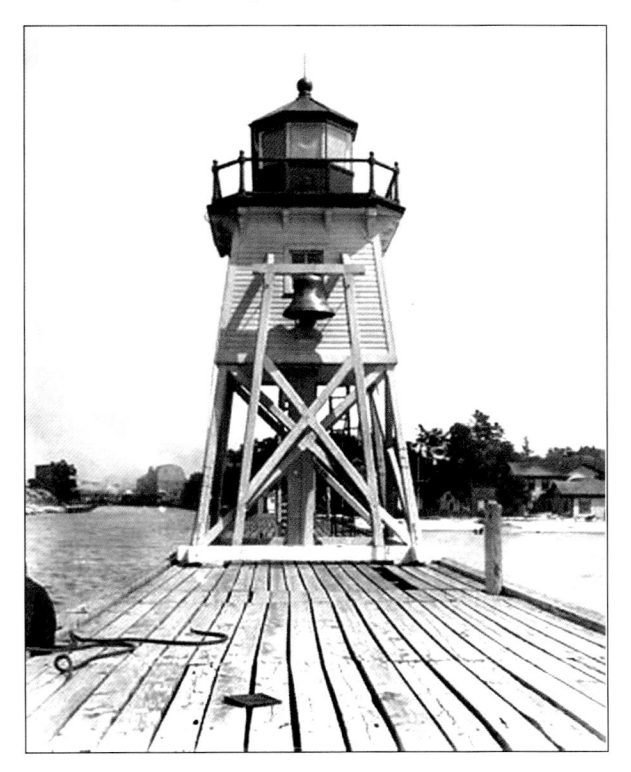

A fog bell was installed on the lakeward side of the beacon in 1909. It rang out its warning to mariners for 28 years during thick weather. In 1937–1938 the bell was removed and replaced with an electric diaphone signal. (USCG)

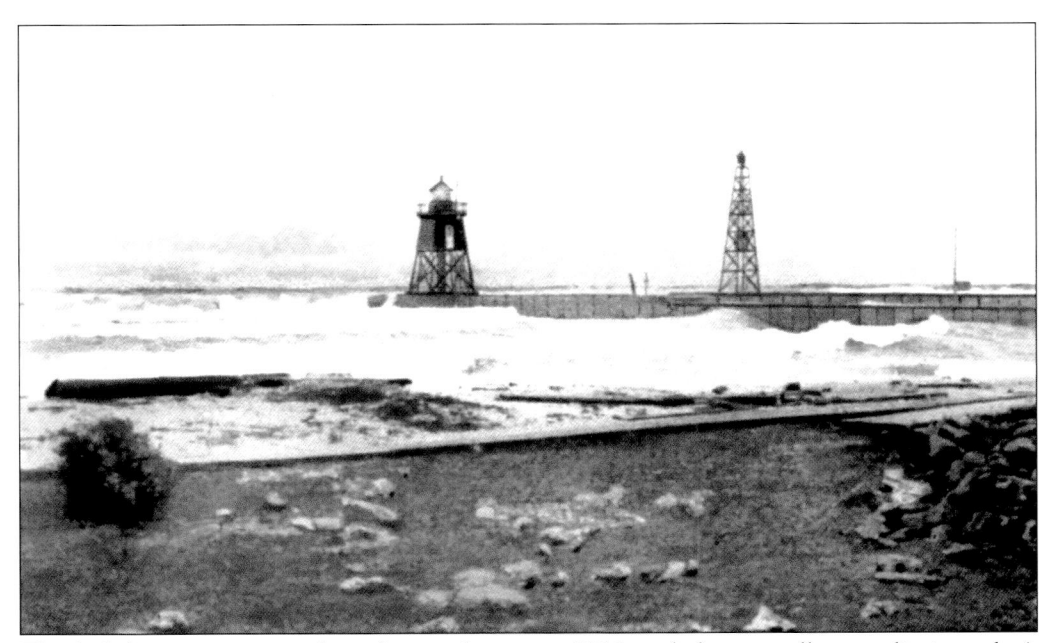

The lighthouse was moved to the south pier c. 1911 and the catwalk was eliminated. A 61-foot-tall open frame tower with a white blinker light was then placed on the end of the north pier. (CHL)

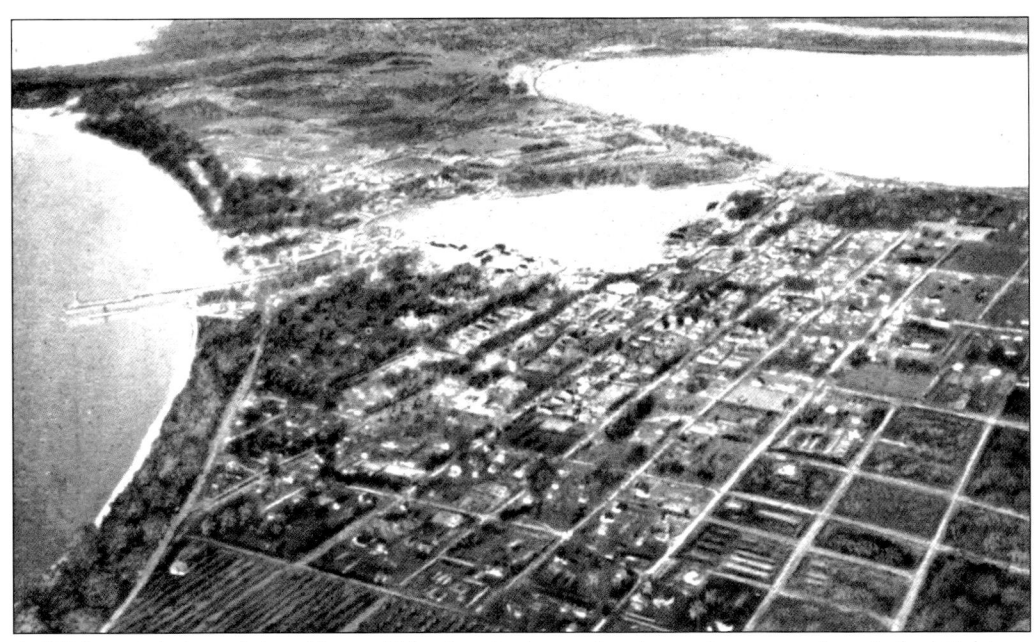

A 1920s aerial view of the village of Charlevoix shows the channel entrance from Lake Michigan on the left, followed by Round Lake and the larger Lake Charlevoix in the rear. (CHL)

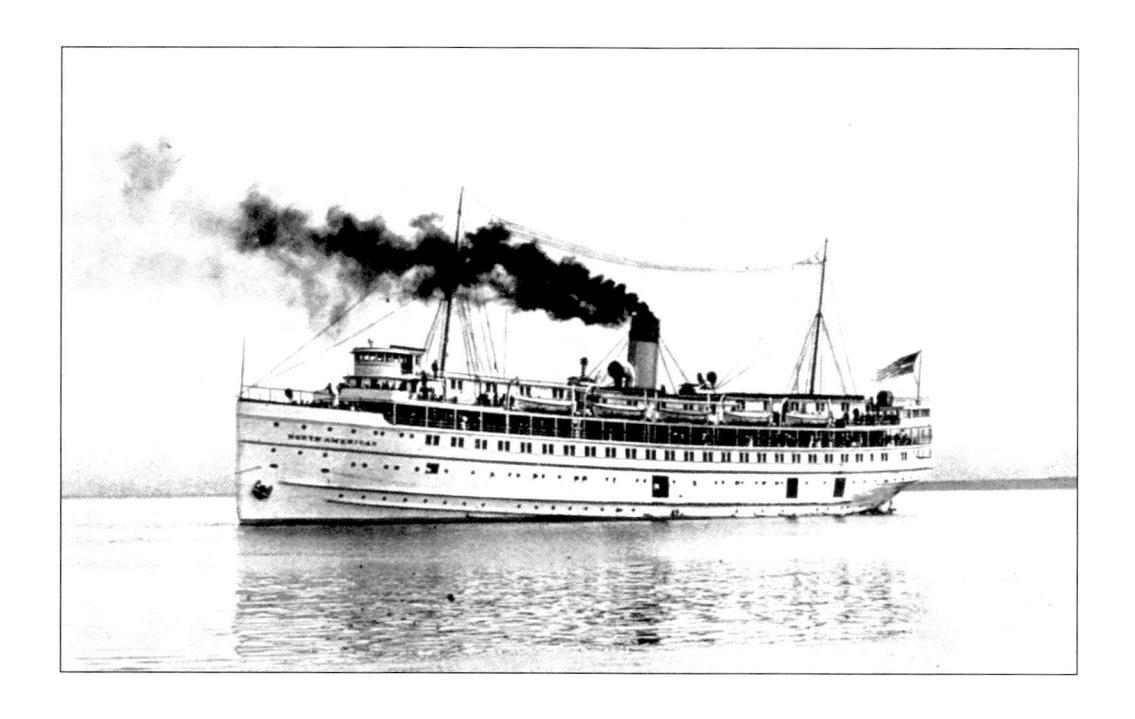

In 1912 Robert C. Davis incorporated the Chicago, Duluth and Georgian Bay Transit Company to form a passenger only inter-lake cruise line. His desire was to service his passengers with comfort and without the exigencies of freight travel. In 1913 the *North American*, the first of his cruise ships, went into service. One year later a near sister ship, the *South American*, was built. Local children were thrilled when the ships came to Charlevoix, since it was the custom of passengers to throw coins onto the dock as they entered Round Lake. (MAPL, MMM)

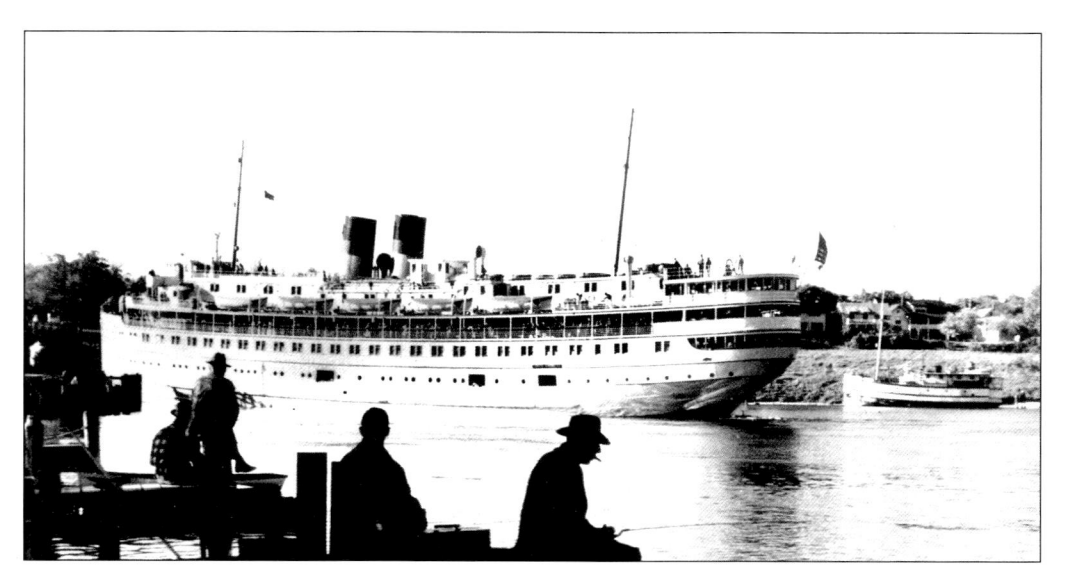

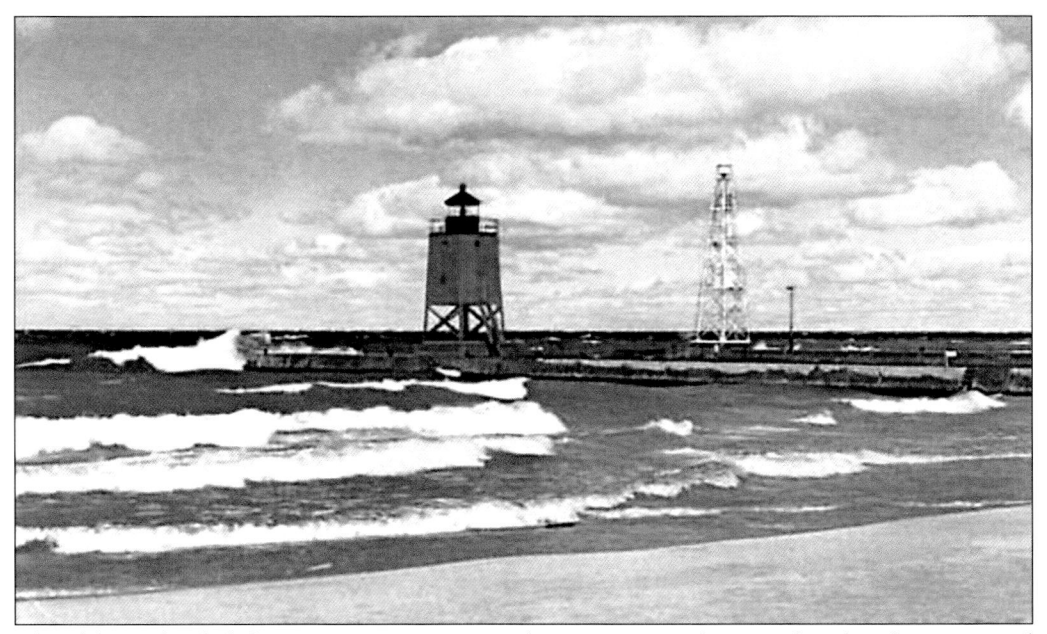

The old wooden lighthouse was giving way to deterioration and was replaced with a new steel light in 1948. It was similar in appearance to the original light; however, it had a longer trunk on top of the open framework. The lens and lantern were taken from the old light and placed in the new tower. This light was painted red and remained that color until the 1980s, when it was repainted white.

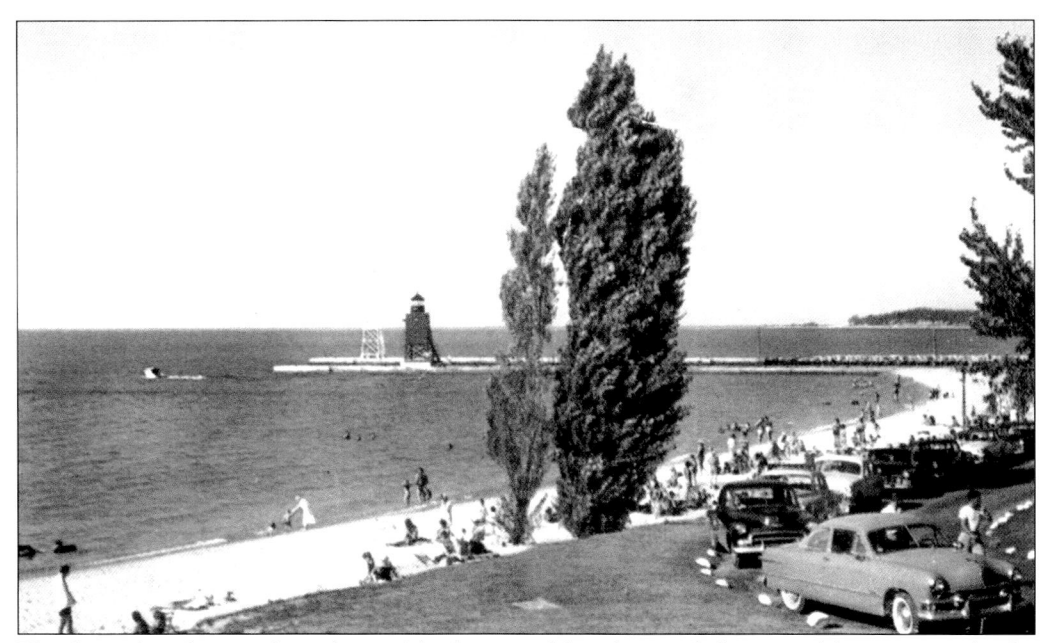

The long shoreline with its beautiful white sand beaches and the azure blue waters of Lake Michigan enhanced by the brilliant color of the lighthouse define the city's nickname, "Charlevoix the Beautiful." (MMM)

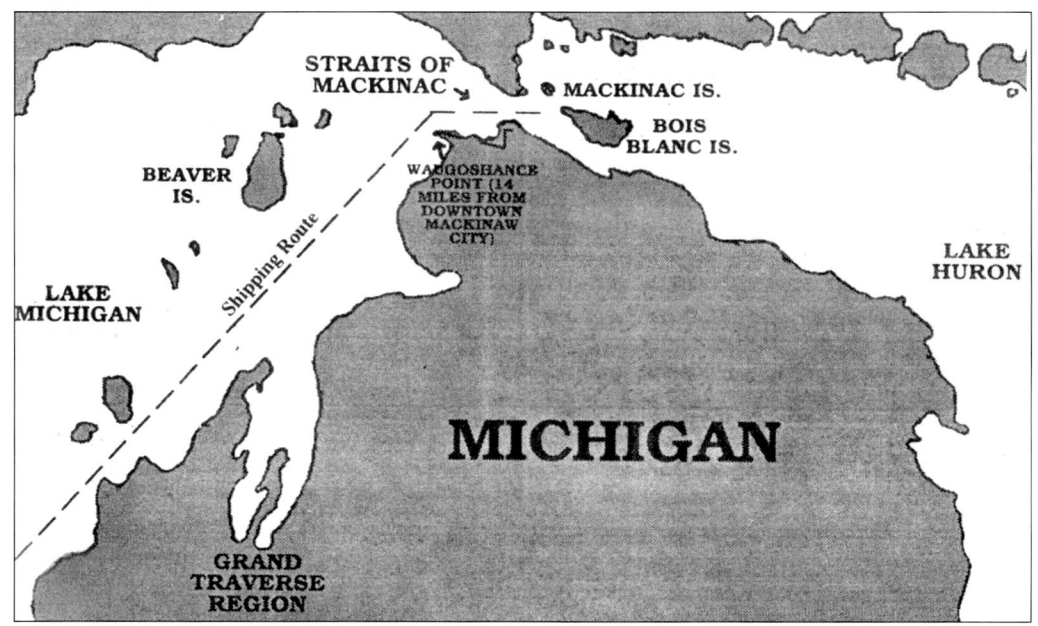

The Beaver Island Archipelago is a group of islands that extend along the shipping route from South Manitou Island northeast to Garden Island. Beaver is the largest of these islands, measuring 13 miles long from end to end. Early economy included thriving lumbering and fishing businesses—so much so that by the mid-1880s, Beaver Island was the largest supplier of fresh water fish in the country. (NC)

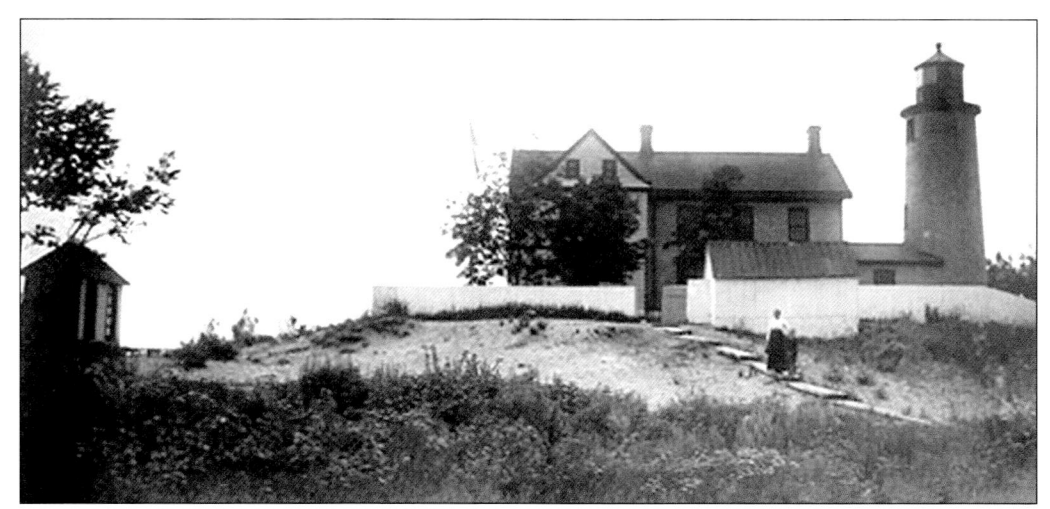

Beaver Island was home to two lighthouses, the Beaver Island Light (Beaver Head) and the St. James Light (Beaver Island Harbor Light). The Beaver Head light, above, was built on the island's southern end in 1852 to mark the western edge of the approach to the Straits of Mackinac. Although the government had purchased land for the light, it was built in the wrong location on non-government-owned land. It took 95 years of legal struggles before the government was able to acquire the land on which the lighthouse sat. In spite of these difficulties, the light remained operational. In 1866 a matching brick keeper's dwelling was constructed and connected to the tower by an enclosed passageway. (USCG)

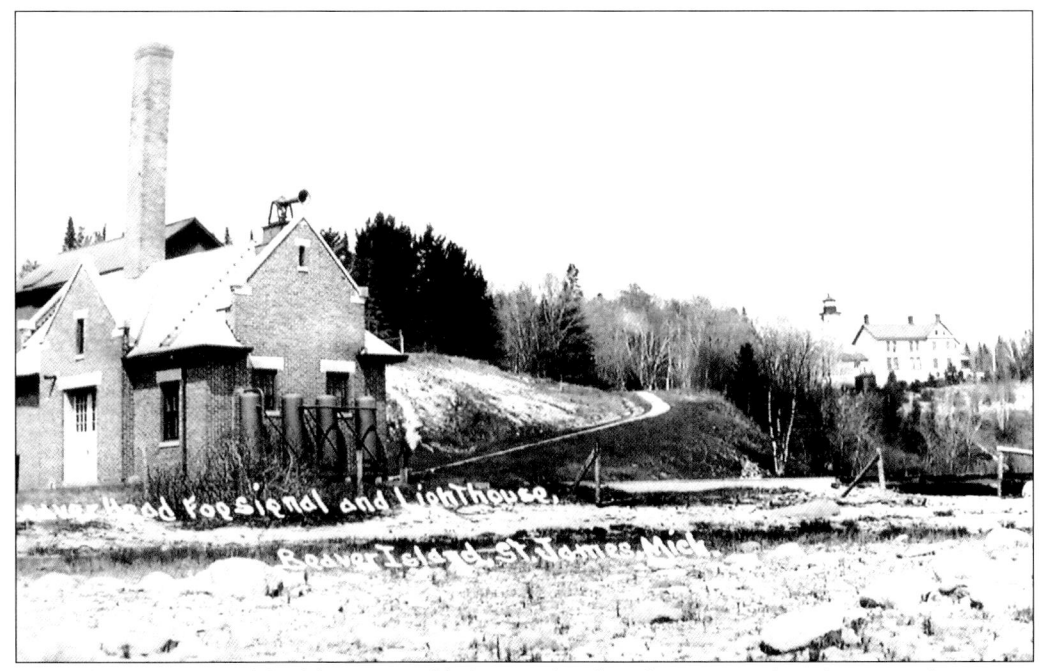

A red brick fog signal building was added near the shoreline in 1913 and a second assistant was hired to maintain the new steam-powered signal. To provide the new assistant with living quarters, a wood-framed addition was added to the dwelling. (BHL)

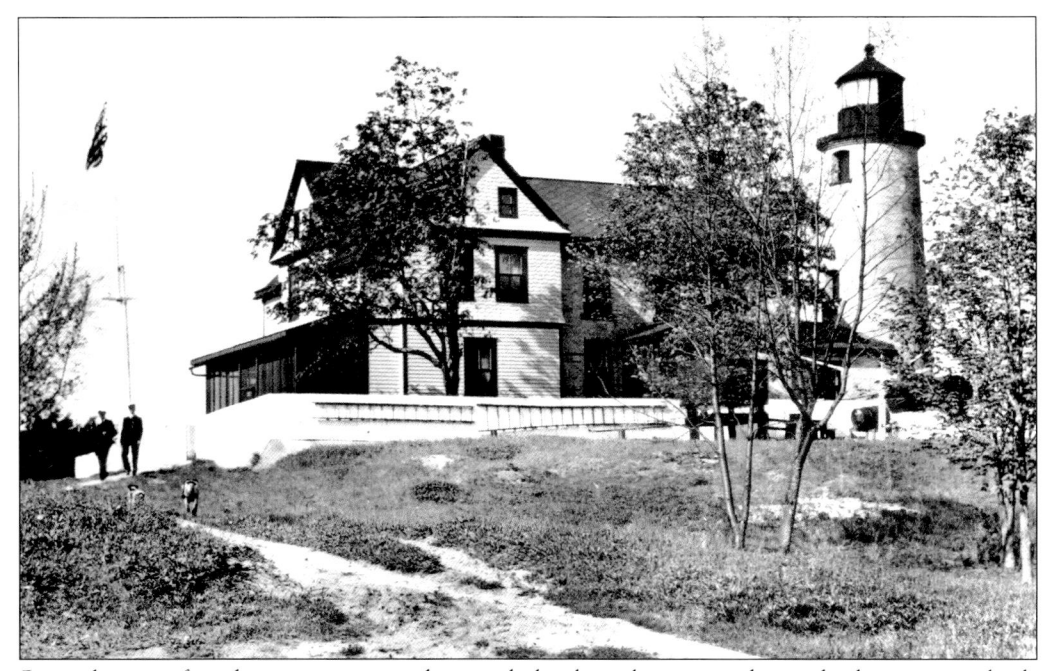

Several years after this picture was taken, a skeletal steel tower with a radio beacon was built on the property. With the addition of this automated light, the lighthouse became obsolete and was decommissioned in 1962. (SAM)

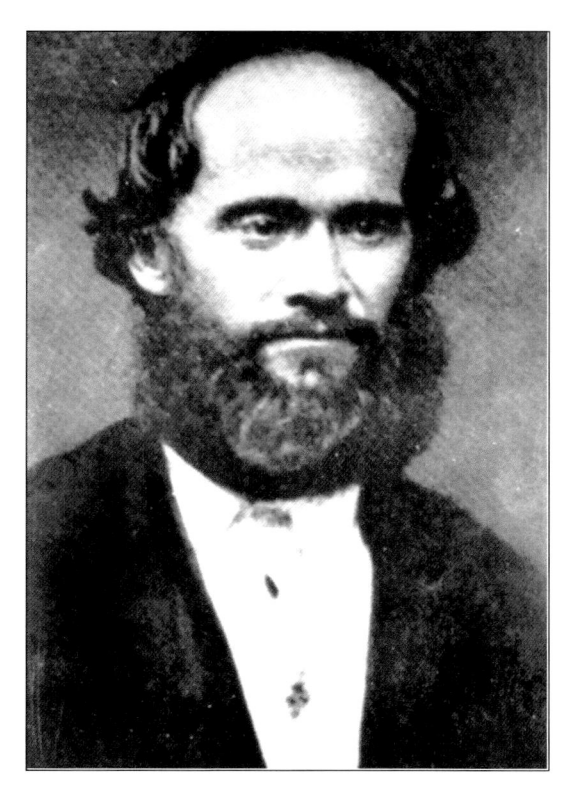

Little is known of the first St. James light, built in 1856 on the natural harbor on the northeast end of the island. It was constructed in the same year of the demise of the self-proclaimed Mormon king of the island, James Strang. Having arrived on the island in 1848, Strang sought to establish his kingdom by building the Mormon population and terrorizing and exiling the "gentiles." His ruthless ways finally caught up to him when he was assassinated by some disgruntled followers. (BHL)

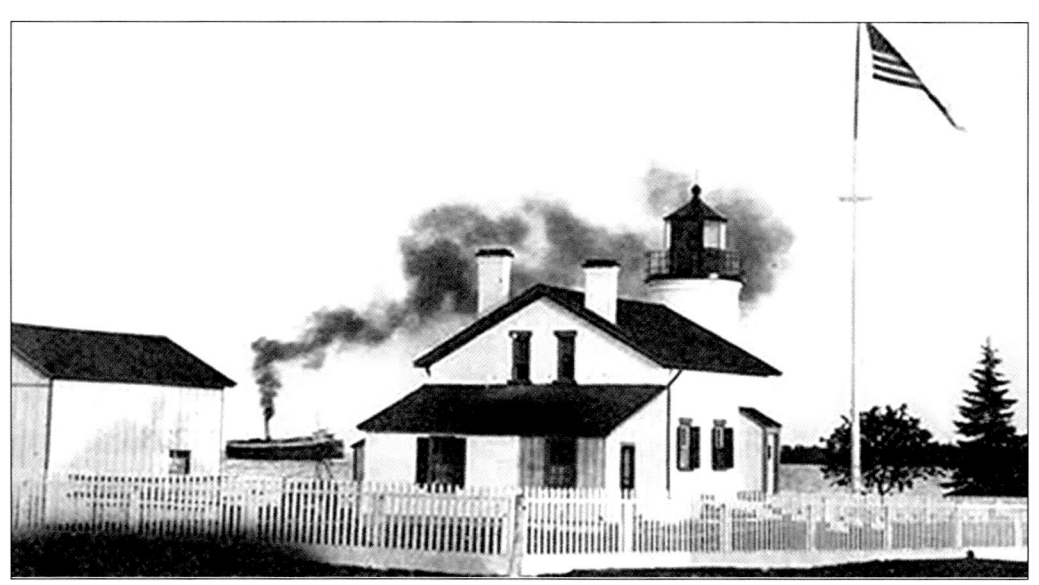

In 1867 the Lighthouse Board recommended that a new larger light be built on the harbor. Congress responded by granting $5,000 for the new lighthouse that was built three years later on Whiskey Point. This structure consisted of a brick keeper's dwelling with a circular tower on the water side and an attached summer kitchen on the back side of the dwelling

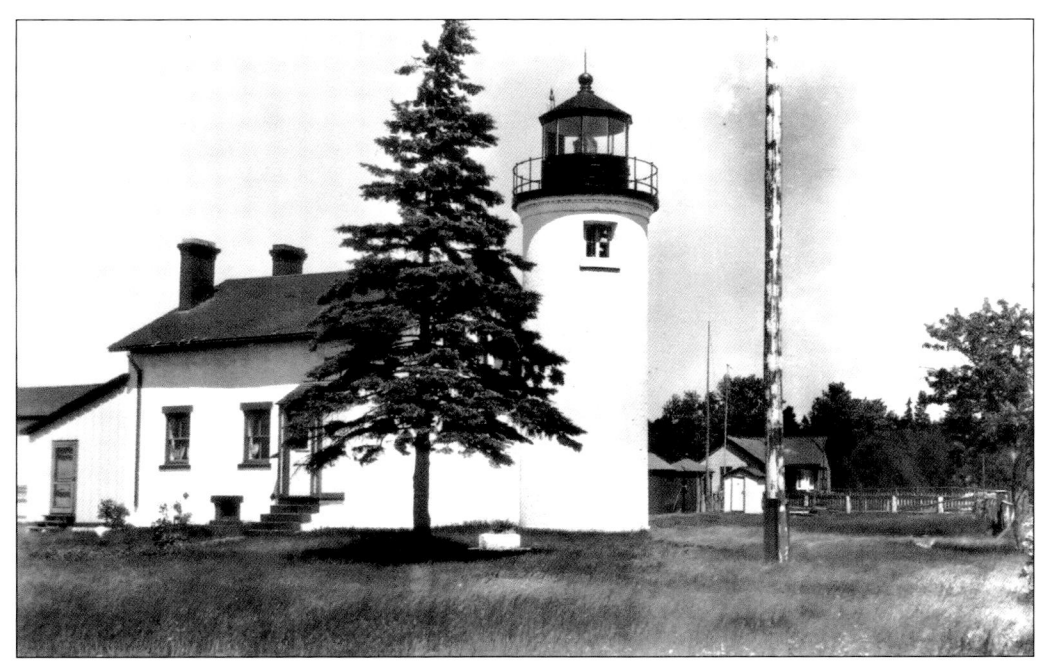

The cylindrical tower stood 41 feet tall and was topped with a black cast iron parapet that held a Fourth Order lens. The tower was attached to the dwelling by a covered passageway. An oil storage and other outbuildings were added to the property in the mid 1880s. (SAM)

The most famous keeper at the St. James Light was Elizabeth Williams. Having spent much of her life growing up on the island, Elizabeth and her family were intimately acquainted with the way of life under King Strang. At age 18, Elizabeth married Clement Van Riper who became keeper of the light in 1869, shortly before the new station was completed. Elizabeth and her husband worked together maintaining the light until Clement disappeared in 1872 while rescuing survivors from a sinking ship. Although grief stricken, Elizabeth rose to the occasion and dedicated herself to providing help to mariners by keeping the light burning. She remained at the light for 12 years until she was transferred to the Little Traverse Light where she served for another 29 years and wrote her autobiography, *A Child of the Sea and Life Among the Mormons*.

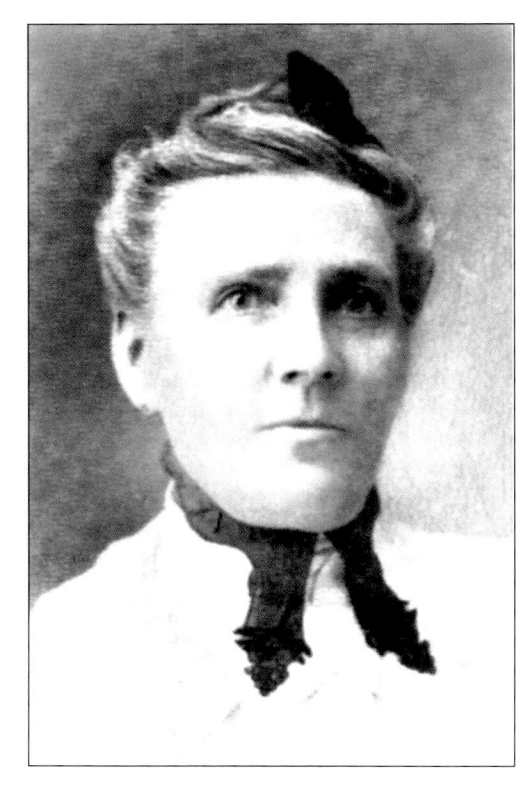

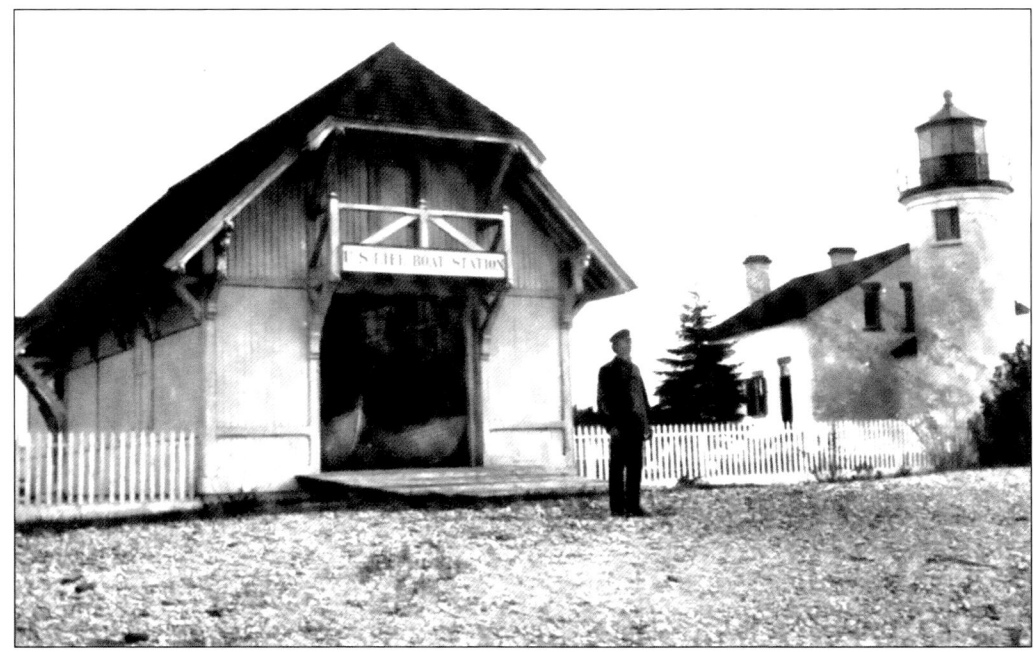

A Lifeboat Station was established next to the lighthouse in 1875. In this clipped gable style station, the lookout consisted of a simple open platform above the boat room doors. At this time the station was equipped with two surfboats, seen inside the building. (CHL)

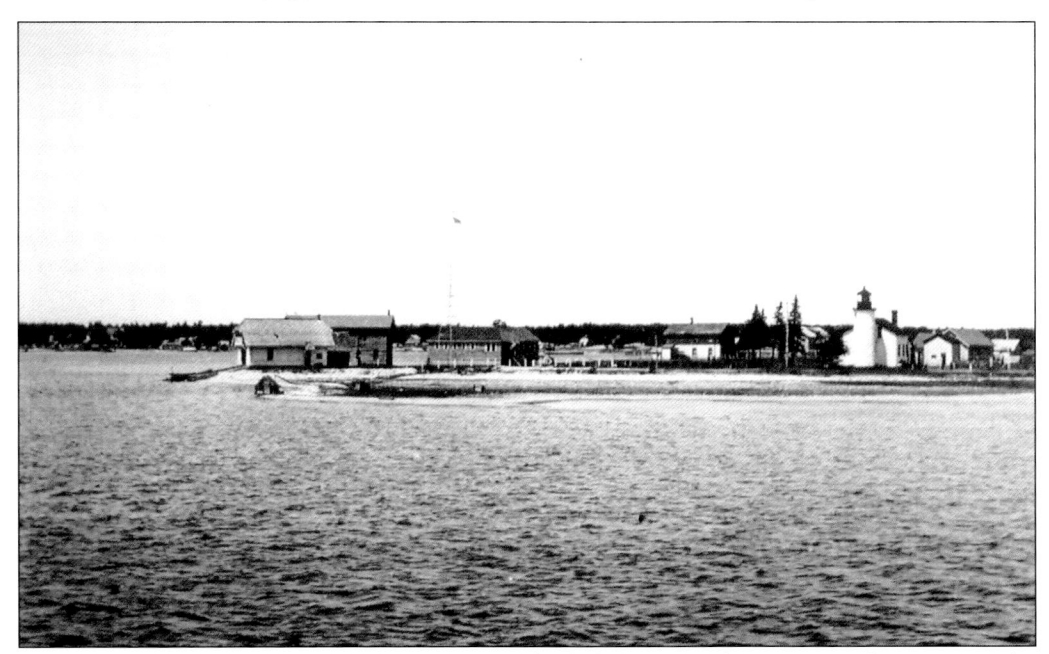

Approaching the harbor from Lake Michigan, the lighthouse and Coast Guard station can be seen on Whiskey Point with the Beaver Island business district in the background. In 1927 the lighthouse was automated, and in the early 1940s the Coast Guard razed the dwelling, leaving only the tower standing. (BHL)

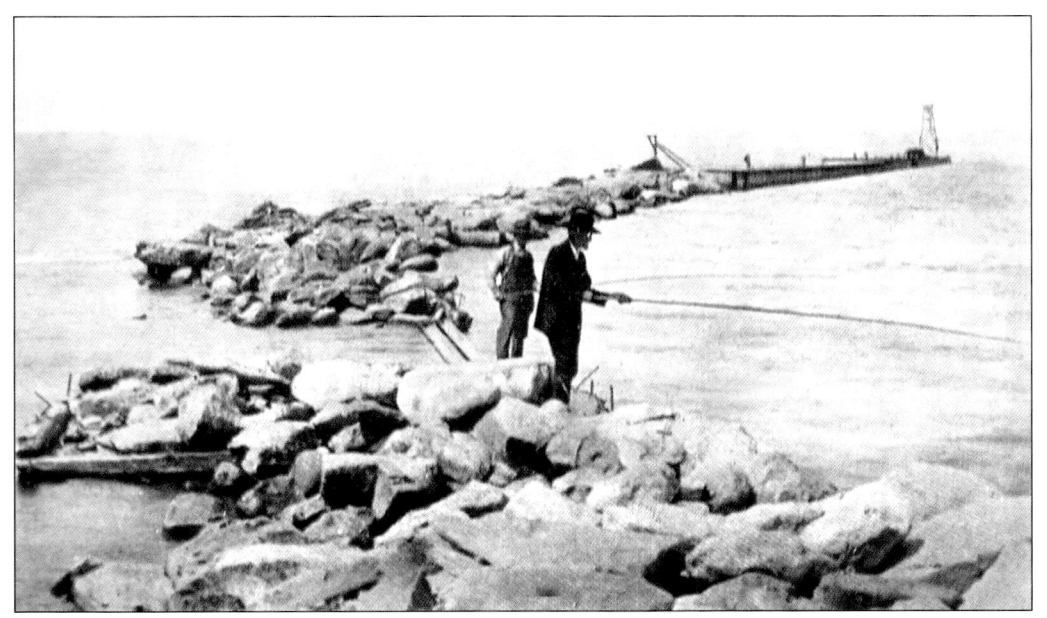

Named after Ottawa Chief Pe-to-se-ga, the town of Petoskey lies on the southeast corner of Little Traverse Bay. Westerly winds traveling the length of the bay often produced rough waters along the exposed waterfront, making it difficult to discharge freight and passengers. In 1895 a breakwater was extended out from the shoreline in an effort to help calm the waters near the loading area. (BHL)

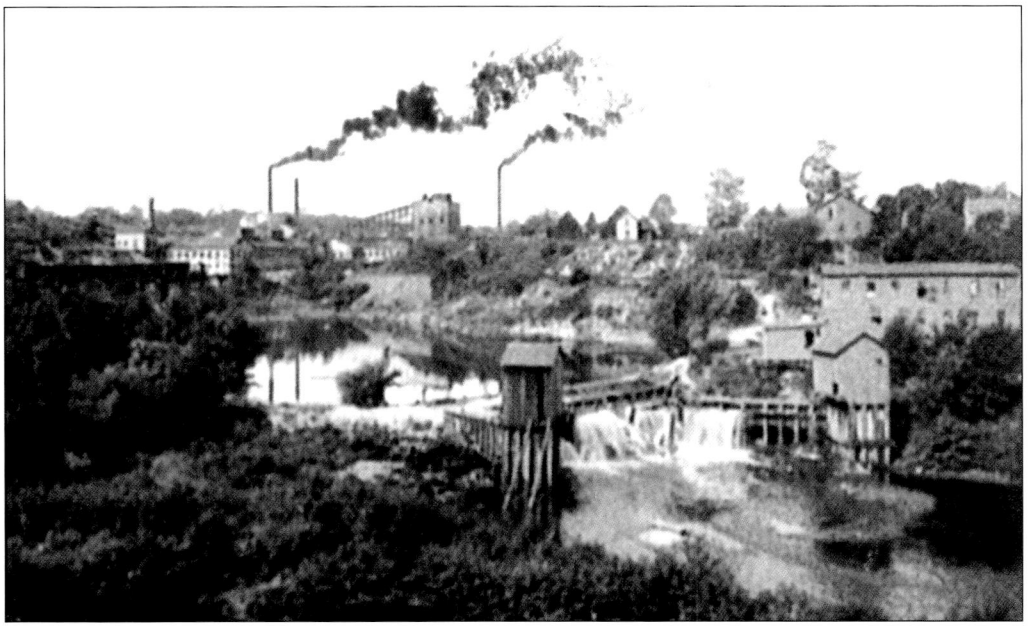

Like most of the harbors along the northeastern Lake Michigan shoreline, Petoskey was a lumbering port during the last half of the 19th century. Sawmills sprang up, meeting the demands of an expanding nation by providing lumber to establish homesteads, businesses, and the growing railway system. (LC)

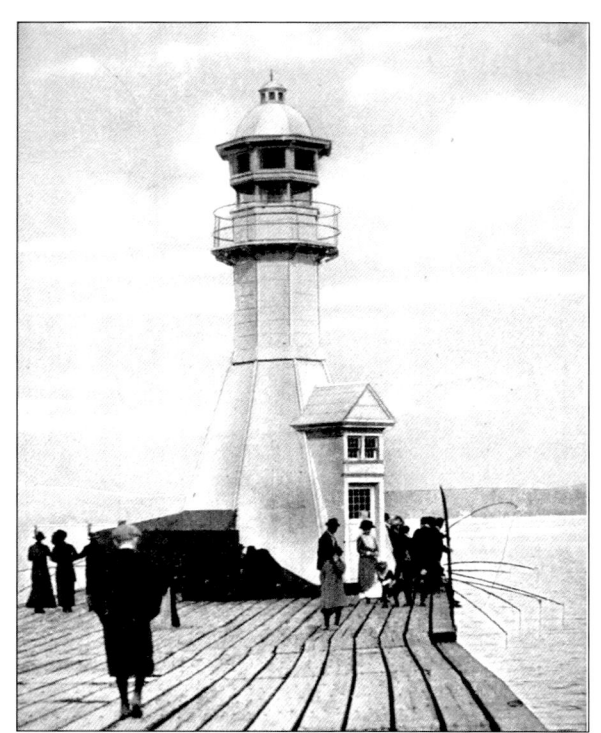

The first light at Petoskey was established on the pier in 1899. The unusual "Pagoda" design consisted of a metal-sided hexagonal tower with a lantern room that held the lowest order lens. This light stood for 25 years before it was washed away in a storm in 1924 and replaced with a modest skeletal tower. (BHL)

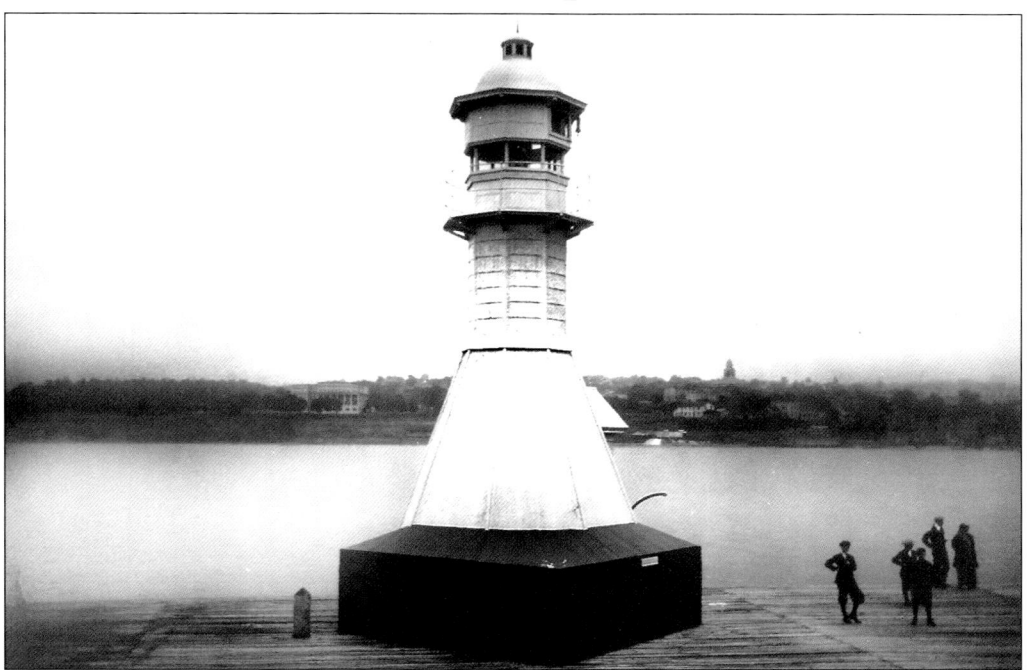

Tourism steadily grew throughout the 19th century until Petoskey became known as a resort town. The *North American*, *South American*, and other steamships brought summer residents who enjoyed living near the waterfront and viewing the "million dollar" sunsets. The beautiful bay area offered fine hotels and diverse activities to entertain these seasonal visitors. (NA)

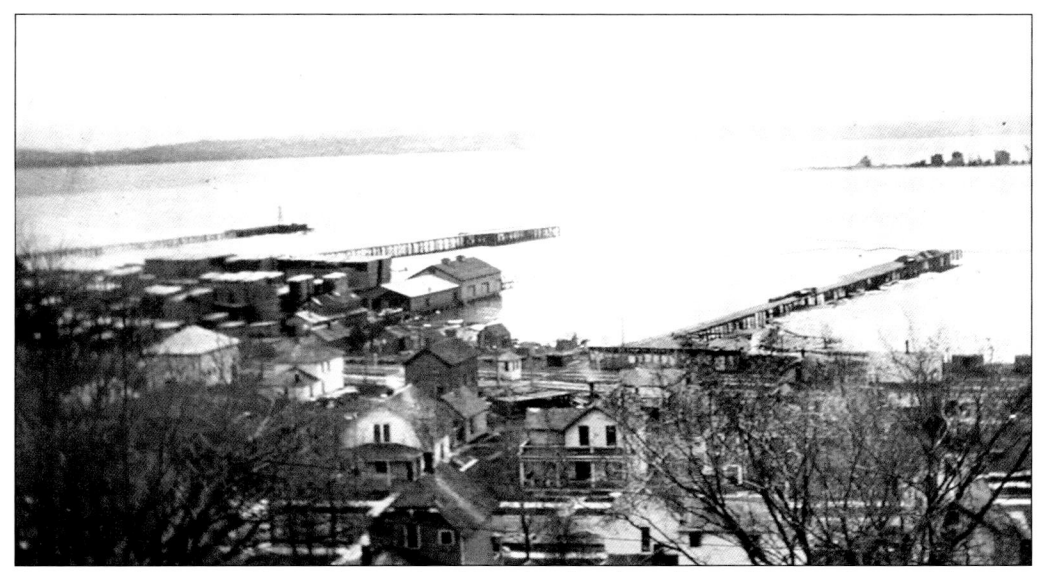

Across Little Traverse Bay to the north of Petoskey lies the village of Harbor Springs. The deep waters of the harbor and its protection from the wind made it a natural harbor of refuge. When land was opened up to settlers c. 1875, a huge influx of lumbermen came to the area to make their fortunes by taking advantage of the bountiful forests. As word of the beauty and healthy climate of the area spread, the rich came to lay claim to their land as well. While plans had been undertaken in the early 1870s to establish a lighthouse on the arm that extended into the bay (right), Congress never responded with an appropriation of funds for the project. (BHL)

With the ever-increasing amount of shipping traffic entering the harbor, by 1882 Congress was again petitioned for funds and this time granted a request for $15,000 to build a light station on the end of Harbor Point. Construction of the Little Traverse Light Station began on May 4, 1884, with the new light being exhibited for the first time on September 25th of the same year.

The lighthouse consisted of a one-and-one-half story red brick dwelling with a square attached tower on its south end. It was topped with an octagonal lantern room that was fitted with a Fourth Order Fresnel lens. (NC)

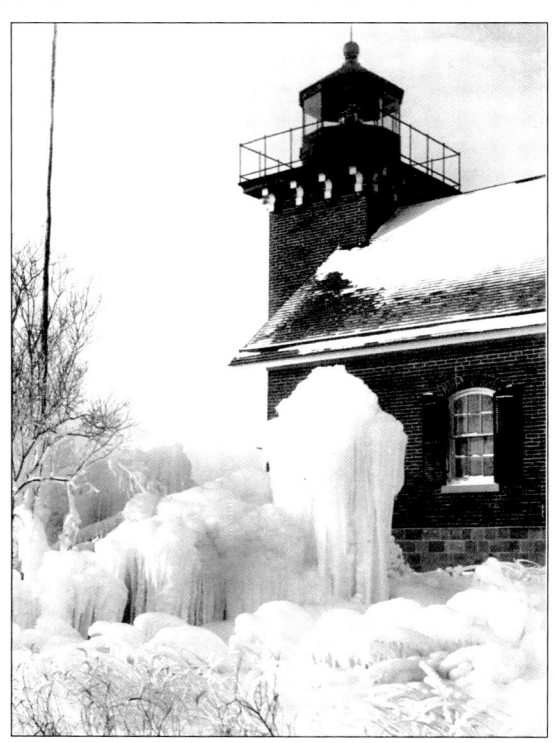

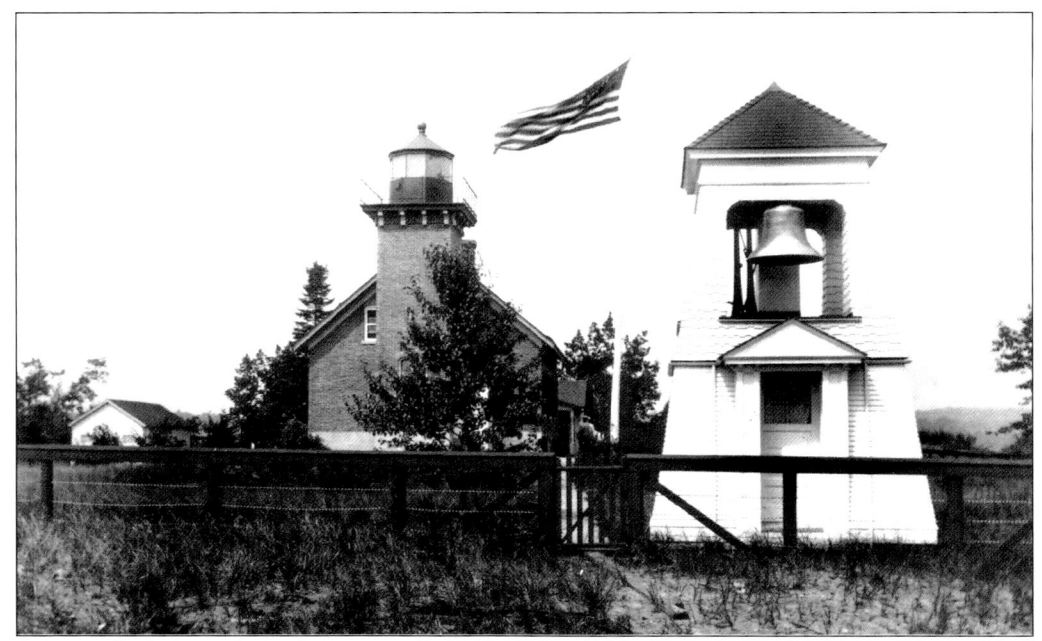

A fog signal was built in front of the light in 1896. The 20-foot-tall tower had an enclosed base with access for the keeper and an open upper section where the bell hung. The signal's modern Steven's bell striking mechanism enabled the bell to be struck 10,000 times before it needed rewinding. At two strikes every 30 seconds, this meant the keeper only needed to wind the bell once a day. (SAM)

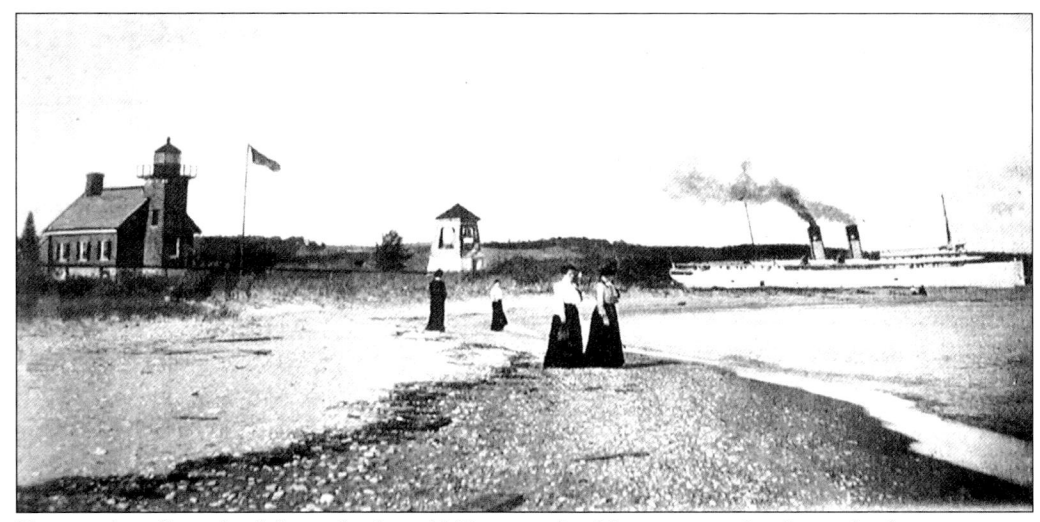

Tourism has flourished from the late 1800s into the 21st century. In the early days, steamers brought passengers from Chicago and other ports to enjoy the beauty of this region. Many wealthy families including the Fords, Upjohns, and Gambles built large summer homes in the resort communities of Harbor Point, Wequetonsing, and Roaring Brook.

When the Coast Guard assumed responsibility for lighthouses in 1939, this light was deactivated, in an effort to cut costs, and later replaced with an unmanned steel skeletal tower. (BHL)

Six

Lights of the Mackinac Straits
Waugoshance Shoal Light, Ile aux Galets Light, Gray's Reef Light, White Shoal Light, and St. Helena Island Light

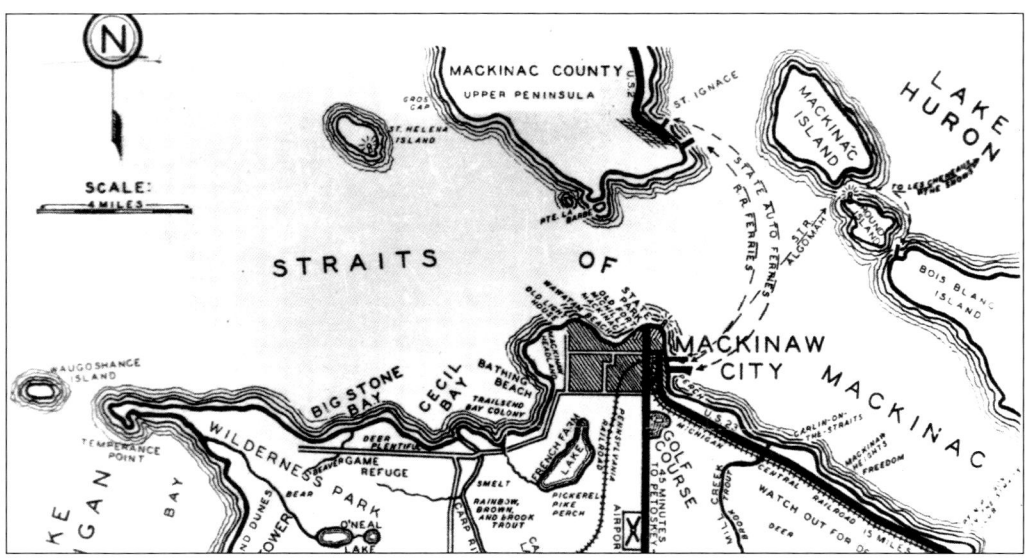

Vessels traveling from southern Lake Michigan ports to upper Michigan, Lake Huron, and Canada passed through the converging waters of Lake Michigan and Lake Huron, known as the Straits of Mackinac. These waters were laden with shoals, reefs, and islands that made passage through the area treacherous. While a light was established on Bois Blanc Island in 1829 to mark the eastern entrance to the Straits, no marker existed on the western side.

In the early 1820s, mariners had begun petitioning the federal government for a light to mark the dangerous six miles of shoals near Waugoshance Point on the western approach to the Straits. However, an offshore crib light had not yet been attempted on the open waters of the Great Lakes, and the task appeared daunting. Consequently, a wooden ship was anchored in the water in 1832 to mark these shoals and the turning point into the Straits. This vessel, equipped with a light and a fog bell, became the first lightship to be used on the Great Lakes. She continued her service at Waugoshance Shoal for the next 19 years. (MAPL)

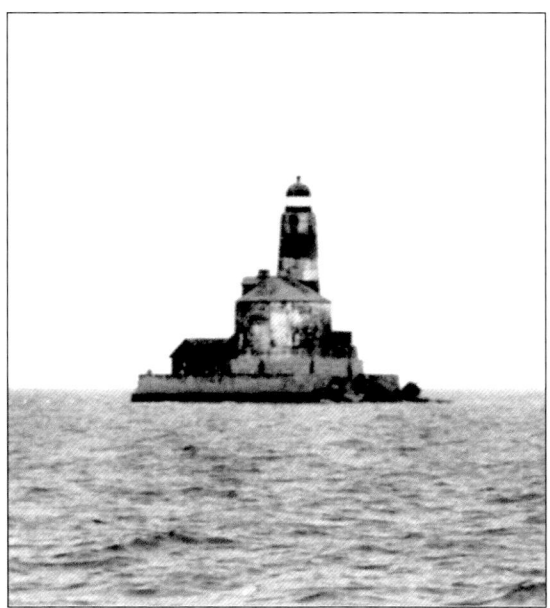

Since lightships were easily blown off-station and were difficult to place into position each spring, the decision was made to build a permanent crib light on the shoal. A wooden crib, constructed on shore at St. Helena Island, was towed to the shoal and sunk in the water by filling it with rocks. The water was pumped out and cement was poured over the shoal to form a flat foundation for the lighthouse. Limestone slabs were then bolted to the concrete and the tower was built on top. Waugoshance Shoal Light was completed in 1851. It stood 76 feet tall and was topped with an unusual birdcage-style lantern room. While underwater cribs had previously been used for breakwaters and piers, this was the first offshore lighthouse on the Great Lakes to be built on a timber crib. (WPRL)

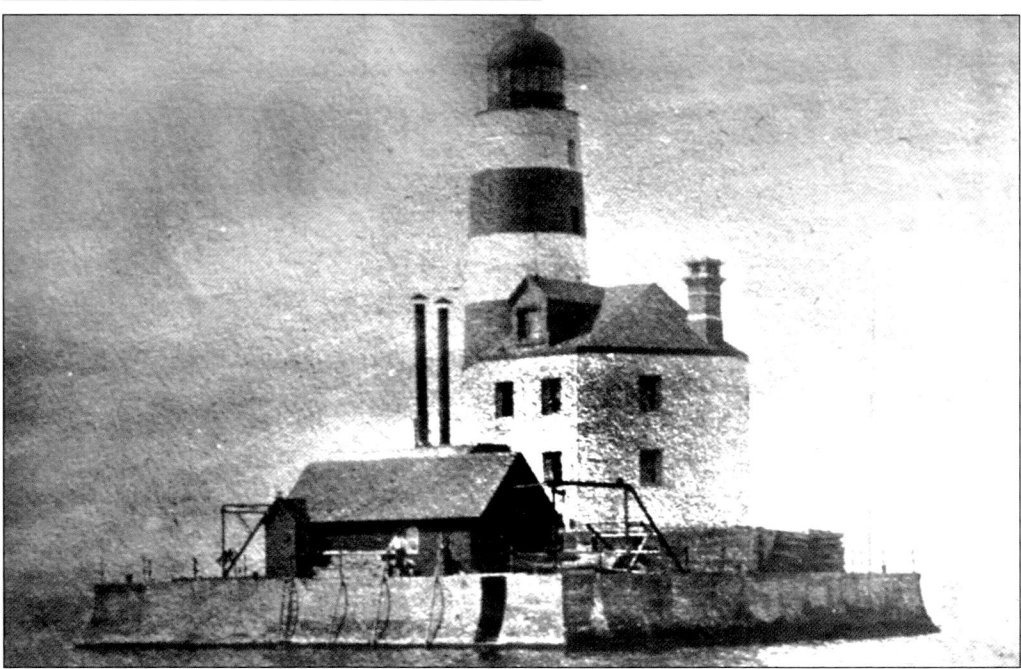

The lighthouse contained living quarters for a keeper and his crew and a fog bell that the keeper manually operated by pulling a rope. During the Chicago fire of 1871, thick smoke, worse than fog, blew up the lake and covered the light. Assistant keeper James Davenport, who was alone at the lighthouse at the time, kept the fog bell ringing non-stop for several days until the smoke cleared. To accomplish this feat, he sat in a chair with the rope in his hand and a dishpan full of smaller pans in his lap. Each time he dozed off the pans crashed to the floor and woke him up. Despite his valiant efforts, once the smoke blew away, he found seven schooners aground on the reefs. (NA)

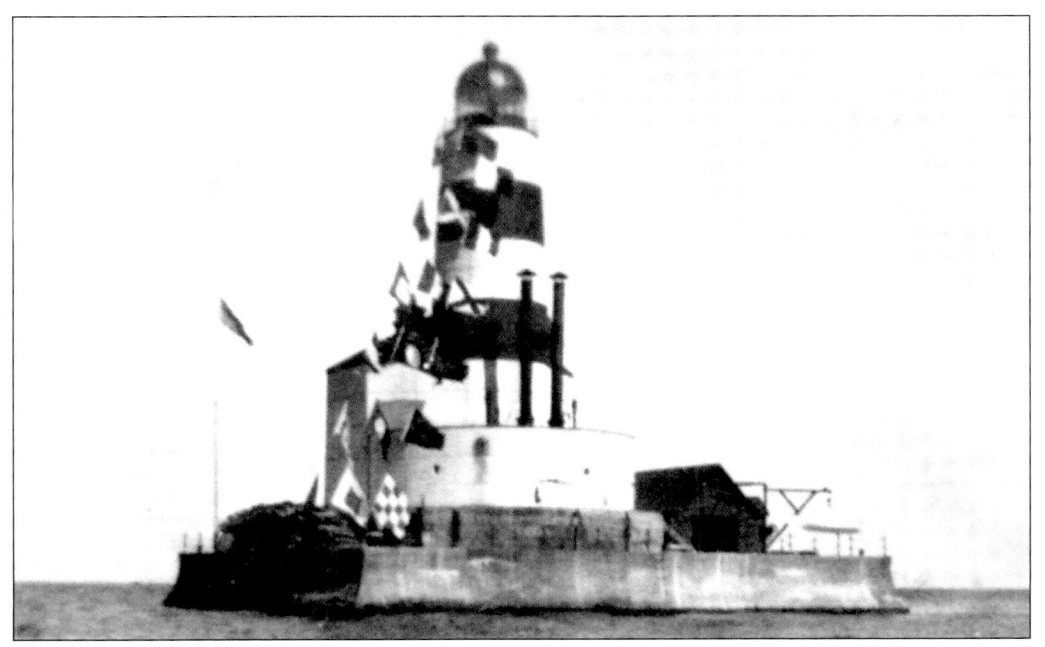

Direct exposure to the furious wave and ice action of the lake caused the light continual deterioration problems. Major renovations took place on the crib in 1865, 1896, and 1902. In 1883 the tower and dwelling were encased in cast iron plating to protect the brick from further erosion. Alternating red and white stripes were then painted around the tower. Also at this time, a steam-powered fog signal and a circular building to house its equipment were added to the crib. (MAPL)

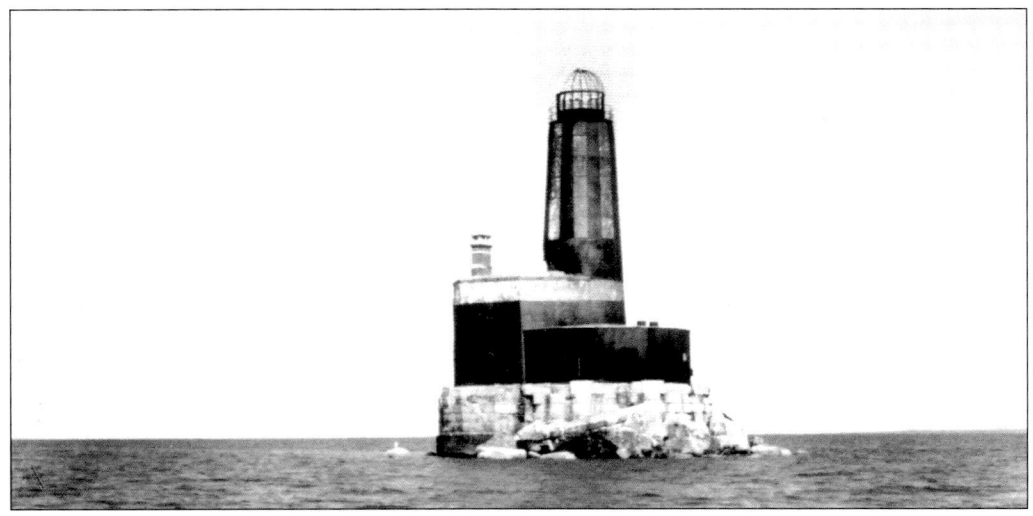

As larger vessels came to the area, they began entering the Straits through the deeper waters north of Waugoshance. Since White Shoal sat very close to this passage, the Lighthouse Board eventually established a light there. When White Shoal Light began shining, Waugoshance was considered redundant and was decommissioned and abandoned in 1912. During World War II, Waugoshance Light was used for target practice. Sadly, a resulting fire completely gutted the house and tower. (NC)

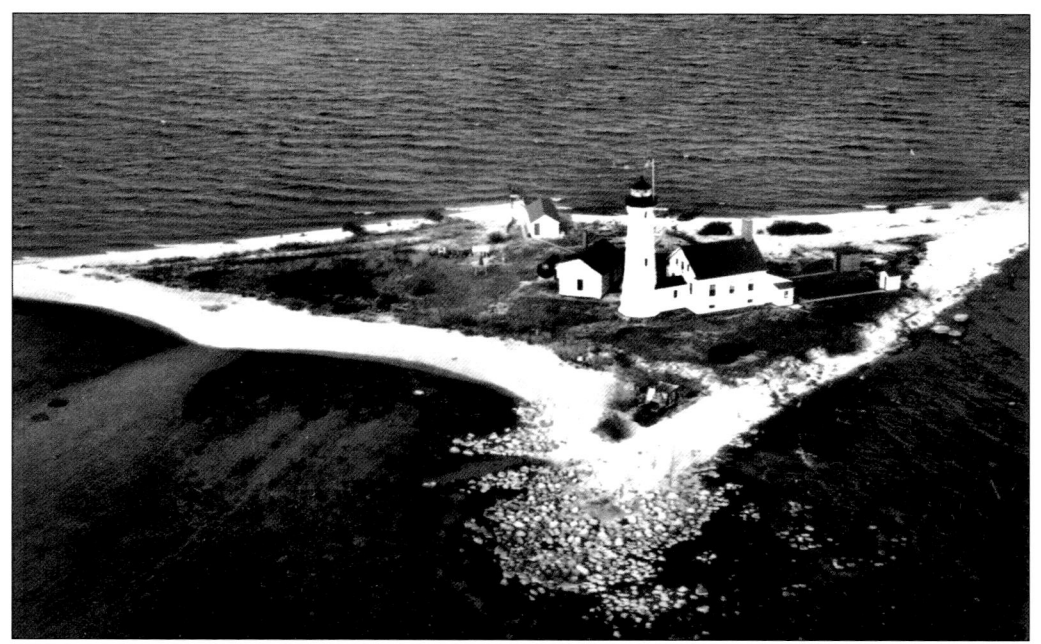

Recognizing that Waugoshance Shoal Light in itself was not sufficient to mark all the hidden dangers in the nearby waters, additional lights were added to assist mariners. Ile Aux Galets, or "Island of Pebbles," is a small flat island located a little over seven miles southwest of Waugoshance Shoal. Originally named by the French, its English pronunciation deteriorated to the name Skillagalee, by which it is known today. (SAM)

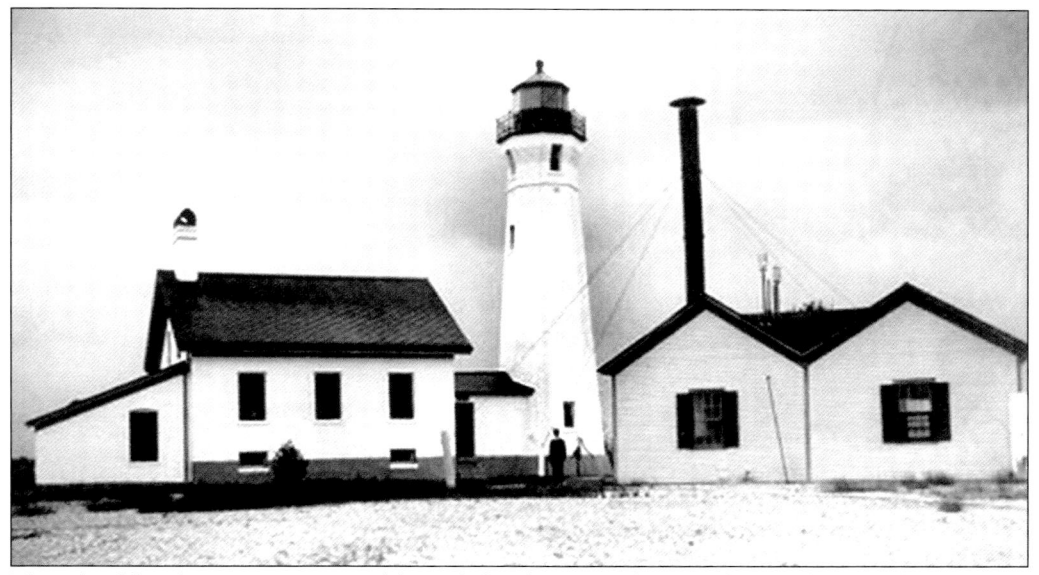

The island has been a navigational hazard that has caused many shipwrecks over the years. Its visible size that changes with the lake's fluctuating water levels, together with its flat surface, makes it almost impossible to detect on the horizon. To warn mariners of its presence, a light was established on the island in 1851. Subject to damage by exposure, it was completely rebuilt in 1868 and again in 1888, resulting in the octagonal tower pictured above. (USCG)

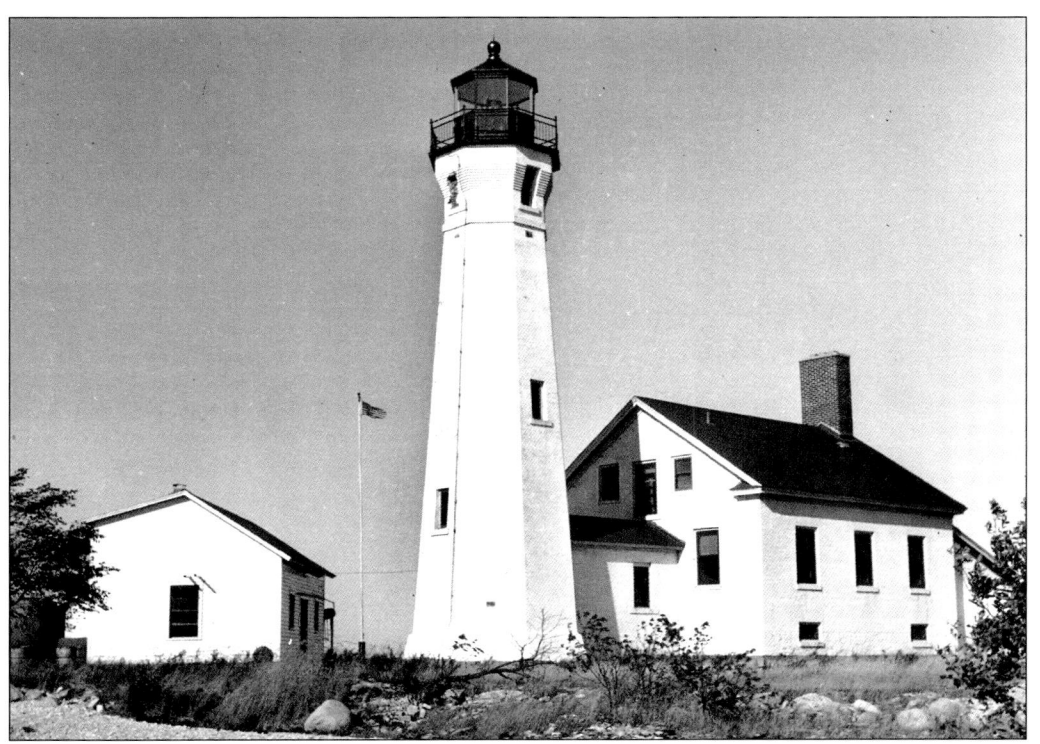

The brick tower stood 58 feet tall and was fitted with a Fourth Order Fresnel lens. It was joined to the one-and-one-half-story keeper's dwelling by a covered passageway that gave protection to the keeper during inclement weather. (MMM)

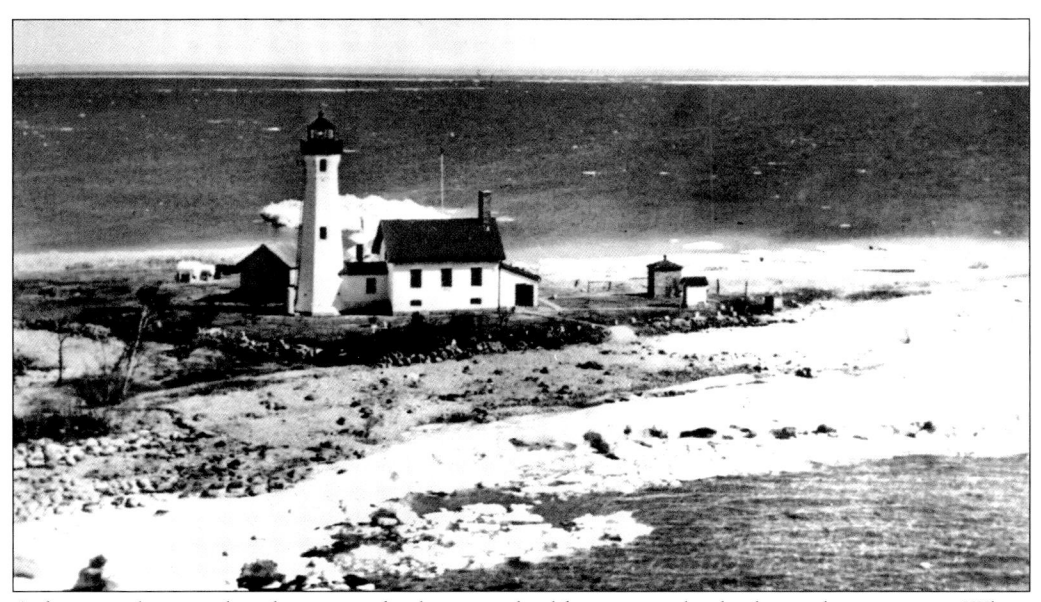

A fog signal, privy, boathouse, and oil storage building were also built on the premises. When the light was automated in 1969, the Coast Guard demolished all buildings except the tower, which remains standing to this day. (SAM)

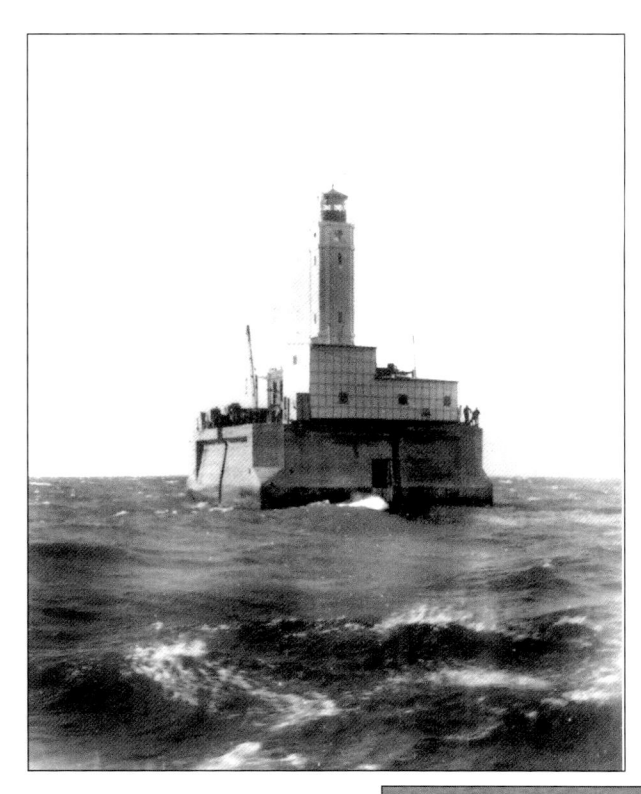

As vessels increased in size, the deeper waters near Gray's Reef became more suitable for their passage into the Straits. In 1891 lightship *LV 57* was anchored on Gray's Reef to mark the eight miles of shallow rocky water on its western side. The lightship continued to mark the shoal for the next 32 years until her hull rotted and she was replaced. In the 1930s, as large ore carriers were making their way through the passage, the government enlarged and deepened it to accommodate these vessels. Six years later a permanent light station with a fog signal was constructed on the site by the Greiling Brothers Company, who had done significant work on the Ludington breakwaters a few years earlier. (NC)

The new Gray's Reef tower was a steel structure covered with riveted steel sheeting. Since it was built later than most of the other lighthouses on the lake, this station was complete with electricity, hot water heat, and plumbing. In May of 1937, a radio beacon was installed. Its signal synchronized with the fog signal so that mariners could pinpoint their exact distance from the station by calculating the differential between receiving the radio signal and hearing the fog signal. The light was fully automated in 1976. (USCG)

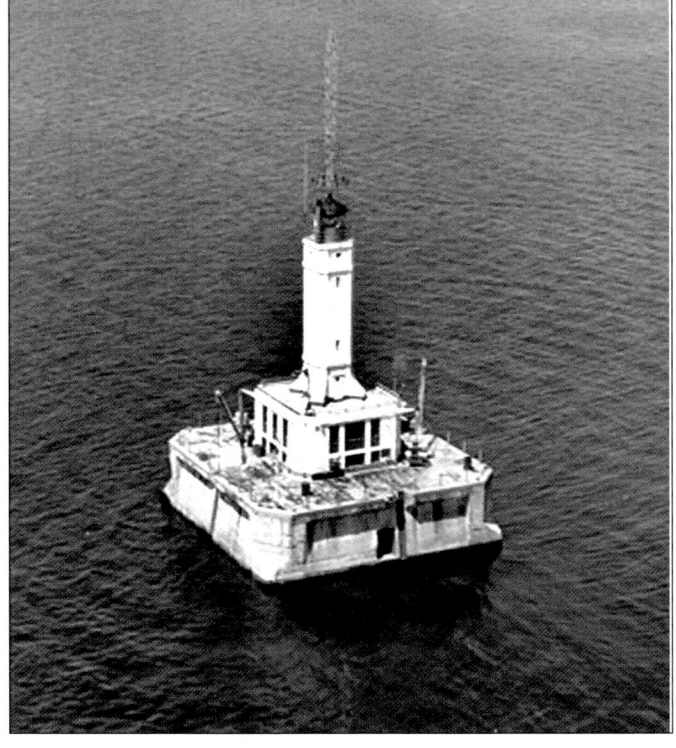

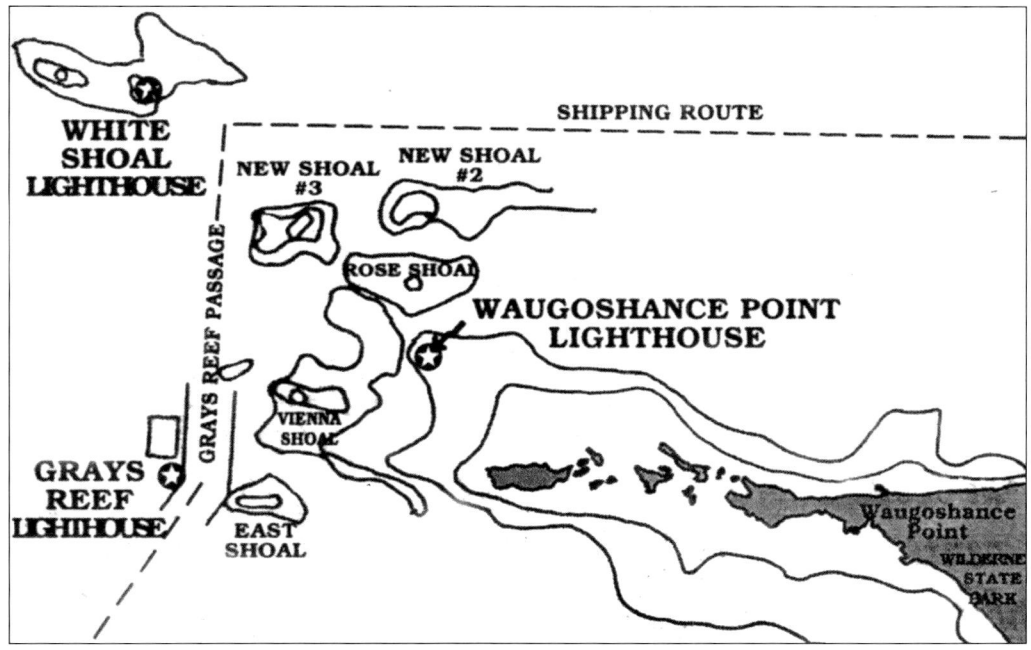

White Shoal is located approximately three miles northwest of Waugoshance Shoal and 20 miles west of Old Mackinac Point. The shoal is almost two miles long and so shallow at its west end that it protrudes through the water's surface. Viewing this as a significant hazard to shipping, the government anchored lightship *LV 56* on the shoal in 1891. (NC)

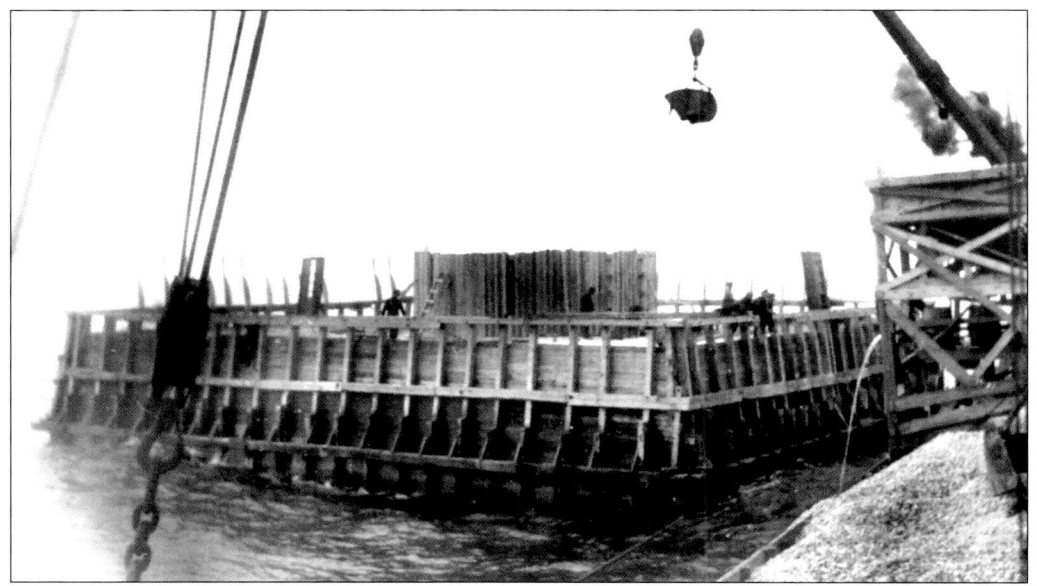

In 1906 the Lighthouse Board requested funds to establish a permanent light on the shoal. Congress responded the following year by granting $250,000 for the project, which began in the spring of 1908. The timber crib, seen above, was constructed on shore to a size of 72 feet square and 18 feet high. It was floated out to the shoal and sunk into the water to form a solid base for the lighthouse tower. (NA)

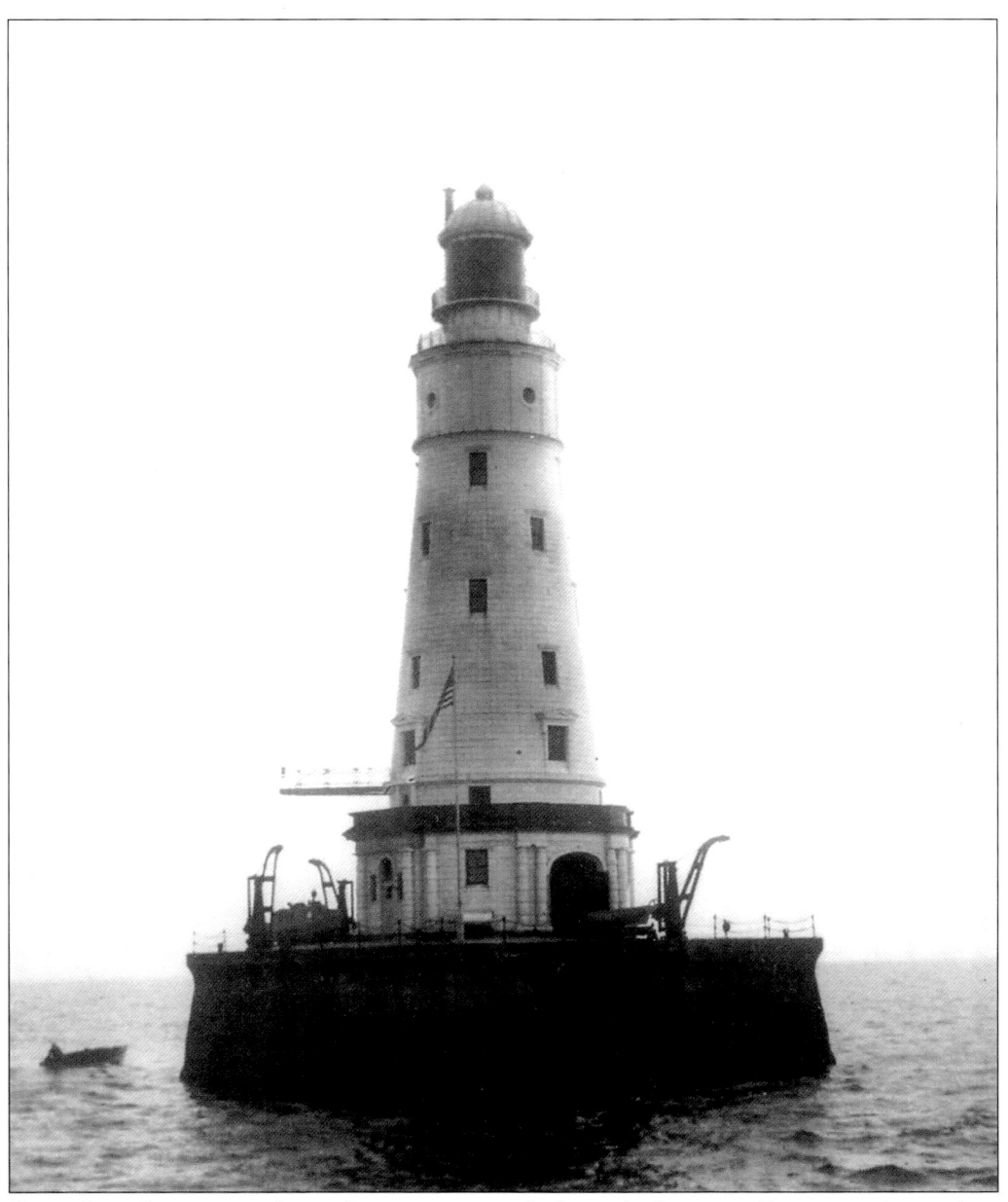

Once the crib was securely in place, a concrete deck was laid on top. On-site work was then suspended for the winter while tower parts were prefabricated on shore. The following spring the parts were shipped to the light and tower construction began.

The conical tower consisted of a skeletal steel framework lined with brick and covered with dark terra cotta blocks. It stood 121 feet tall and held eight levels of living and working space inside. With the addition of the diaphone fog signal the following year, the station was complete and the light began shining on September 1, 1910. Since the lightship was no longer needed, it was removed and placed on North Manitou Shoal.

The steam-powered cranes, seen on the sides of the base, were used for unloading supplies and raising and lowering the keeper's boat. (United States Coast Guard)

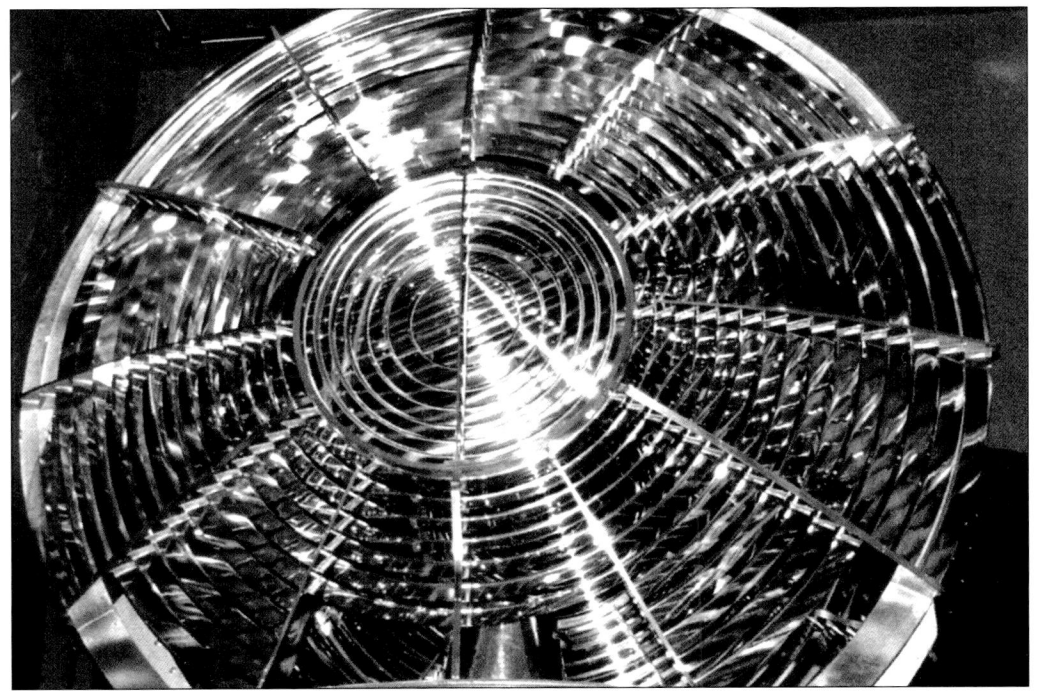

The lantern room housed a Second Order Fresnel Lens. The "clam-shell" design lens measured more than nine feet in diameter and gave the light visibility up to 28 miles. Only four other locations on the Great Lakes were equipped with this large size lens.

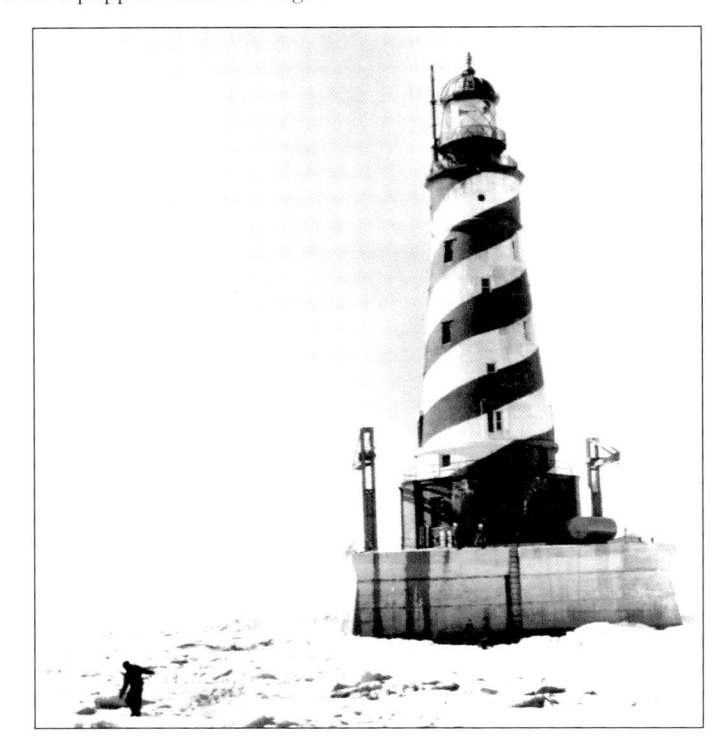

To make it a more effective daymark, the White Shoal Light was painted with distinctive red and white stripes in 1954. In 1976 the light was automated and seven years later the Fresnel lens was removed from the tower and was later placed in the Great Lakes Shipwreck Museum. (SAM)

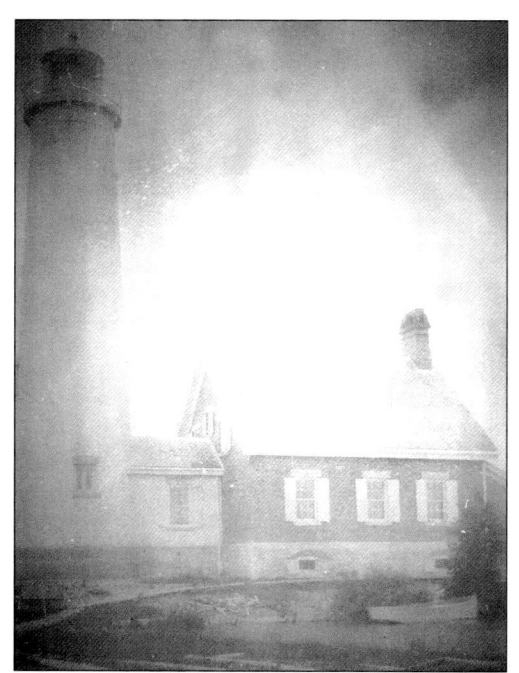

The 240-acre St. Helena Island is located about six miles west of the Mackinac Bridge. A natural harbor on its north side provided shelter for lake vessels and contributed to the birth of a substantial fishing village. While the waters of the harbor were deep and clear, dangerous shoals marked the eastern and western sides of the island. As an aid to vessels crossing the Straits or entering the harbor, the Lighthouse Board requested $14,000 to construct a lighthouse on the island's southeast side. Congress responded five years later on June 10, 1872 with an appropriation of the requested funds.

Construction began in the fall of the same year and continued until the light was first exhibited in September of 1873. The tower and keeper's dwelling, made of red brick, were connected by a small covered walkway. A cast iron spiral stairway in the tower led to the light that was illuminated by a fixed red Third-and-a-Half-Order lens. (NA)

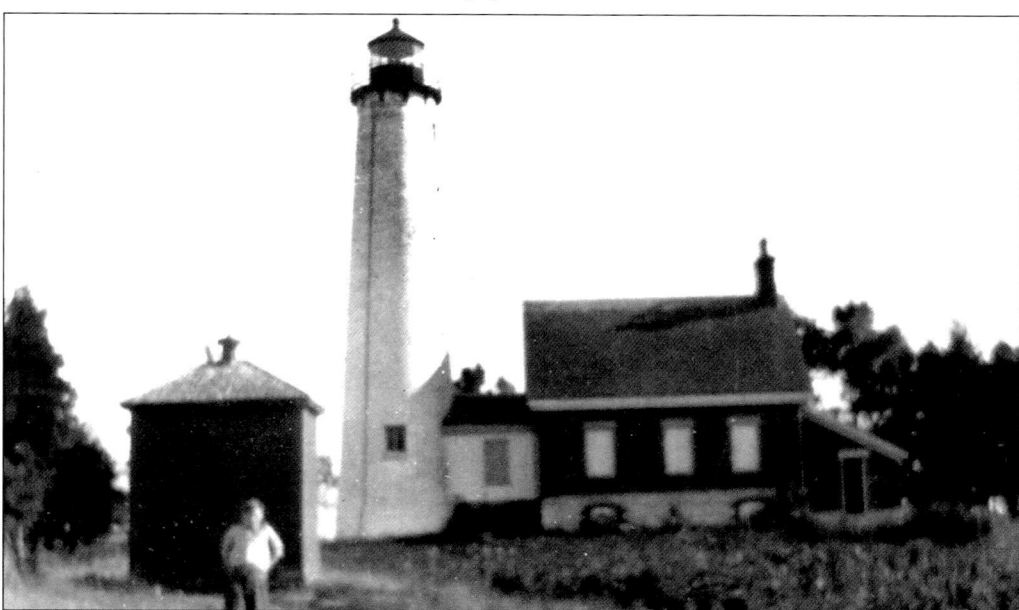

The spacious keeper's dwelling contained a dining room, parlor, kitchen, and office on the first floor and bedrooms on the second floor. A summer kitchen was added to the end of the building and a privy was built behind it. In 1895 a boathouse and dock were built on the grounds, and the following year a 360-gallon brick oil storage building was constructed near the tower.

The light was automated in 1922 with an acetylene gas lamp. A sun valve regulated the lamp to turn on in the cool of the evening and turn off in the heat of the day. Consequently, a keeper was no longer needed, so he was transferred to another light and the dwelling was boarded up. Periodic maintenance fell to the keepers of the Old Mackinac Point Light thereafter. (SAM)

Seven

MACKINAC AREA LIGHTS
McGulpin's Point Light, Old Mackinac Point Light, and Mackinac Bridge

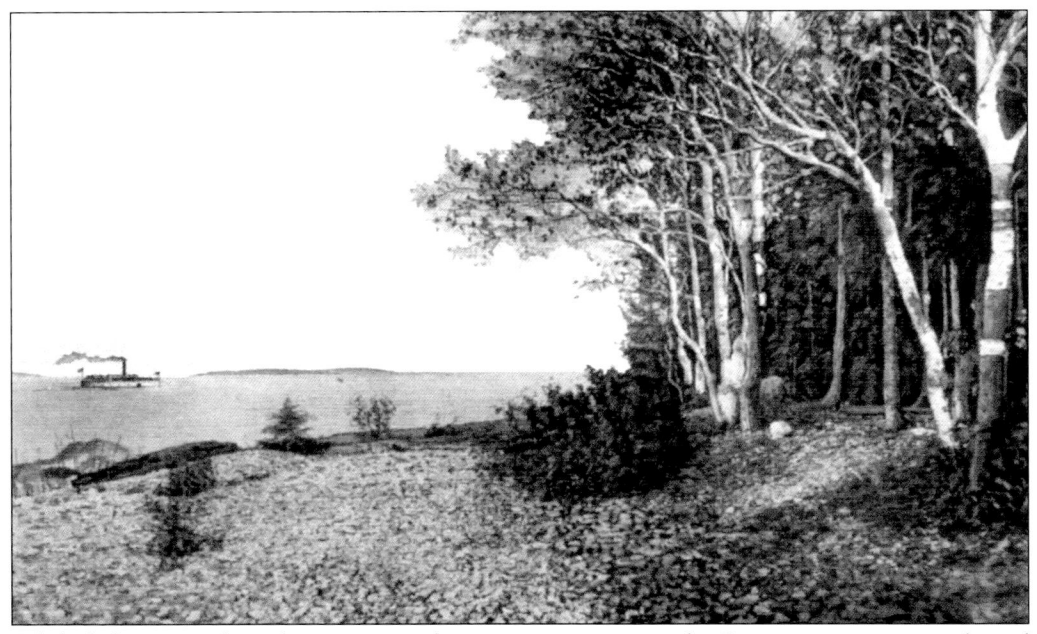

While lights existed on the eastern and western entrances to the Straits, mariners complained that there was no light to guide them into the narrow channel between the upper and lower peninsulas. Finding their way safely through this area was especially hard at night and during storms. To remedy this situation, the Lighthouse Board petitioned Congress for funds to establish a lighthouse on McGulpin's Point, three miles west of Fort Michilimackinac in Mackinaw City. Congress responded by granting $6,000 for the project in 1854; however, for reasons unknown, construction was never begun. Twelve years later, after more than 30 ships had gone down in the passage, Congress was again petitioned and granted funds and this time construction was begun. (MAPL)

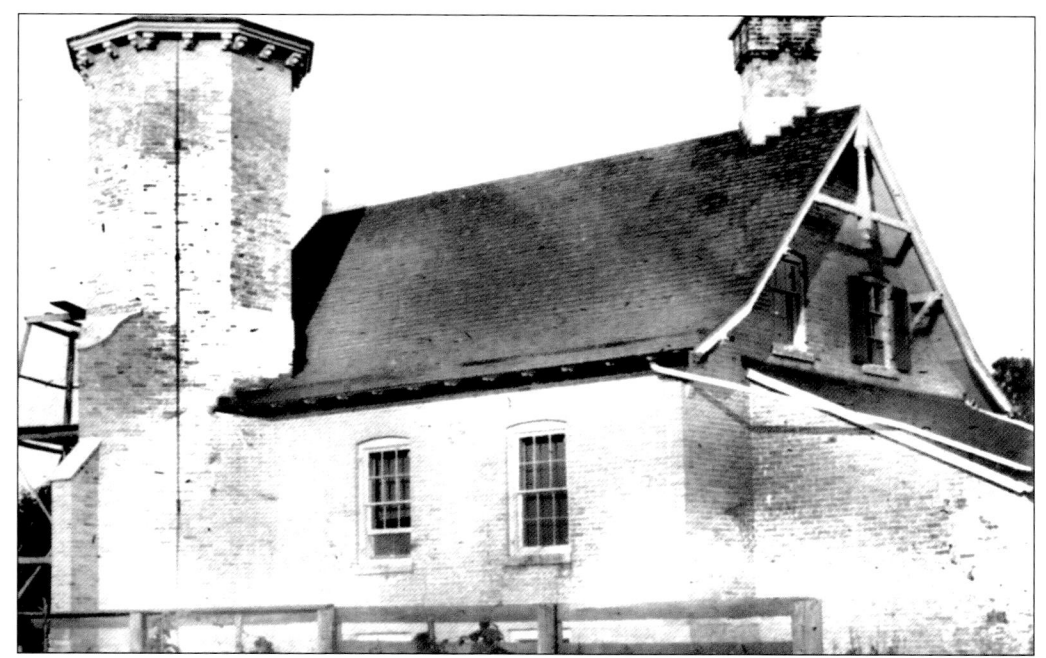

McGulpin's Point Lighthouse consisted of a two-story brick dwelling with an attached octagonal tower placed at an angle on the northwest corner. The main floor living area contained five large rooms and the second floor held three bedrooms that were accessed by climbing the spiral stairs of the tower. (NC)

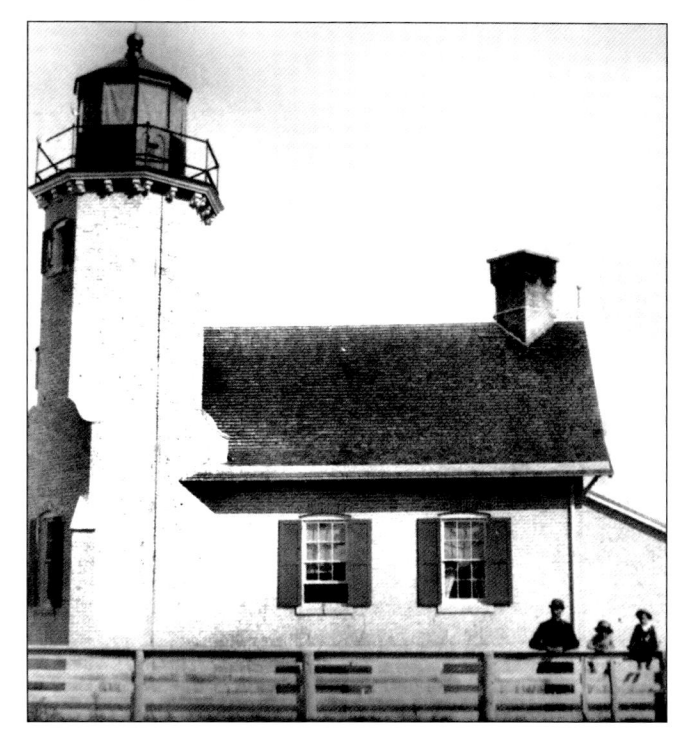

A cast iron lantern room on top of the tower housed a Third-and-half Order Fresnel lens that was lit for the first time in 1869. Left, keeper James Davenport is pictured with two of his nine children. Before coming to McGulpin's Point, Davenport served at Waugoshance Shoal Light and Little Sable Point Light. While serving at Waugoshance, Davenport's wife died in childbirth. It had been her desire to be buried on Mackinac Island, so as the other children watched, James and his oldest daughter loaded his deceased wife and baby on a sled and pulled them across the frozen water to the island. Eight years later (in 1879), James began serving at McGulpin's Point and remained there until the light was discontinued 27 years later. (MAPL)

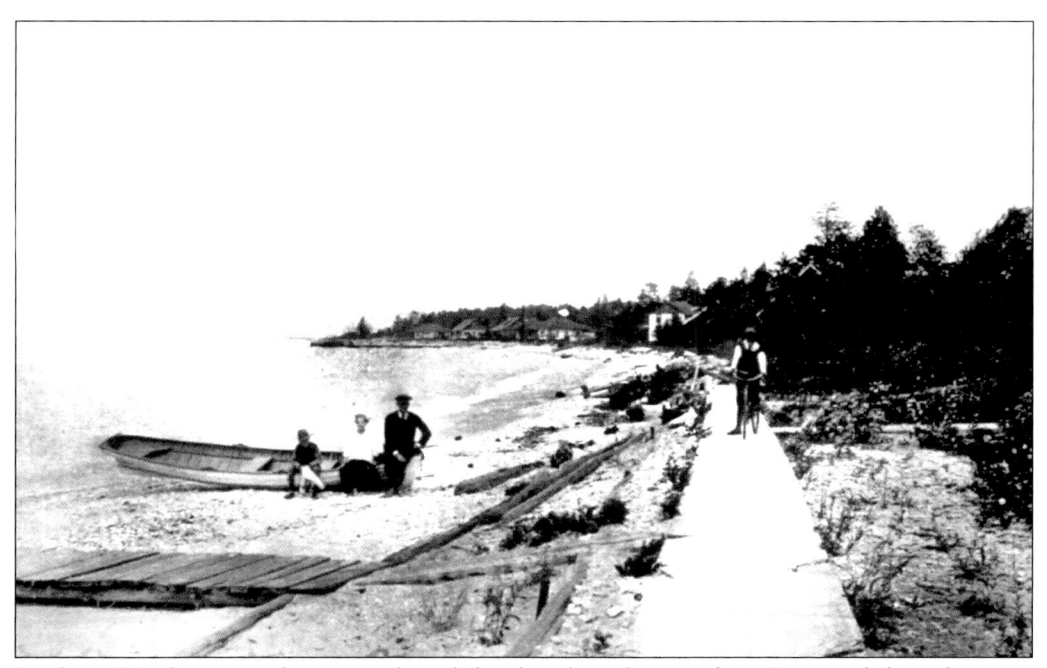

By the 1900s, homes and cottages dotted the shoreline that ran from Fort Michilimackinac to McGulpin's Point. Wawatam Beach, along the boardwalk, was a favorite place for the locals to picnic, swim, and enjoy corn roasts. (MAPL)

Shortly after the light was put into operation, mariners complained that it had been placed in a poor location to aid them in preparing to go through the narrowest part of the passage. In spite of this problem, the light remained in service for many years before it was replaced by the more visible Old Mackinac Point Light. In 1906 the light was decommissioned and the lantern room was later removed from the tower. (NC)

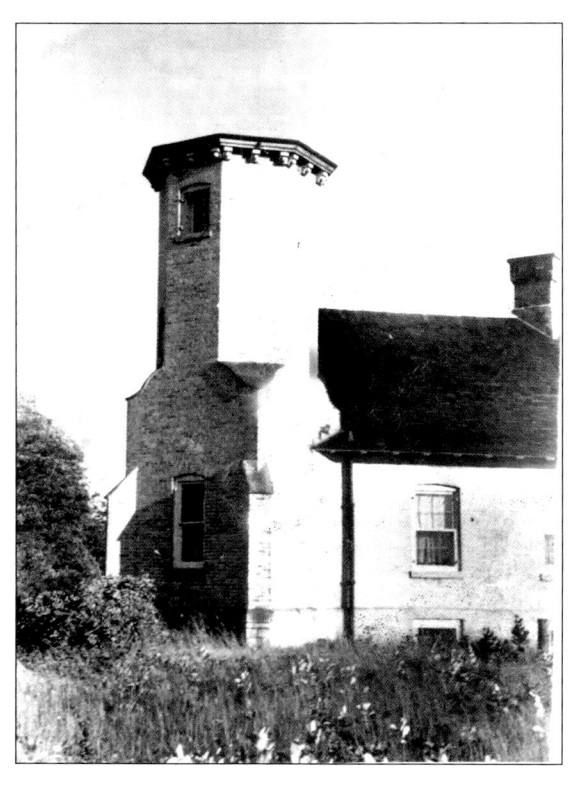

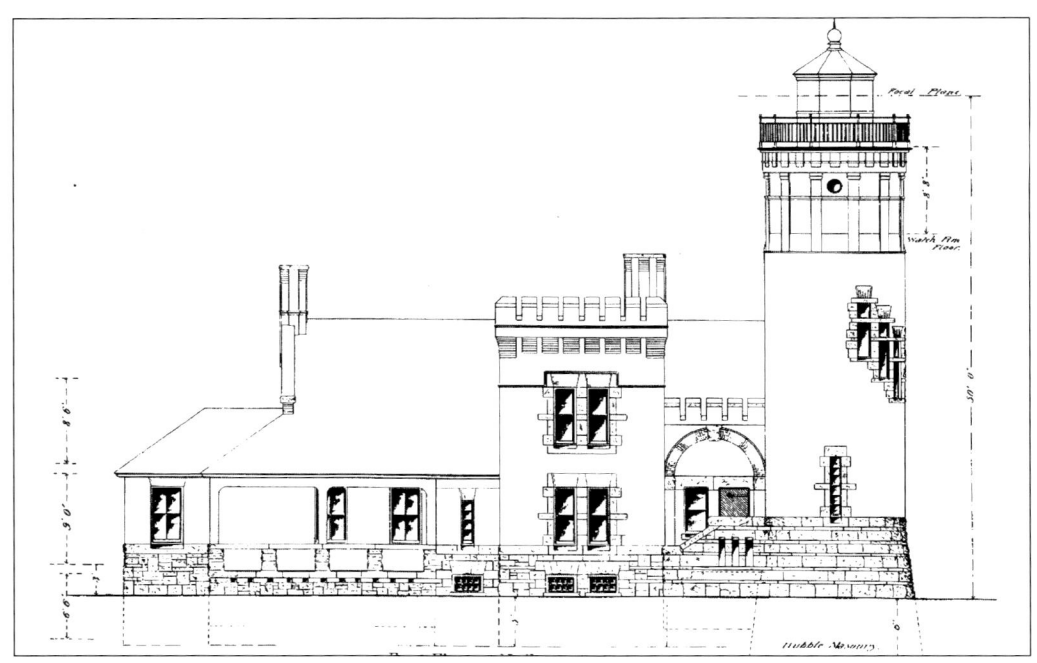

Throughout the existence of McGulpin's Point Light, mariners traveling from the west had difficulty spotting the beacon. Many requests were made to remedy the problem, but it wasn't until 1888 that a decision was made to build a light on Old Mackinac Point, in the center of the Straits, to replace the McGulpin's Point Light. The new light plan called for a 50-foot tower with an attached two-story keeper's dwelling made of Cream City brick and limestone. (NC)

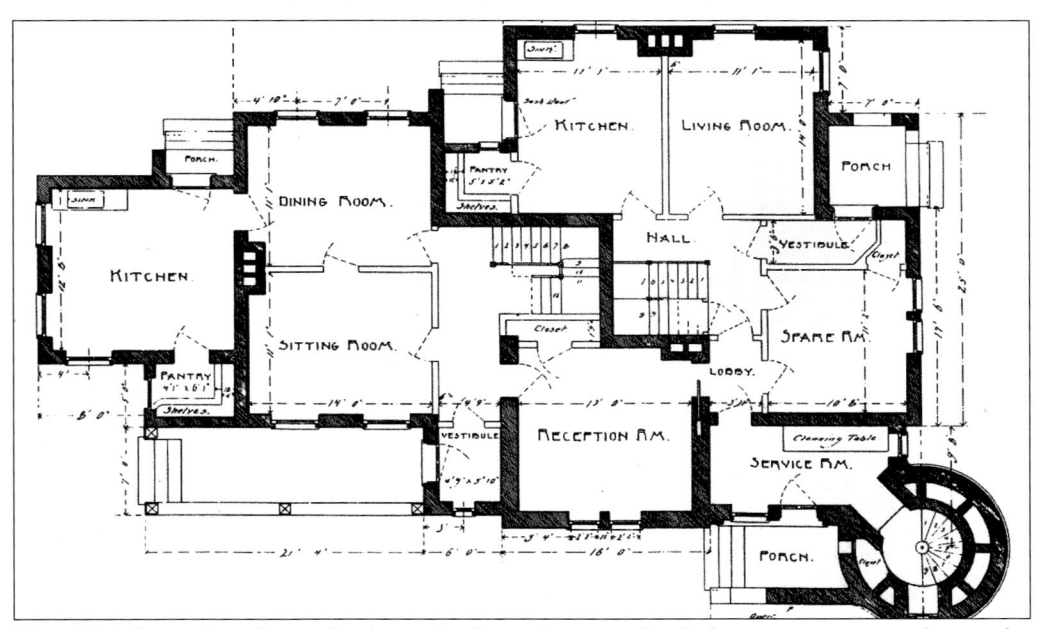

The 1891 floor plan shows the large dwelling that was divided into two parts to house the families of a keeper and an assistant. A connecting doorway between the two sides of the dwelling allowed both men access to the service room and the light tower. (NC)

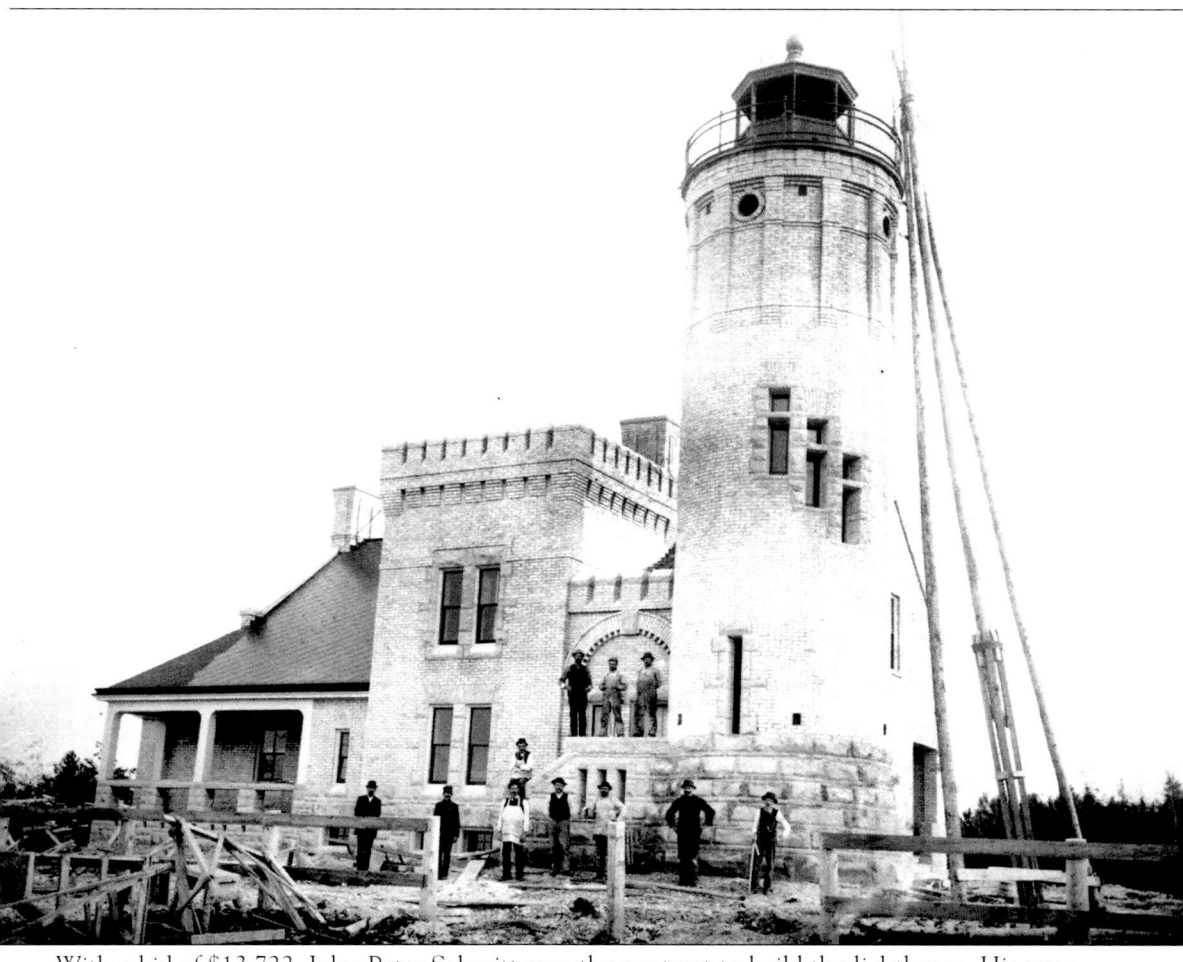

With a bid of $13,722, John Peter Schmitt won the contract to build the lighthouse. His crew and materials arrived from Detroit on the lighthouse tender and construction was begun in May of 1892. Work progressed quickly and the Old Mackinac Point Light began shining on October 25th of the same year.

When the project was completed, the crew posed for a picture in front of the lighthouse. First keeper of the light, George Marshall, who was already tending the fog signal and who helped build the light, is seen standing second from the left. The tall wooden poles on the right of the picture were used to hoist the cupola and railing to the top of the tower. The metal roof was painted bright red to make it a more visible daymark for mariners.

In 1960, Mackinac State Historic Parks purchased the lighthouse property and currently maintains it as a museum. (MSHP)

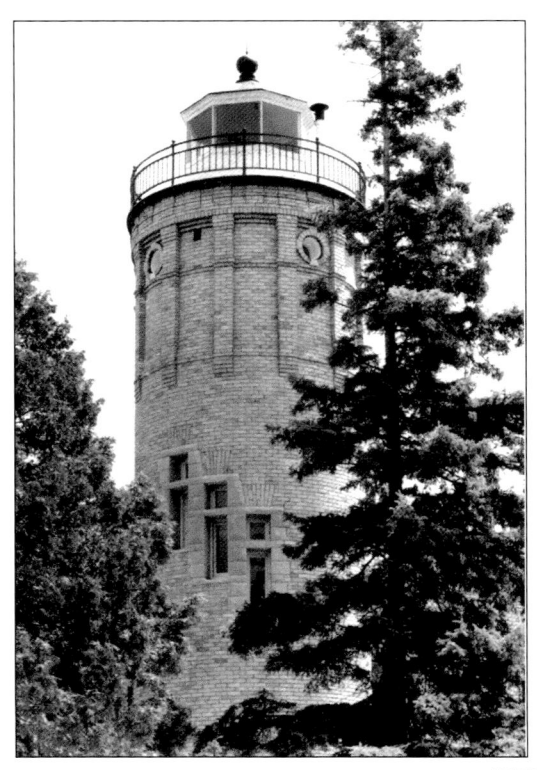

A close-up of the tower shows the intricate detail of the structure. The porthole-like windows amid the corbeled brickwork around the top of the tower and the stone lintels of the lower windows contributed to the tower's architectural beauty. (NC)

The tower was capped with a lantern room that held a Fourth Order Fresnel lens. According to the 1902 *Instructions to Light-Keepers* manual there were 14 rules regarding the cleaning of the light apparatus that were strictly followed. The keeper wore an apron when performing these duties so none of his clothing could come in contact with the lens. Before cleaning the lens, he brushed it with a feather brush to remove all dust. Then he wiped it with a soft linen cloth and polished it with buff-skin. If there was oil or grease on any part, it had to be removed with a soft linen cloth dipped in wine spirits and polished with a buff-skin. Under no circumstances could a skin that was wet or damp be used. This cleaning process could take two to three hours of the keeper's time each day. (NC)

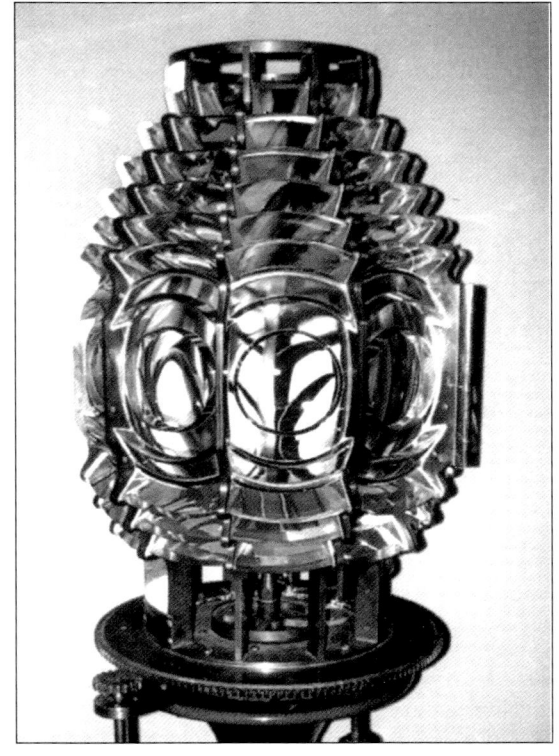

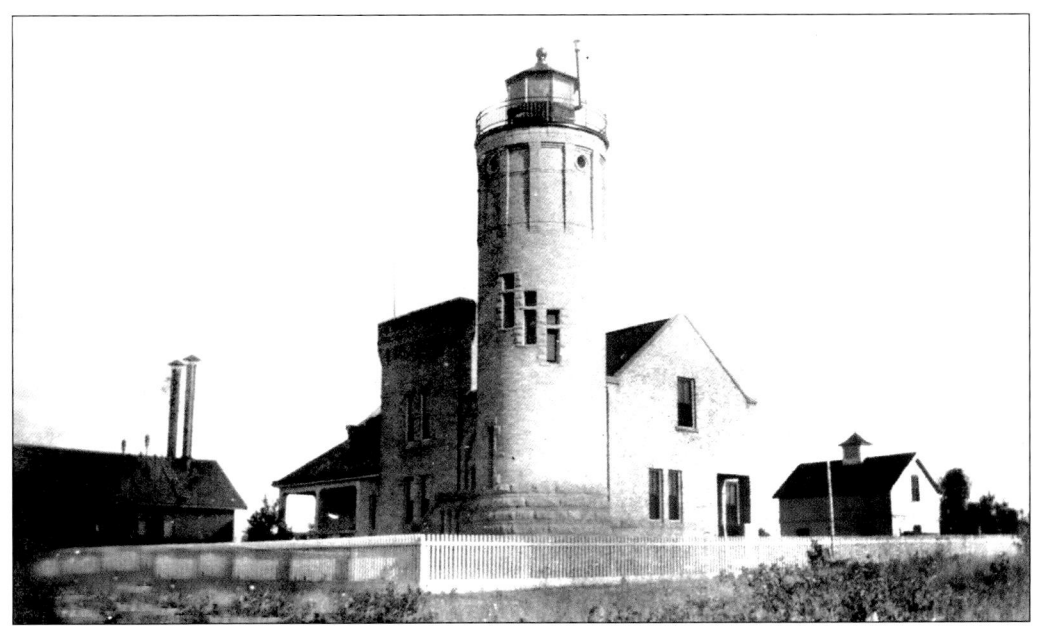

Funds for a fog signal building (left) were acquired before the funds for the lighthouse, which resulted in the fog signal becoming operational about two years before the light was built. The exterior of the wood-frame fog building was sheathed in corrugated iron while the interior walls were sheathed with smooth iron. The fog horn began operating on November 5, 1889. (MMM)

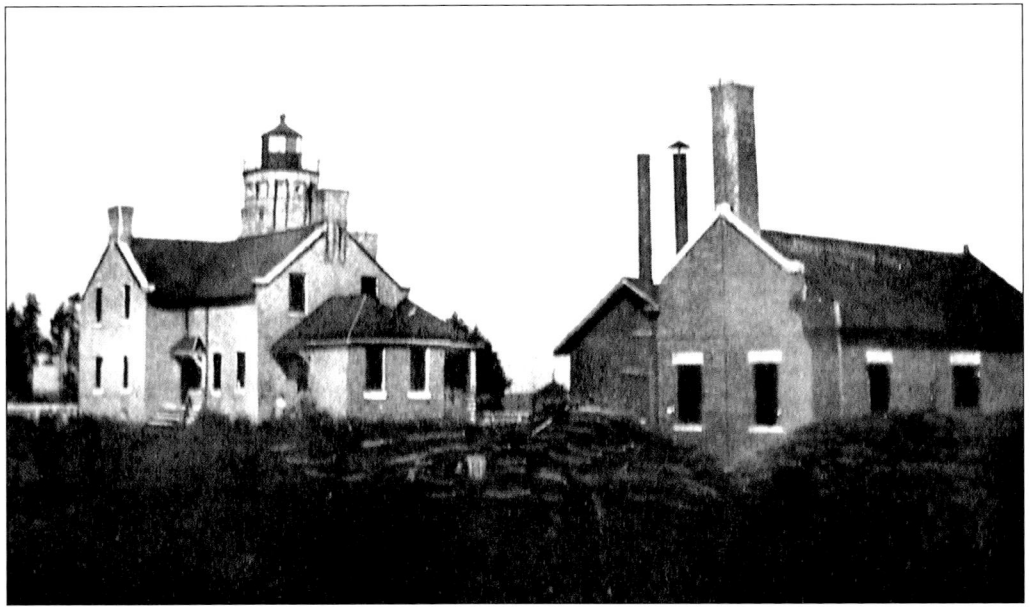

Soon after the lighthouse was completed, it became apparent that the fog signal and the light were built too close together. A recommendation was made to move the fog signal 50 feet to the east. However, that land was owned by Mackinaw City, which was unwilling to sell. After lengthy court proceedings, the Lighthouse Board was allowed to purchase the land whereupon they decided to build a new fog signal (right) and retain the old one as a warehouse. (BHL)

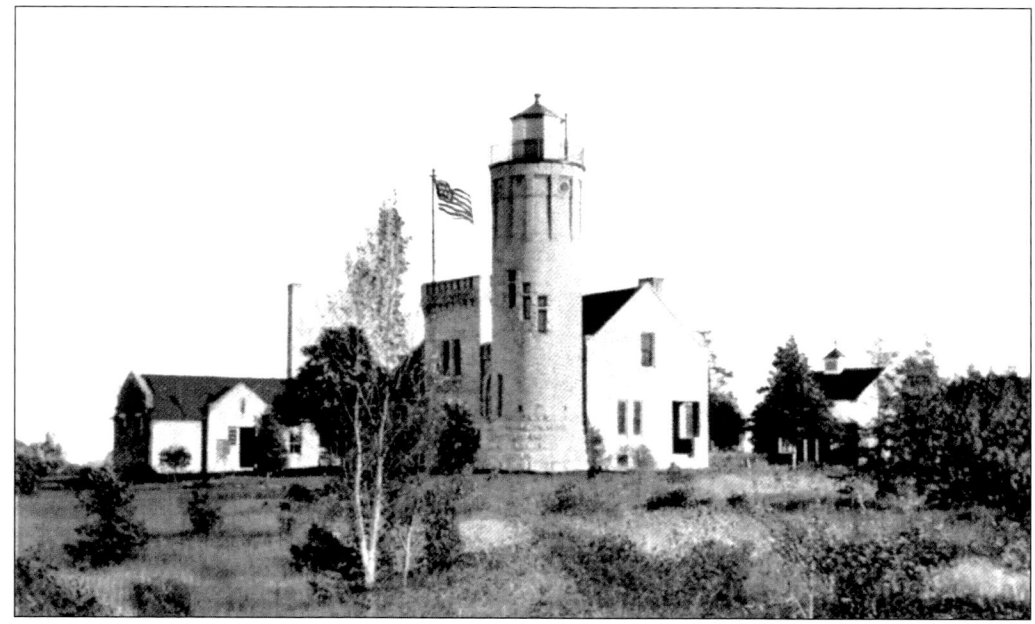

The new fog signal building (left) was completed in 1907. It was a red brick gable-roofed building with a tall square chimney rising from its south end. The steam whistles, boilers, and engines were transferred from the old building for use in the new structure. (MAPL)

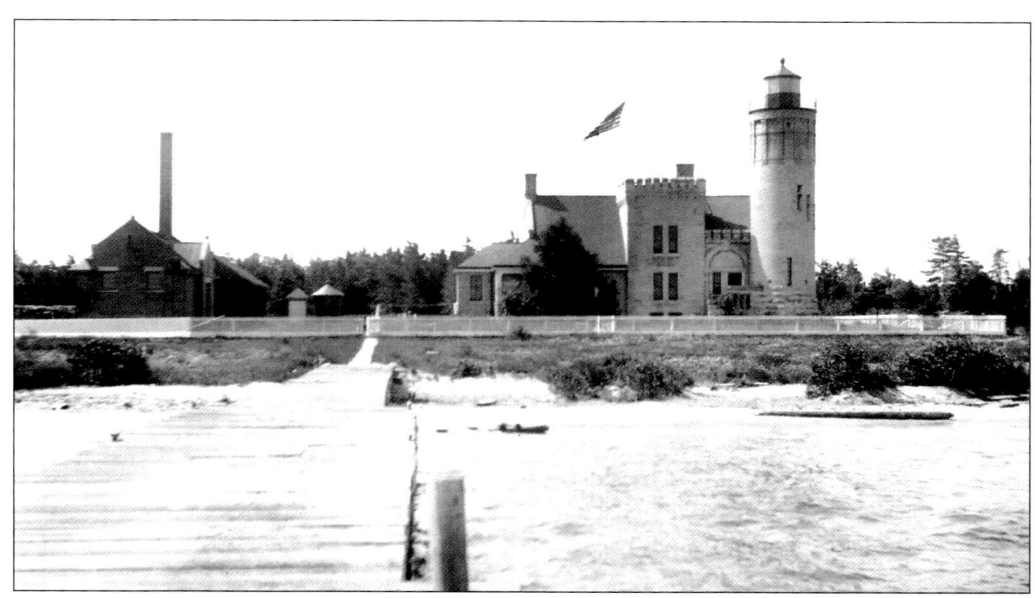

A view from the water shows the lighthouse grounds as they appeared after the new fog signal building was constructed in 1907. The old fog signal (warehouse) was moved adjacent to the new building and can be seen behind it on the left side of the picture. A circular oil storage and privy are located to the right of the warehouse. (NC)

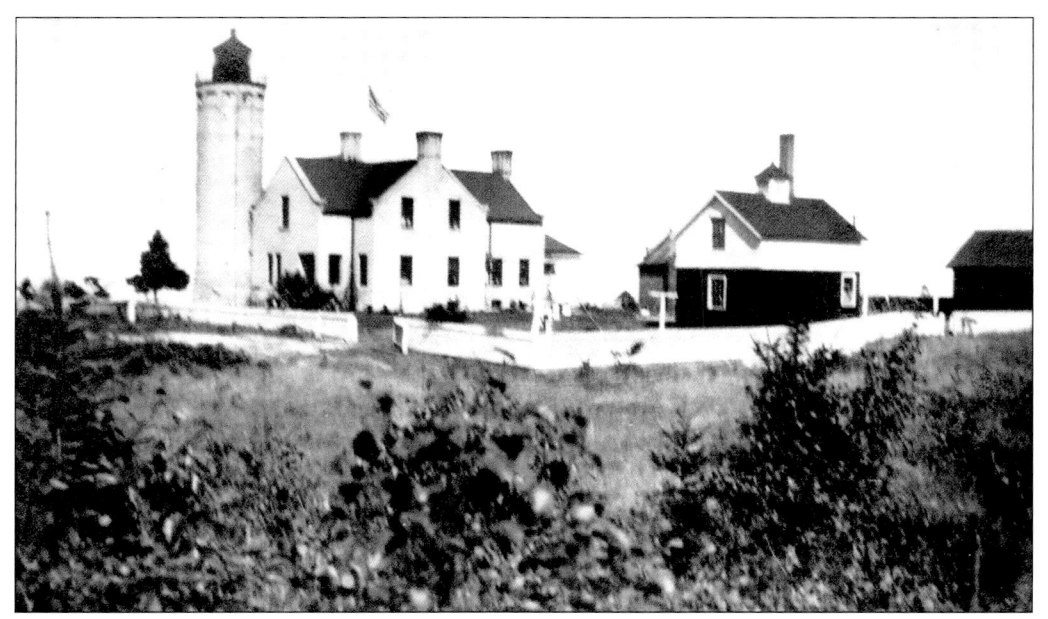

Looking from the south side of the property toward the lake offers a view of the back of the lighthouse, the old and new fog signal buildings, and the barn. (NC)

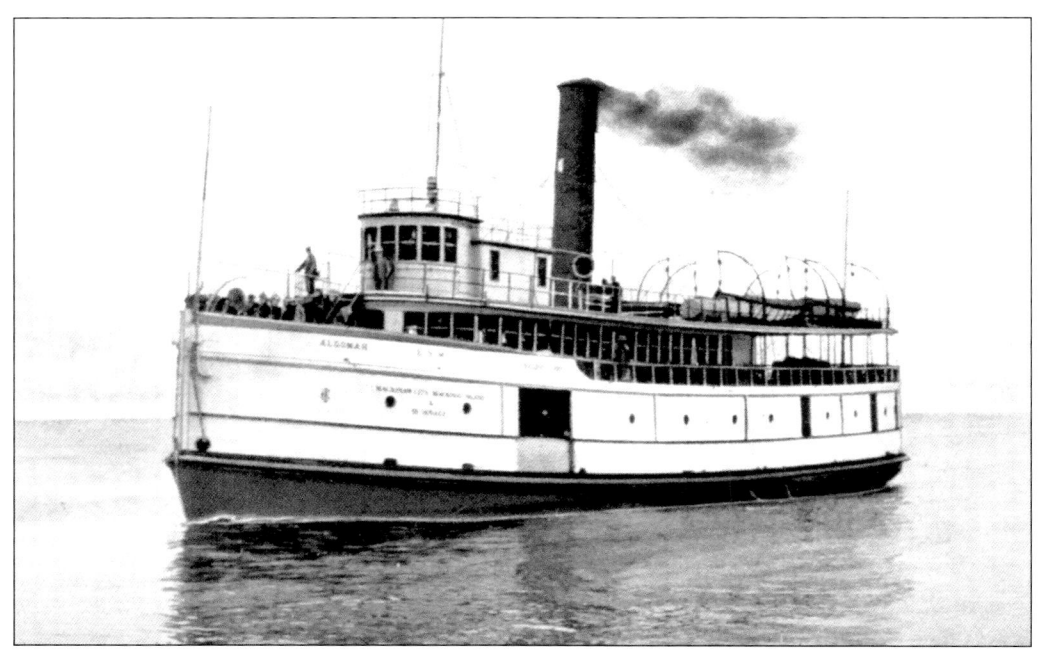

From the arrival of the earliest settlers in Mackinaw, crossing the Straits to reach the Upper Peninsula had presented a problem. Strong winds and currents often produced rough waters and huge swells that made crossing dangerous in the summer. Winter travel was often stalled by unpredictable ice conditions. In 1882 the first steam ferry and ice breaker, the *Algomah*, was put into service to carry mail, passengers, and railroad cars across the Straits. (MMM)

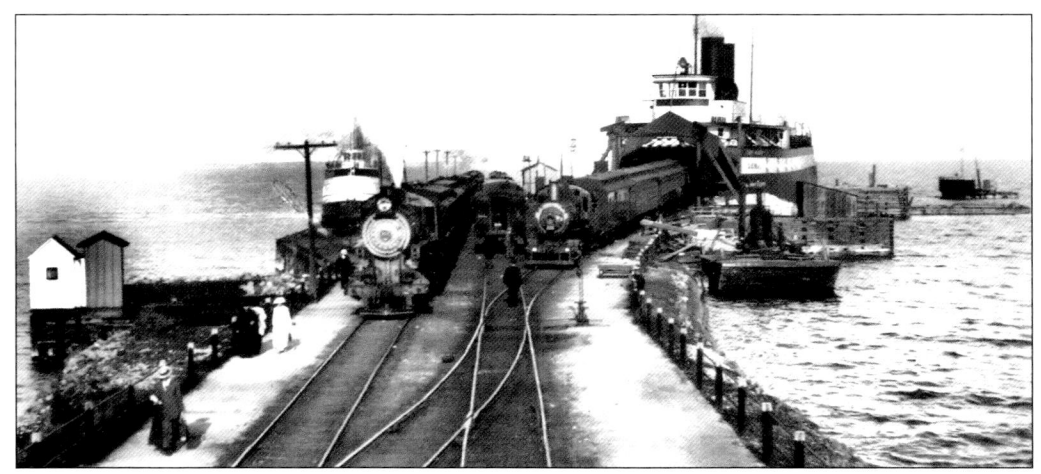

In 1911 the Mackinac Transportation Company had the steel carferry *Chief Wawatam* built to cross the Straits. Seen at the right loading dock, this ship was over 350 feet long and could carry up to 26 railroad cars at one time. The flat-bottom bow design of the *Chief Wawatam* allowed it to run on the ice by pushing the ice down. This capability combined with its steel hull made it proficient at forging through the frozen surf and resulted in the ferry becoming world renown for its excellence as an ice breaker. (MAPL)

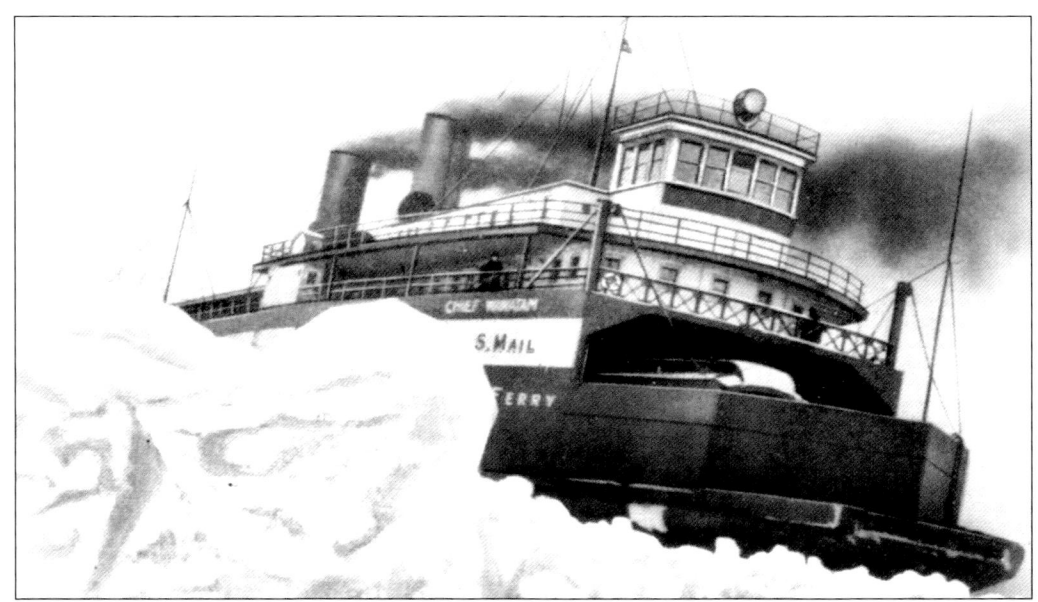

The *Chief Wawatam* and her sister ship, *Sainte Marie*, worked together for nearly 50 years keeping a channel open through the ice of the Straits. This was often a difficult task since the waves and currents could blow the ships out of the channel and into ice piles along the edges of the channel. Some of these piles were known to have risen up to 20 feet high, making it difficult to break through. Despite her ice breaking prowess, the *Chief Wawatam* was stuck fast in the ice for five days during the severe winter of 1922. Huge ice piles prevented her from making any headway and efforts by the passengers and crew to remove the ice failed. After several days, a group of railroad men came with 500 lbs. of dynamite and blew away enough ice enough to allow the ship to move. The next morning she headed toward St. Ignace and arrived there by evening. (MAPL)

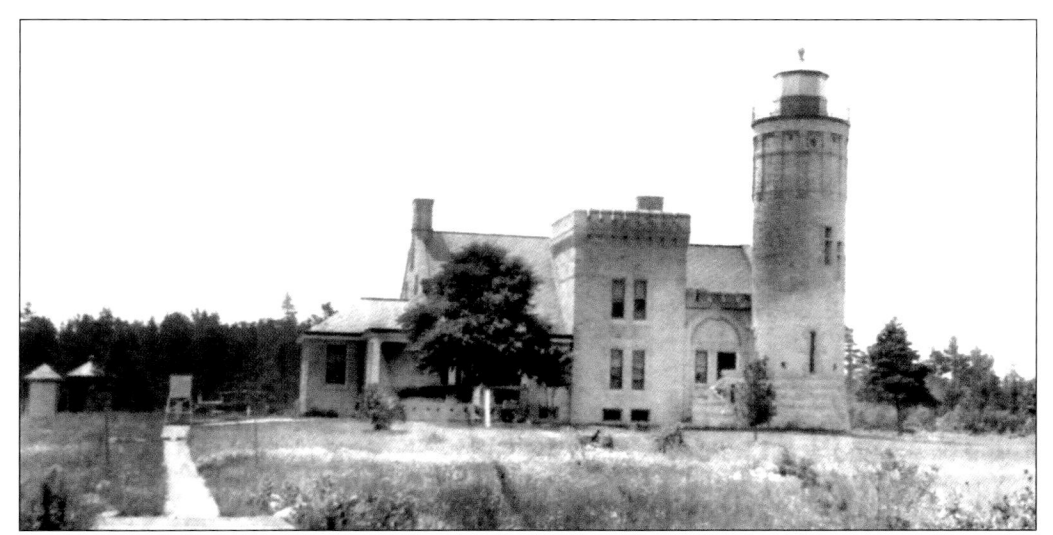

U.S. Weather Bureau observation equipment was added to the property at the end of the boardwalk in 1920. While recording data was not part of the keeper's required responsibilities, it was something he enjoyed doing. (NC)

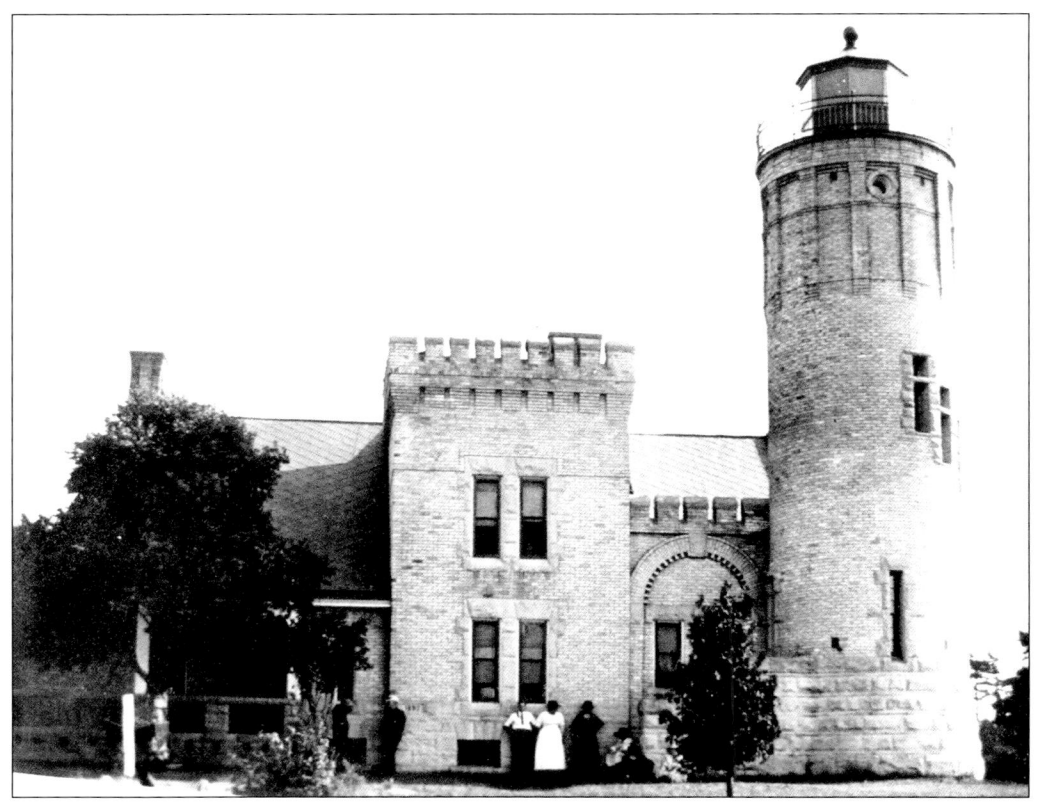

In the 1920s electricity reached the lighthouse and the oil lamp was replaced with an electric light. Since electricity burned cleaner than oil and didn't have to be refueled on site, the keeper was able to spend less of his work day in the tower. (NC)

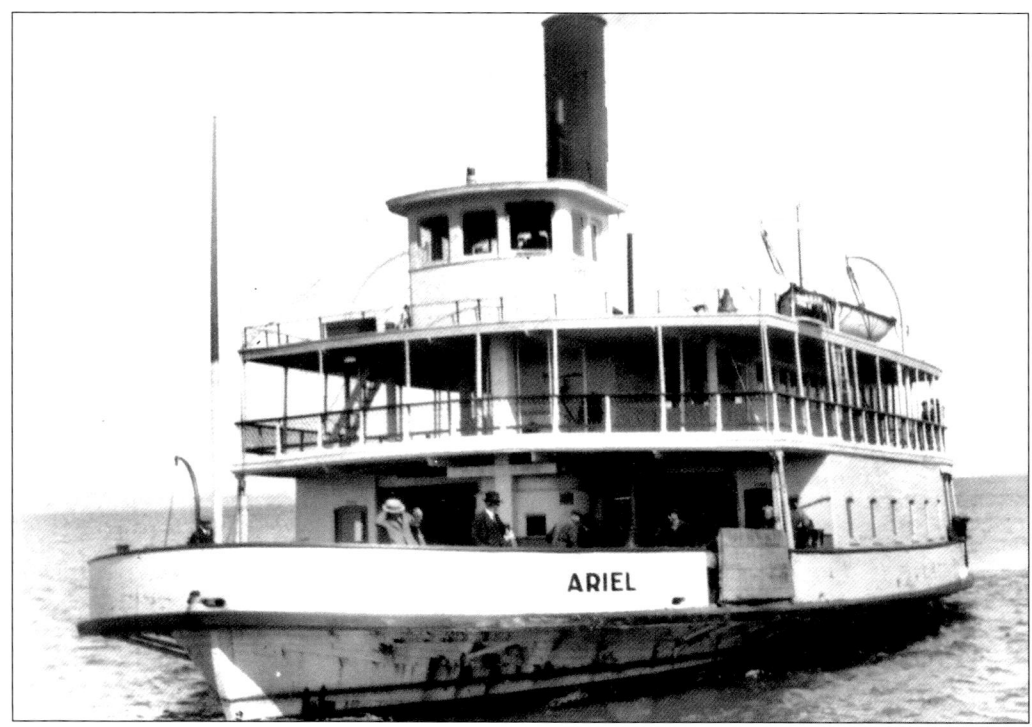

The increasing popularity of the automobile and the improvement of state roadways brought more tourists and hunters to the area. The demand for a cheaper ferry system to connect the highways of the Upper and Lower Peninsulas was heard by the State Highway Department, who established the Michigan State Ferry fleet in 1923 to accommodate this need. The small wooden vessel, Ariel, was the first ferry purchased for the State fleet. Her maiden run on August 2, 1923, went from St. Ignace to Mackinaw City. Since she was small and shallow and not able to handle the rough waters or ice of the Straits, she operated seasonally from spring through fall and stayed in port during strong winds. In spite of these drawbacks, she transported over 10,000 vehicles across the Straits in her first year of operation. (NC)

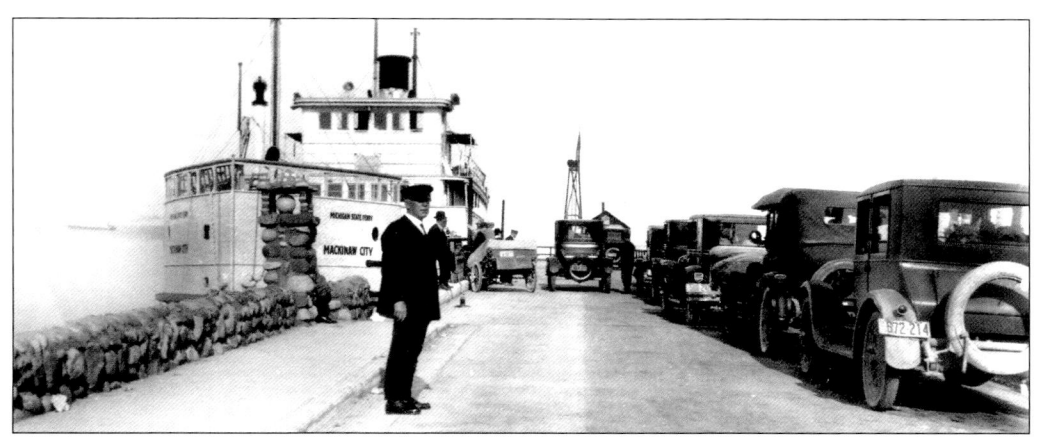

When the ferry system first began, the State of Michigan rented dockage on the Mackinaw City railroad dock. In 1923–1924 water frontage was purchased and a ferry dock that extended 1,400 feet into the water was built in Mackinaw City. (MMM)

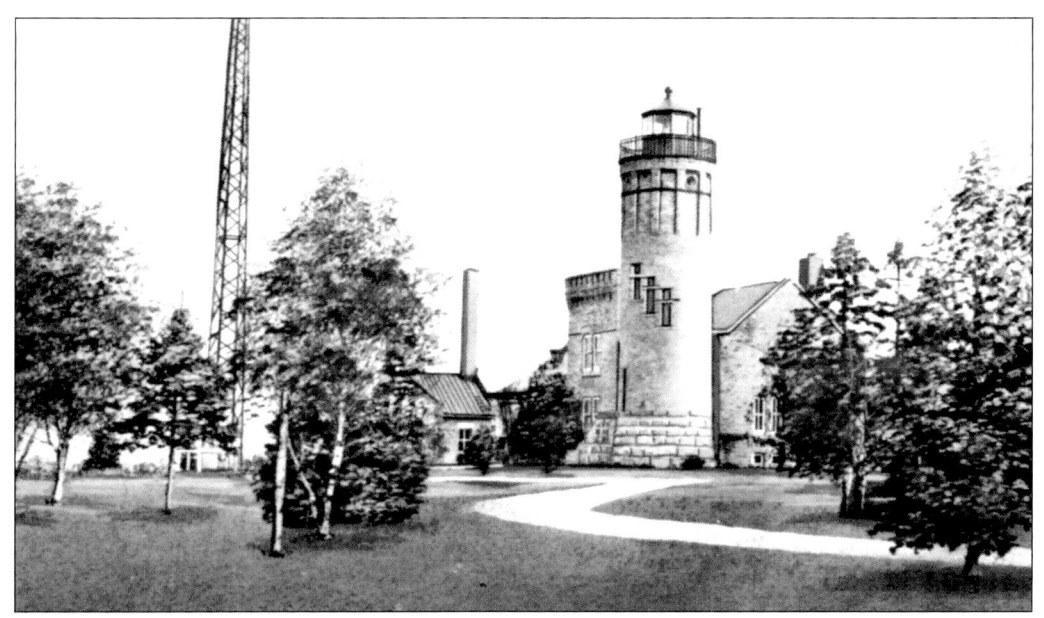

During the 1930s many lighthouses were becoming equipped with radio apparatus. By triangulating signals sent from beacons along the shoreline, a captain could easily determine his position on the water. In the late 1930s a radio tower was constructed on the Old Mackinac Point Lighthouse property and a room was set up in the fog signal building to handle the necessary radio equipment. (MAPL)

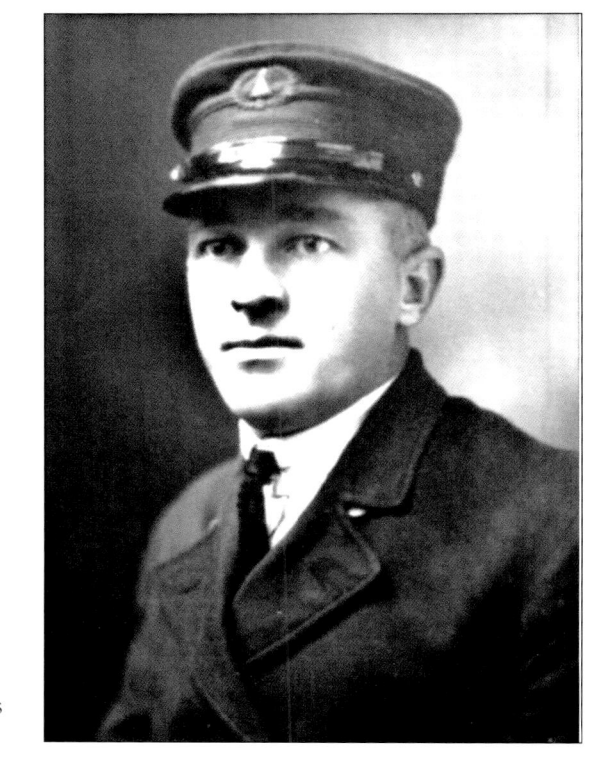

Henrik Olsen served as assistant for seven years under second keeper James Marshall. When Marshall retired in 1940, Henrik became the keeper and remained in that position until his retirement in 1951. Presumably, Henrik was the first keeper at Old Mackinac Point to own a car. He stored it in the old fog signal building until the barn was converted into a garage. (OCHGS)

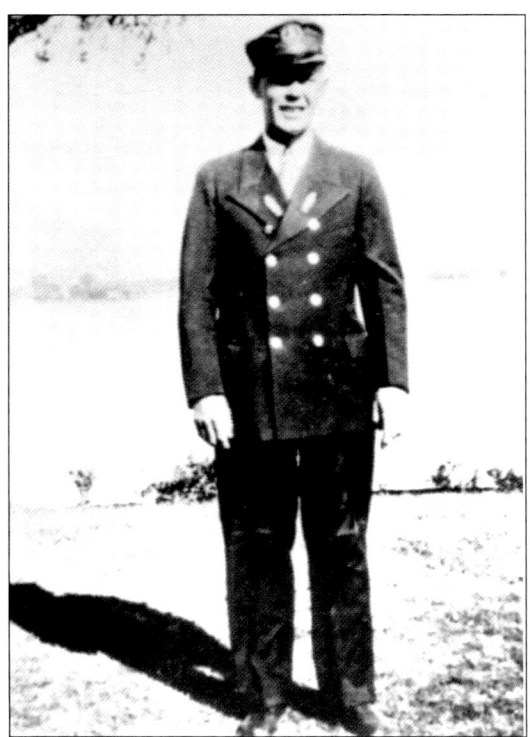

John Campbell was assistant keeper of the light from 1944 until keeper Olsen retired. Campbell served as keeper from 1951 until the station closed. He then transferred to the Point Betsie Light Station where he served for nearly six years before he died. (NC)

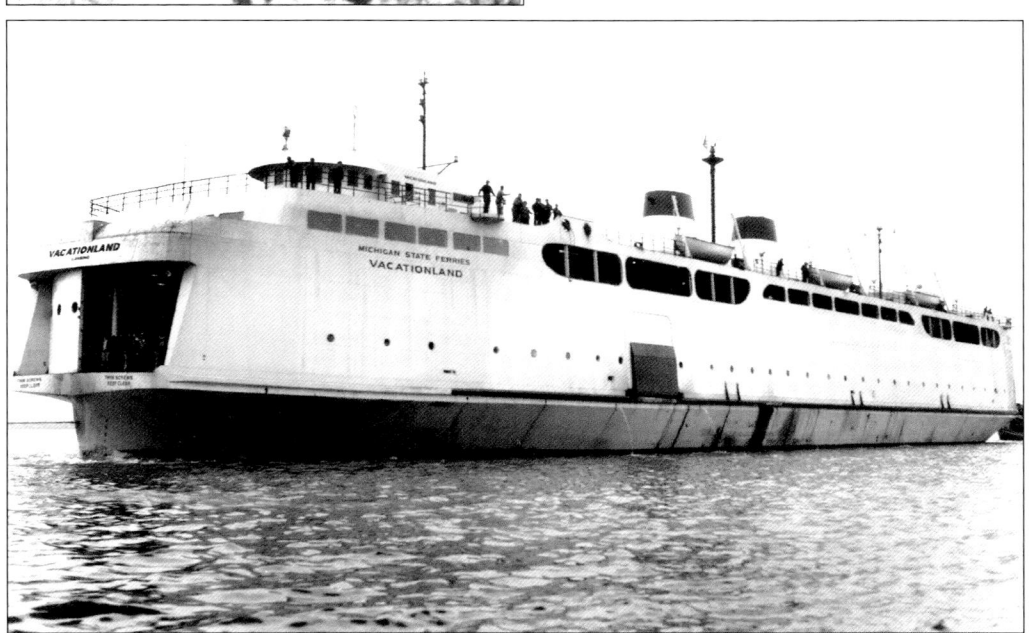

The Highway Commissioner made a proposal in 1947 to build a 150-vehicle capacity ice breaker ferry for the Straits. At $4.5 million, many questioned spending that sum of money on a ship when talk of building a bridge across the straits was growing stronger. The *Vactionland* was built, however, and was a great boost to the state ferry line until the system closed down in the late 1950s. (MAPL)

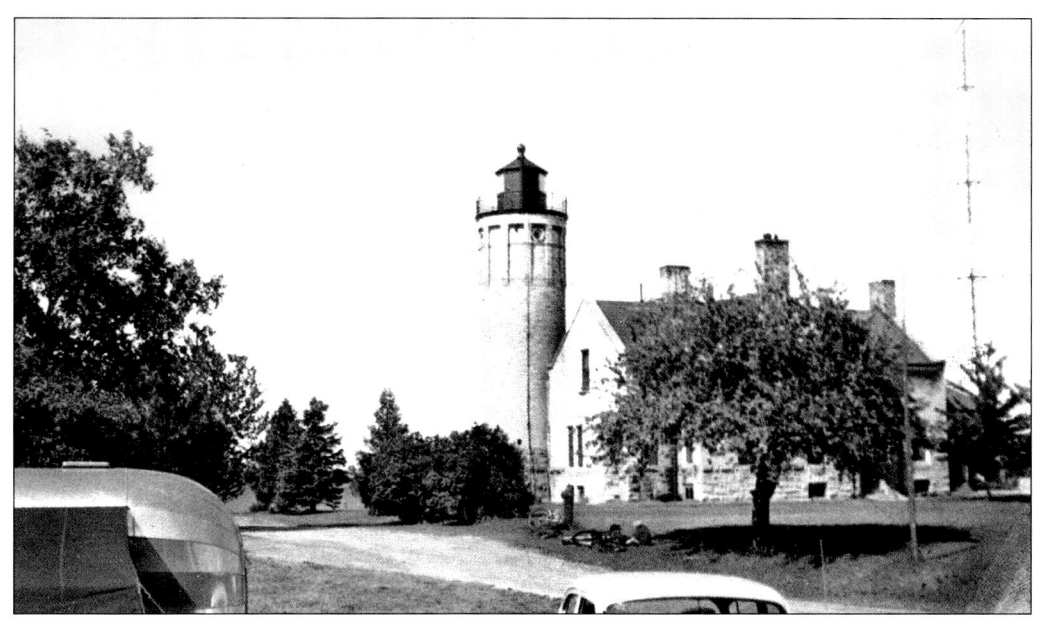

A photograph from the 1950s offers a view of the grounds from the rear of the station. A public campground was located near the lighthouse at this time. The Old Mackinac Point Light remained an active aid to navigation, guiding the heavy volume of commercial ships and carferries through most of the 1950s. (MAPL)

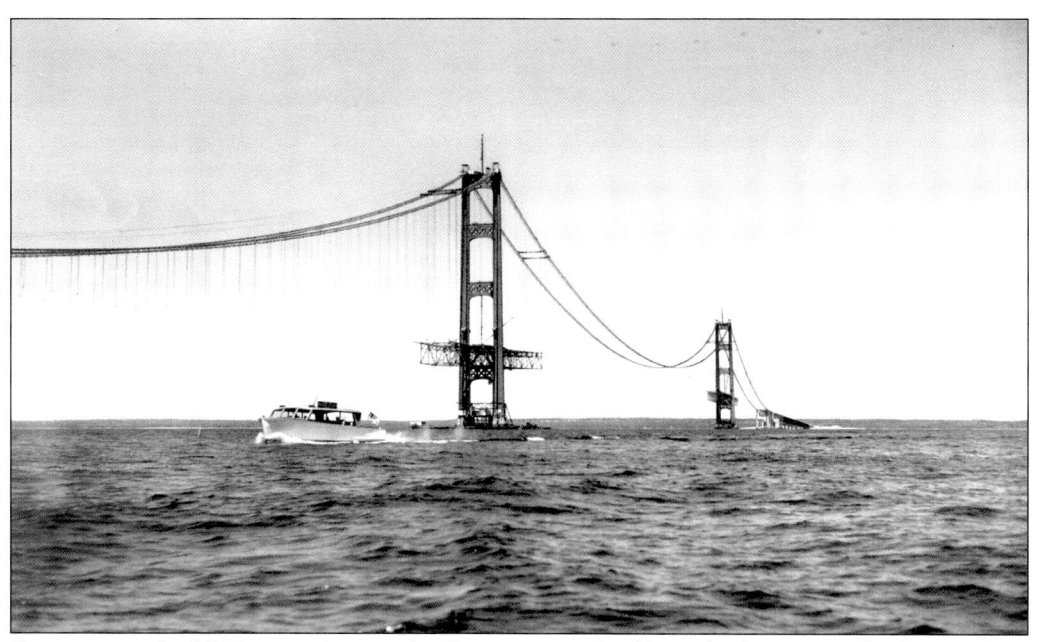

Beginning in the 1880s, consideration had been given to building a bridge to span the Straits. Over the years, many discussions—both political and economic—took place regarding the feasibility of such a project. While progress kept moving forward, it was delayed several times by those in opposition to it and by the nation's involvement in various wars. Finally, on May 7 and 8, 1954, ground-breaking occurred on each peninsula and construction began soon after. (CHL)

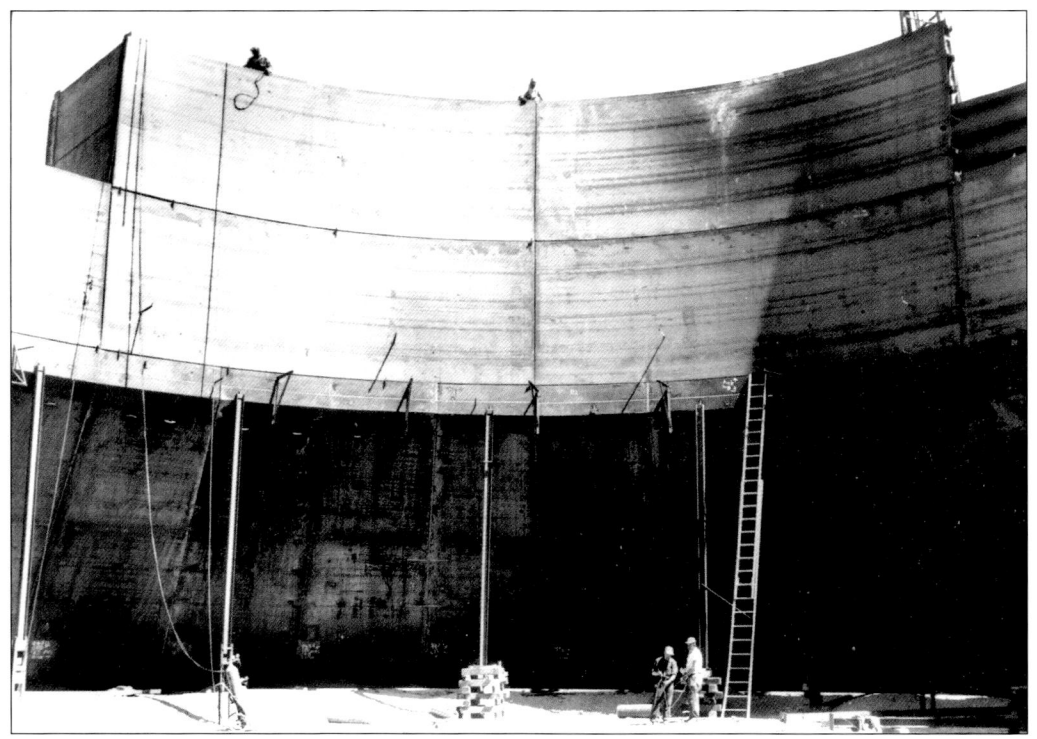

The construction crew's first task was to build two large caissons that formed the major foundation for the bridge. Steel sections were floated to the bridge and welded together to form the chambers that were sunk to bedrock and then filled with stone and concrete. The picture above looks inside one of the 116-foot diameter caissons. (CHL)

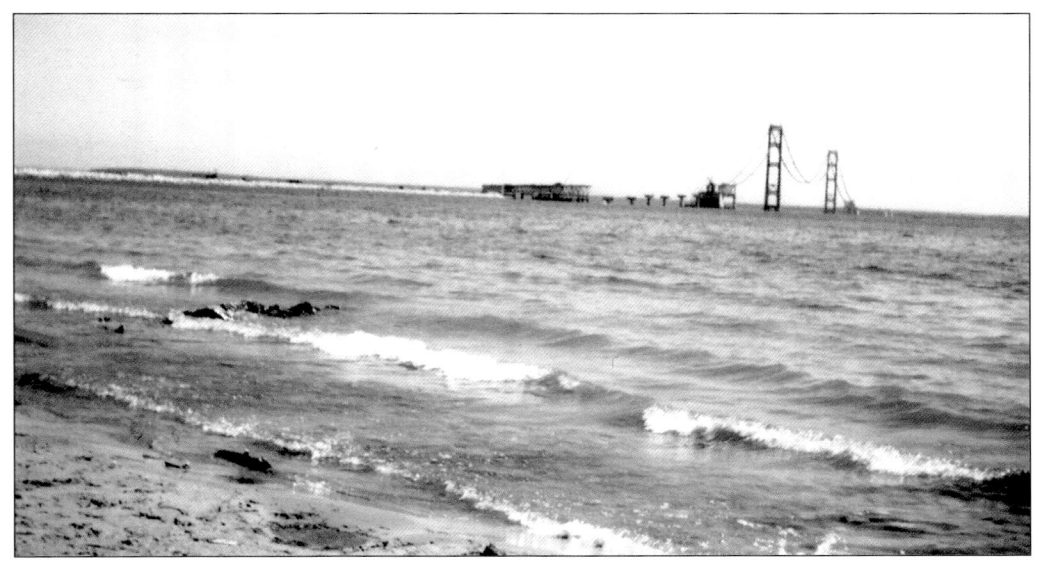

In 1955 the minor foundations running from land to the anchor piers on either side of the bridge were completed. The towers were constructed on land and floated out to the bridge and erected to a finished height of 552 feet above the water.

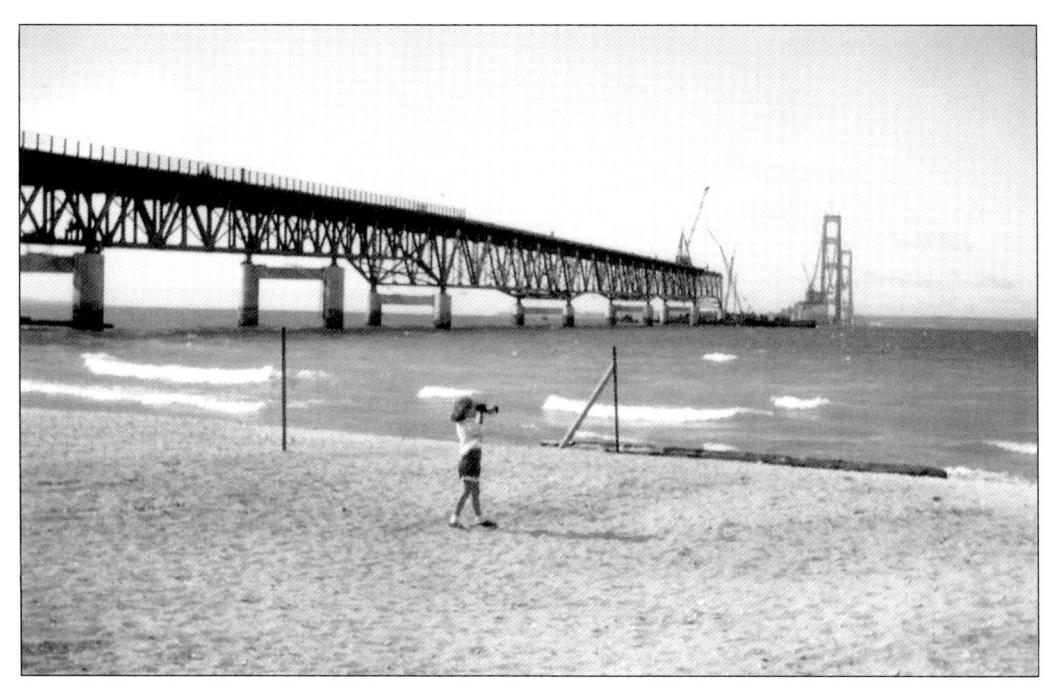

As a child, author Susan Roark Hoyt watches the progress of the bridge as the steel superstructure is completed and preparations are made to attach the last truss spans to the suspension cables near the towers.

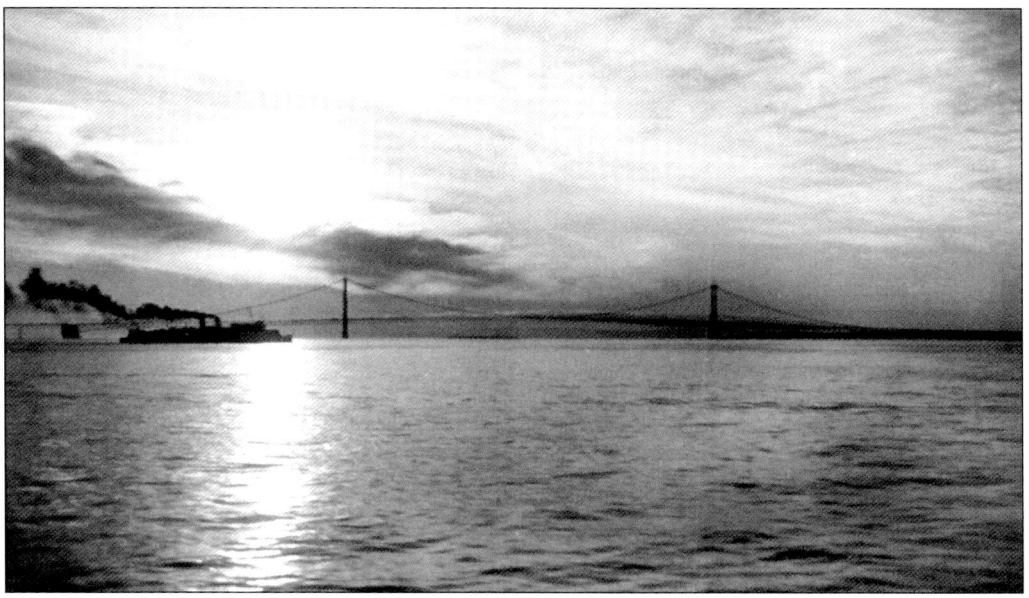

With the final truss spans in place and the 41,000 miles of cable spun, the Mackinac Bridge was complete. On November 1, 1957, the $100 million suspension bridge—the world's largest at the time—was officially opened. No longer dependent on public transportation, people were free to cross the Straits at will and this freedom naturally brought an end to the state-run ferry system. Pictured above is one of the ferries making its last trip across the Straits. (MAPL)

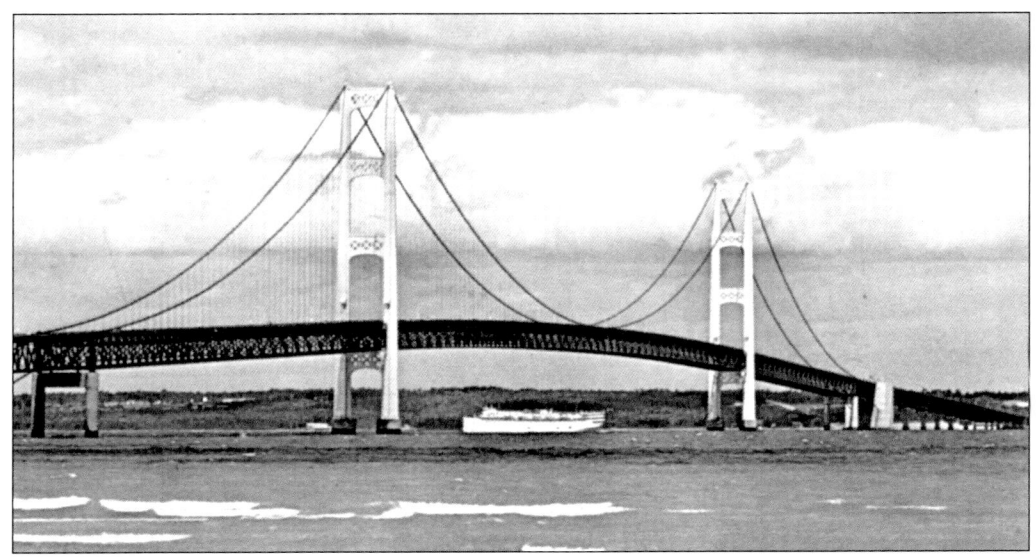

The size and location of the bridge, along with the navigational aids placed on its towers, made it an excellent marker for mariners. Although it was not intended to be a lighthouse, the bridge proved to be a more effective marker than either McGulpin's Point Light or Old Mackinac Point Light had been. (MMM)

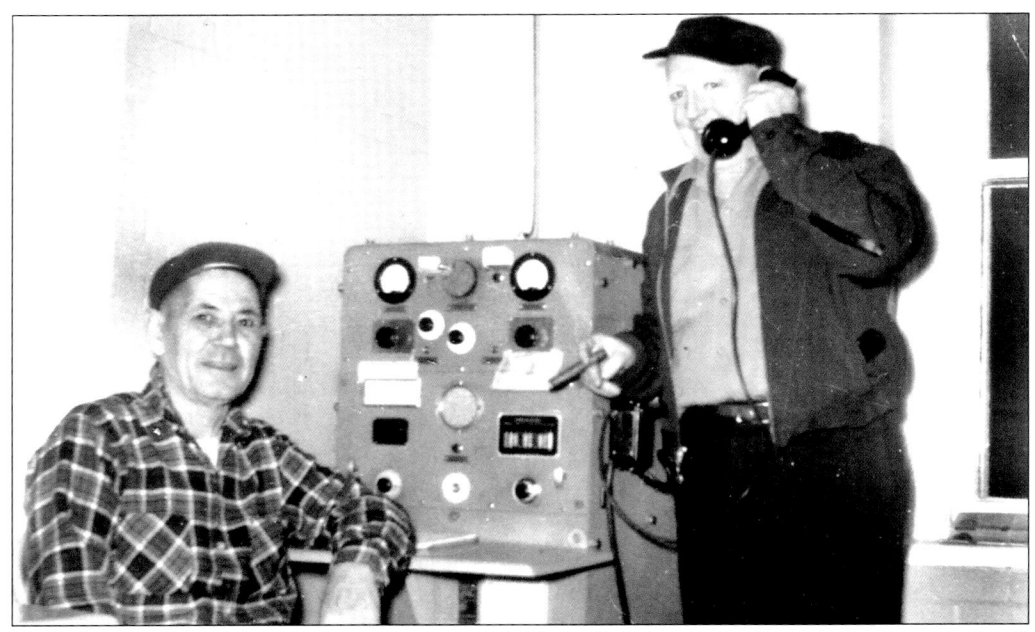

With the opening of the Mackinac Bridge in 1957, the lighthouse on the mainland was declared surplus. After 65 years of service the Old Mackinac Point Light was closed and its signal lights were transferred to the new bridge. On December 20, 1957, keeper John Campbell (left) and assistant keeper John Marken sent the last radio message from the station before it closed. The dawning of a new era in transportation across the Straits was exciting but came with mixed emotions. While many people cheered at the opening of the Mackinac Bridge, the families of the lighthouse keepers wept. (NC)